Steven Redgrave's
COMPLETE BOOK OF
ROWING

PARTRIDGE PRESS

LONDON · NEW YORK · TORONTO · SYDNEY · AUCKLAND

TRANSWORLD PUBLISHERS LTD
61–63 Uxbridge Road, London W5 5SA

TRANSWORLD PUBLISHERS (AUSTRALIA) PTY LTD
15–23 Helles Avenue, Moorebank, NSW 2170

TRANSWORLD PUBLISHERS (NZ) LTD
3 William Pickering Drive,
Albany, Auckland

Published 1992 by Partridge Press
a division of Transworld Publishers Ltd
Revised edition published 1995
Copyright © **Steven Redgrave 1992, 1995**

The right of **Steven Redgrave** to be identified
as author of this work has been asserted in accordance
with sections 77 and 78 of the Copyright Designs and
Patents Act 1988.

A catalogue record for this book is available from the British Library

ISBN 185225 2308

Human Function Curve p.135 from *Changing Ideas in Heath Care*, edited by
D. Seedhouse and A. Cribb © 1989 John Wiley. Ch 2. Human functions and the heart,
P. G. F. Nixon, Charing Cross Hospital.

Flexibility tests p. 192–4 reproduced from *Fitness for Sport* by Rex Hazeldine.

Appendix II: ARA Water Safety Code courtesy of Amateur Rowing Association.

Typeset in Plantin by Chippendale Type, Otley, West Yorkshire, England.

Printed and bound in Great Britain by
Butler & Tanner Ltd, Frome and London

To all those who have played a part in the success of my rowing career.

Acknowledgements

I would like to thank everyone involved in the publication of this book, but in particular Fiona Johnston for her clear line drawings, Peter Spurrier for the photographic plates, Patrick Sweeney, Bob Michaels and Alison Gill for contributions to the text, and my sister Christine for help with typing the manuscript.

Thanks must also go to my wife without whose help and patience this book would remain a figment of my imagination.

CONTENTS

1

THE ORIGINS OF ROWING

The credit for developing the *rowed boat* seems to belong to the Egyptians. The first recorded boat with oars appears in a relief on an ancient stone wall erected in Egypt between 3300 BC and 3000 BC.

History has been shaped in part by oars and the men who pulled them. Roman warships, Viking longboats and Venetian galleys all relied heavily on oar power.

Traditionally, with each form of transport, there comes the desire to race, and rowing boats were no exception. In England, racing in rowing boats evolved from the times when the only bridges crossing the River Thames were London Bridge and Chelsea Bridge. Those who wanted to cross the river elsewhere had to call upon the services of the ferry craft. The watermen who plied this trade became the subjects of wagers developed between the gentry, among whom high stakes were a major pastime.

It was for these watermen that the Doggett Coat and Badge race was instituted. The eighteenth-century Irish comedian, Thomas Doggett, founded this race to improve the quality of rowing by the professional Thames watermen and also to celebrate the first anniversary of the coronation of King George I. On his deathbed, Doggett requested that the race be staged on 1 August 'for ever'.

The first of these sculling races took place in the year 1716 starting at The Old Swan pub at London Bridge. It was rowed over a course of nearly 5 miles to The White Swan pub at Chelsea. This race is the oldest documented race in the world and still takes place today. Although largely unchanged, it is now an amateur instead of a professional race.

The race is open to watermen who have completed their apprenticeship and taken up Freedom of the Company within the twelve months preceding the day of the race. The prize is a luxurious red garment (the Doggett Coat) and a victory badge. In the early days of the race not only did these items bring status to the winner, they were also far beyond the purse of the average labourer of the time.

Today, the two most well-known sporting occasions in the rowing calendar are the University Boat Race between Oxford and Cambridge and, of course, Henley Royal Regatta.

English gentlemen eventually came to the sport of rowing in the early nineteenth century, the first University Boat Race taking place on Wednesday 10 June 1829 at 7.56 p.m. This race between Oxford and Cambridge was rowed from Hambleden-Lock to Henley. The favourites, Cambridge, won the toss and chose the Berkshire shore, but Oxford won easily by five to six lengths in a recorded time of 14 minutes 10 seconds.

Until outriggers came into vogue, the Henley course proper – from island to bridge – was never rowed in under 8 minutes. This race is now rowed every spring on the Tideway, from Putney to Mortlake. The students still rule their race a private affair, conducted under conditions agreed upon by themselves in secret correspondence, known otherwise only to the umpire of the day.

The University Boat Race was first televised and broadcast to the nation in 1938. History was made again when in 1981 Susan Brown became the first woman to take part in the Boat Race, successfully steering Oxford to the winning post.

Regatta, the Italian word for a boat race held in grand manner, exactly describes Henley Royal Regatta, which was first held in 1839. Henley did not attain its royal status until twelve years later in 1851, when Prince Albert granted his patronage, graciously contributing £50 to the Regatta's ailing finances.

Since its beginnings the course has been changed four times in attempts to avoid giving unfair advantage to either station. Now, the 'Straight course' is described as being 'about one mile 550 yards' in length.

Henley is the most prestigious event in the rowing calendar and it has always been the desire of international oarsmen to win there. Imitation is said to be the greatest form of flattery, and there are now several 'Henley Regattas' held world-wide in countries such as America, Canada and Australia.

The original Henley Regatta was designed 'for the amusement and gratification of the neighbourhood'. The present day Henley Royal Regatta has been described as 'The Best Organized Picnic in Europe' but to the serious oarsman the chance to compete there is all.

In 1984 the number of Regatta entries exceeded 300 for the first time, and so in 1986, to cope with this increase, the stewards extended the event to five days. The event is always held to include the first weekend in July. Racing commences on the preceding Wednesday and finishes on the Sunday afternoon. Before the Regatta commences the swans are carefully collected and removed from the course, as it would not be appropriate for swans, which are after all royal property, to come to any harm during the Royal Regatta.

Rowing became an Olympic sport in 1900, the Olympic regatta being held in Henley for the Games of 1908 and 1948. The 1908 Olympic Games were originally given to Rome but two years prior, in 1906, Vesuvius erupted and caused many deaths as well as ruin to the Italian economy thus causing Italy's withdrawal as the venue. The British Olympic Association was asked to step in and the rowing events took place at Henley, the home of the famous regatta. Rowing was one of twenty-one sports represented at the Games, and for the first time gold medals were given to the winners. Olympic rowing in this year was notable for a tremendous race in the eights in which Leander, representing Great Britain, just beat the formidable Belgian crew. And in the single sculls final, forty-year-old Harry Blackstaffe was twice the age of his opponent, McCulloch, yet he was able to finish more strongly and win by one-and-a-quarter lengths.

In 1948 the International Olympic Committee was anxious to stage the Games as soon as the Second World War was over, and the Games were awarded to London. The British public were still on rationing, and there was a shortage of materials and supplies, but the Olympic spirit survived the war. The rowing and canoeing events were again held outside London on the Henley course and Great Britain took two gold medals. Herbert Bushnell and Richard Burnell won the double sculls, and John Wilson and Stanley Laurie 'The Desert Rats', back in the country after ten years in the Colonial Service in the Sudan, won the coxless pairs.

It is interesting to note how the rules of racing have changed since the early 1900s for if London were to host the Olympic Games again, the Henley course would not be considered for the Olympic regatta as international racing now requires *still* water.

In his 1897 book *Rowing* R. C. Lehmann said:

> Consider for a moment the modern racing ship. It is a frail, elongated, graceful piece of cabinet work, held together by thin stays, small bolts and copper nails and separates you from the water in which it floats by an eighth of an inch of Mexican Cedar. Most builders will turn you out a sculling boat for from £12–£15, a pair from about £20, a four for £33 and an eight for £55.

Today's cost for a single scull is in the region of £2,000 and an eight would be around £10,000.

The early races were rowed in boats similar to the barges of the previous century. These were wide, heavy, planked craft with fixed seats and their oarlocks on the gunwales. In 1846, Oxford developed the outrigger, allowing their crew to mount their oarlocks outboard of the gunwale. This permitted a narrower, lighter hull, while still achieving the same leverage. In 1870 Yale oarsmen appeared with greased leather pants. With their feet locked in place, they slid back and forth on smooth wooden planks, incorporating the power of their legs into the rowing stroke. It was only a year later that the rolling (now called 'sliding') seat was invented. The racing shell was now complete – a narrow, easily driven hull, wide outriggers to spread the oarlocks, foot blocks to anchor the feet and a sliding seat to allow every muscle in the body to be used to drive the oars through the water. Since then, the design of the basic racing shell has only been refined in construction. The main changes have been in the use of new materials and construction techniques. In the last century the racing shell has become lighter, stiffer, narrower and longer, all in the search for speed.

The search for increasing speed using modern technology in the design and construction of racing shells continues. The cost of research and development is formidable, and beyond the economy of some of the countries that participate at the World Rowing Championships. For this reason FISA, the International Rowing Federation examines closely any changes in boat design, banning those which through cost may introduce an element of unfairness. Control over boat design has introduced some standardization to racing boats.

With the standardization of equipment, rowing is becoming a sport in which races are man against man. More time is devoted to training; to developing good technique. Thus success is dependent on ability, not on superior equipment.

2

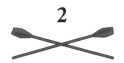

BOATBUILDING AND OAR
CONSTRUCTION

Boat building

There are basically two types of materials from which
rowing boats are constructed. There is the traditional
wooden craft and the more up-to-date composite plastic
boat. Both have their place in the rowing world, both have their
advantages and disadvantages and all rowers have their own
personal preferences.

This chapter gives an insight into the construction of the
boats and the possibility of repair.

Wooden boat construction

The making of a wooden boat is still very much an art, the
quality of the boat that is made being determined by the men
who put it together.

A wooden boat is assembled piece by piece on a frame that
predetermines the final shape. First the skeleton is constructed
and then the flesh of the boat is added. The boat is assembled
upside-down until the point when the canvasses are to be
attached, then it is turned the right way up and finished off.

The first step in constructing a wooden boat is to lay out the
stocks on a long wooden bench called the plate. The stocks are
wooden supports around which the frame of the boat is shaped.
The stocks are placed crossways on the bench and levelled up
using wedges if necessary. Levelling is done each time the
stocks are used as wood is a living substance and settles with
heat.

The frame or inwale of the boat is made from the best North American spruce. Once the frame has been laid down, the cross bracings made of Brazilian cedar are glued and screwed into position. The cross bracings take the brunt of the strain of the rowing stroke that is exerted on the boat. Following this the seat beams on which the seat is sited are glued and the uprights and the keel are fitted. The keel is lined up by eye between two upright posts at each end of the plate and a line is drawn down the centre of the plate to help site the keel. The internal skeleton is completed by fitting the shoulders.

The saxboards are attached before the skin is applied. The saxboard is a piece of mahogany-faced plywood that has been made lighter by cutting holes along its length. It is fastened to the shoulders and inwales of the boat to provide stiffness to the upper edge of the skin.

The exposed surfaces of the internal skeleton are varnished at this stage when easy access is possible.

Moulding of the skin begins at the same time as the construction of the skeleton of the boat. The inner skin is one long piece of plywood whereas the outer skin is moulded in quarters. The skins are usually made from mahogany plywood faced with cedar, but more recently a white wood called Koto has been used in place of the mahogany.

The mould over which the plywood is eased into the shape of the boat is constructed in a similar manner to the boat itself. The mould is made from half-inch timbers so that it can withstand the colossal pressures used to shape the skin without distortion. It takes two men a month to make a mould for an eight, and two weeks to make a mould for a four. The inner skin is laid over the mould, flexed into position and then a second layer of plywood is glued to it. The two layers are held together under high pressure until the glue has dried. Glueing, as a rule, is done at 6 a.m. In the summer the glue will be dry by 10 a.m., but in the winter, even with the aid of a hot-air blower, it will not be dry until about 3 p.m. The whole process is repeated until the ply of the skin has been formed.

As the skin is applied to the frame of the boat formers are used inside the boat hull to obtain trueness of shape.

The skin is glued to the saxboard and pinned to the keel. An effort is being made to eliminate the use of pins and to do this the glue join of the keel may have to be changed back to the older T-shape joint.

Stretching the skin over a male mould.

Applying the skin is a fairly easy task and takes three men only half an hour to do.

The stern and bow posts are laminated with strips of ash to provide a stronger resistance to the knocks which the ends of the boat are inevitably subject to.

The boat is turned the right way up for the canvasses to be fitted. The canvas can be hard or soft, a hard canvas is preferable as it adds strength to the construction of the boat. Before the canvas is attached the inside of the hull is varnished – four coats of varnish are used to ensure the boat is watertight.

The next stage is essentially cosmetic and involves the

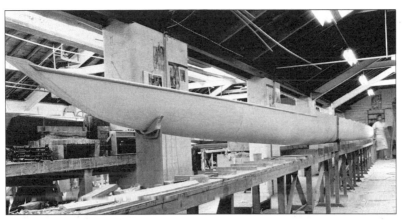

After construction, the boat is turned upright for finishing. Note the stocks laid out on the plate.

Preparing a smooth finish for varnishing.

chipping out of any excess glue. This can be very time-consuming but gives a better finished product. A mahogany strip is ironed on to the endgrain of the top edge of the saxboard to protect against trailer damage during transit. Damage to the endgrain would allow water to seep into the substance of the boat and may lead to rotting.

Finally the boat is cleaned out and varnished, by hand on the inner surface and by spraying the outer surface.

The fitting of riggers etc. is not really a job for the craftsmen who make the boat: their time is better spent starting the next piece of craftsmanship, for it takes twelve man-weeks to build a wooden eight that will have a lifespan of twenty years plus if it is well maintained. Maintenance of the boat varnish is needed to keep the boat watertight. A wooden boat should be revarnished at the end of its first year of life and then once every three to four years.

Repairing a wooden boat

Repairing a wooden boat requires the skills of carpentry. It is possible to patch a hole or reconstruct the end of a damaged boat but this should be done by the experienced boat builder only. For most clubs this means returning the boat to the manufacturer for repair.

The construction of a composite plastic boat

The construction of a plastic boat starts with the making of a female mould. This mould can be made by the boat builder, or bought from a company who specialize in making boat moulds. Essentially, when using a female mould you make a boat in reverse, lining the mould rather than working over the mould as in wooden boat construction.

The condition in which a boat builder keeps his moulds is very important to his business. After all, with a plastic boat the surface of the mould determines the surface of the finished product if no paint is to be applied. A good boat builder will ensure that his moulds are looked after and if necessary, regularly changed. The mould has to have a nice clean, smooth and shiny surface. Like baking a cake in a cake tin, you want to be able to turn it out in one piece when the time comes. To ensure that this happens a wax is used to line the mould just as you would grease the cake tin. There are many expensive waxes specifically available for this job but a basic traffic wax can be used, like the type you would use when polishing around the house. With this type of wax you also need to use a release agent – an alcohol-based solution which has a non-stick property.

When the mould is prepared, it is lined with a gell coat of epoxy resin. This is mixed from powdered epoxy to create a non-runny substance which can be rollered on to the inside of the mould, on top of the release agent. The gel is used to create a waterproof barrier between the cloth material that is to be used next and the water in which the boat will sit when in use. Some boat builders choose to use a coloured gel coat, which then becomes the final external colour of the finished product. At present the colour range of these gels is rather limited and some of the colours are not totally colourfast. There have been a few problems with colour change and the development of a 'chalky substance' on exposure to ultraviolet sunlight. New products are constantly being developed and it should not be long before these problems are overcome.

When the gel is applied, the experienced boat builder will ensure that it goes on at the correct thickness. Too thick and it will be adding unnecessary weight and wasting material; too thin an application and 'pinholes' will appear on the finished shell surface, making it difficult to achieve a smooth finish without going through the time-wasting process of filling and sanding before the paint can be applied.

In the early days of plastic boat building, the original *carbocraft* were black. As dark colours attract and retain heat, these boats would often go soft in the sun due to the resin only being able to withstand temperatures of 70–80°C. Today, the modern resins used can withstand temperatures of up to 150°C. Recently in the States a boathouse burnt down, unbelievably, leaving most of the boats almost intact on their racks.

Next the skins are laid up. In a top racing boat, a material called 'Kevlar' is used. Kevlar is a very tough material which is very difficult to break. It is eight times stronger than steel which means for the boat builder, who is always looking for weight saving ideas, that Kevlar is an ideal material because for eight times less weight it will give the same strength to the shell as would steel. The only drawback to using Kevlar is that it doesn't stick very well to other materials and demonstrates what is called 'interlaminate shear'. If a boat made from Kevlar were damaged, you would be able to peel the Kevlar off the honeycomb structure without too much trouble. Despite this, it is still a very useful material that will not easily break or puncture. It comes on a roll, like cloth, and looks very much like shirt material. A width of 92 centimetres is used for the purpose of boat construction. There are many different weaves available but a plain weave is generally used in boat construction, because the fibres run straight down and straight across giving strength to the construction along the line of the fibres. The first layer of plain-weave cloth is laid in one continuous sheet, lengthwise, from one end of the boat to the other, giving strength to the boat, longitudinally and horizontally. Some boat builders choose to lay down their cloth at 45 degrees on the outer skin, this means that there is less stiffness down and across the boat but more torsional stiffness i.e. greater twisting stiffness.

Before the Kevlar cloth is laid into the mould, it is laid out on a bench and to ensure even distribution, the resin is then applied with a roller. This takes place approximately four hours after the gel coat has been applied, when the gel has reached a tacky consistency.

The next process is to apply carbon to the areas that will have the most bending stresses applied to them when the boat is being rowed. Carbon is a stiff material that gives added strength to the weakest areas of the boat such as down the keel, along the saxboards and around the bulkheads. One of the biggest areas of weakness in the boat are the bulkheads, which are made vulnerable by the up-and-down movement of the riggers. The bulkheads should be made to have as little movement in them as possible for a one millimetre movement in the bulkhead will result in as much as 5–6 centimetre movement at the end of the rigger.

Application of a special material called 'over-expanded honeycomb' is next. This is a good name for the material as it explains very well how it is made. A standard sheet of honeycomb material is put into a machine which then stretches the hexagonal honeycomb cells into oblong shapes. This new cell shape is what enables the material to bend round curves.

On to this honeycomb structure a mixture of glass and carbon is applied to the top performance shells, or just glass for the more standard boats.

After this the top edge of the skin is put on which is called the pultrusion. The process begins with the application of a vacuum bag: a plasticine-like substance is put all the way round the mould and a plastic sheet is laid down on to it. This makes the mould airtight. A vacuum pump is then attached to suck out all the air until a pressure of 30 lb per square inch is attained (approx. 13.6 kg per 25.4 mm). This pressure will hold everything in the correct place whilst the resin is drying. The drying process can take up to twelve hours depending on the weather and is usually left to cure overnight. The resin is heat sensitive and although in the summer months it is rock hard in the morning, during the cold winter months the resin could still be jelly-like in the morning. Heat can be used to speed up this process.

When the resin has cured completely, the vacuum bag can be taken off and the whole process started again, this time to form the inner skin. This should mirror the outer skin exactly, the Kevlar and the carbon applied to the same place and in the same quantities. The secret to making a good sandwich structure is to balance the inner skin with the outer skin, this will give maximum performance from the material. A sandwich structure increases the strength of a material by fifteen to twenty times that of a single skin and the stiffness of the material is increased even more. A product made from a sandwich structure will always be lighter, stiffer and stronger than a single-skin material.

Prior to releasing the boat from the mould, all the excess material above the top of the mould is trimmed off. The boat is then released and the hull is checked to ensure that there are no imperfections. It is then placed back in the mould ready for the bulkheads to be attached. The bulkheads are cut out of plywood and put into moulds, then about sixteen layers of carbon are added to them. These are attached to the boat using carbon cloth. Next to go into the boat is the monocoque; this is the decking on which the internal boat fittings sit. The monocoque is made out of a balanced carbon applied to both sides of honeycomb. Instead of using the vacuum method, monocoque is made and put under a press which exerts several tons of pressure on it whilst curing. The monocoque is then taped into the side of the boat using thin carbon cloth. All the joins in the monocoques are clothed over, ensuring that the torsional stiffness is kept at a maximum. After the bulkheads and monocoques are fixed, the rudder tube is inserted. This is done by blocking off the stern with a piece of honeycomb material and using resin to fill the space around the tube to hold it firmly in place.

The boat goes into the finishing shop where the canvasses are attached. The canvasses are made in a semi-circular mould, generally using honeycomb and glass material. In the top-class boats, honeycomb and carbon are used, mainly as a weight-saving exercise but also to increase the longitudinal stiffness of the boat. Some boat builders will put the canvasses on whilst the boat is still in the mould but this can be time-consuming.

When the boat comes out of the mould, two blocks of wood are attached to the hull where the fin is to be placed. The boat is turned over, the skin is cut out above these blocks and the fin is sunk into the hull and secured by being screwed into the wooden blocks. Another much more practical way of attaching the fin is to use a finbox. This is a box containing a slot which is moulded into the boat during the early stages of construction. The fin is slotted into the box and held in place by a small screw. This has the advantage of enabling a quick change of fin at any time if necessary due to damage or a change in course conditions. A deep fin is more advantageous for a straight course and a shallow one for a twisty course. With a finbox construction, this change could be done in a matter of minutes. Before fitting out the interior of the boat the hull is painted.

The painting is done in two stages. The hull is given a good rub down and is checked out so that any blemishes that might be there from the mould can be dealt with and one spray coat of paint is given. When dry, this coat will clearly show up any surface defects which can then be dealt with. The boat is given a final rub down and the final coats of paint applied. When completely dry the boat is polished.

Finally the fittings are attached, with holes drilled in the bulkheads for the attachment of the riggers.

The whole process from start to finish takes a minimum of two weeks, one week in the mould and one week on finishing. On average a single scull will take one man four days to build; a pair will take one man five days; and a four will take two men five days.

To repair a plastic boat

The damaged spot is cut clean and the inner skin is stripped, taking the honeycomb back about 6 or 7 inches from the outer skin. The boat is then placed back in a mould and a gel coat is applied to the hole. The first skins are then laid up to the honeycomb over the existing skin and new honeycomb is laid up to the existing honeycomb, just in the same way as when the original boat was constructed. This area of the boat will now be much stronger than before. The surface is then smoothed over, a filler being used around the edges if necessary and resprayed. If done properly, a repair is almost undetectable to the untrained eye, but a repair can affect the way a boat behaves. A repair to an eight probably wouldn't make much difference, but to a single scull a repair could make a noticeable difference to the way the boat bends as one area of the boat is now stiffer than the rest.

Boat clubs can do their own minor repairs. If there is a hole in a boat which has only damaged the outer skin, some car-body filler can be used to fill the hole as there is still an inner skin. If the hole has gone completely through both skins then some glass cloth must be used beneath the car-body filler. These elastic fillers are useful as they are able to stretch when the boat bends and there shouldn't be a problem with cracking. A reasonably experienced DIY enthusiast could easily effect a minor repair to a plastic boat but a boat that is badly damaged will require expert attention and it is best to return it to the manufacturers.

Oars and sculls

As with boats, there are also two basic materials used in the construction of oars and sculls. These are wood and carbon fibre. Whichever type of blade you choose, both should be treated with respect and care should be taken during their use and transportation. Padded covers can be used to protect your blades from chipping and splintering whilst in transit. The maintenance of your blades is important. You can increase the life-span of wooden blades with regular varnishing and of both wooden and carbon blades by lubricating the sleeves, although with the modern plastic sleeve only the slightest application of silicone is necessary. Never lay your oars on a flat surface; always prop them up to prevent damage. The most important consideration when buying new blades is to make sure they are well built and, in the case of a pair of sculls, matched in weight.

Wooden oar construction

The skills of the dying art of wooden oar making are the same today as they were 100 years ago, with craftsmen doing most of the work by hand.

The timber used to construct the wooden oar or scull is a softwood pine called Sitka spruce. This spruce comes from the west coast of the United States and Canada, the best quality coming from Alaska. Trees from the northern hemisphere have a slower and more regular growth pattern and therefore produce higher quality close-grain timber which is suited to the construction of oars.

The Sitka spruce arrives at the oar manufacturers by the lorry load, usually in five or six standards at a time. A standard is a timber merchant's measurement for a volume of wood.

Out of one standard of timber, 10–15 per cent is unusable. It will not be the required quality for the construction of oars as it may have too many knots and an irregular grain; instead it is utilized for garden posts etc.

If the correct timber is not chosen at this stage the finished oar may have problems with twisting, so careful selection is important and can be done with ease by an oarmaker who has an experienced eye.

Of the remaining 85 per cent of timber, 20 per cent will be of medium quality and only suitable for the cheeks and blocking which will go to shape part of the blade. The final 60–65 per cent will be used to manufacture the shaft or the loom of the oar. The quality of the wood is extremely important, as this part of the oar will take the main load of the stroke and must bend absolutely true.

This selected wood is cut into long fine strips. The strips are paired up and crossbred so that each oar shaft is laminated from four different pieces of wood, guaranteeing a good average for stiffness and weight ratio. If one oar was made from one piece of wood only there would be greater chance of a weight difference in a set of oars, this would lead to an unbalanced boat when they were used by a crew.

The central core of the shaft is made first. It is left hollow to save weight. A sandwich of spruce strips is laminated to the central core giving a boxed effect to the shaft and producing a boxed loom. The loom is then passed through a machine called a thicknesser, which cuts it into an even square shape. Along one side of this is laminated a hardwood strip which adds stiffness to the shaft and also helps it to withstand the compression applied to the loom when it comes under load as the blade is pulled through the water.

The small pieces of wood that will form the cheeks of the blade are added, together with a hardwood strip to the tip of the blade. The tip acts as a ply and helps the blade to withstand wear and tear. In the old days a copper strip was used instead of hardwood and this was tacked into place but unfortunately the tacks allowed water to penetrate the wood, resulting in a weak point.

From this roughly shaped oar blade a template is used to cut the chosen blade shape. There have been hundreds of different blade shapes made over the years but two main types are used today: the needle or pencil blade (32 inches long/approx. 81 cm) which is used mainly for coastal rowing and the Macon or shovel blade (23½ inches long/approx. 60 cm). The Macon blade, which is more squashed and blown out than the needle, was developed by the Germans for use in the 1958 European Championships held that year in Macon, France, hence the name. Until recently, this was considered the most reliable shape for racing blades.

Wooden blades in block form prior to shaping.

The rough looking oar is then shelved and racked for a period of time to allow development of any distortion that might take place. As it is a living material, tension is released when wood is cut and this time on the shelf allows the newly laminated oar to settle before being finally cut to size and finished.

The oars are taken from the rack and finished to the customer's requirements. They are planed and sanded to shape using the hand tools of the trade. The drawknife, a two-handled blade is used to hack off excess wood but can also be used to carve delicate parts of the oar. Wood-smoothing planes are used to carve the face of the blade and shape the back of the neck. Once the loom is shaved by hand to a nominal size, it is finished off by using a router to give it a perfect cylindrical shape.

Using a drawknife to hack off excess wood.

Using a wood-smoothing plane to carve the face of the blade.

The optimum size for a Macon oar is 12 feet 8 inches (approx. 3.86 m). This size is recognized as giving maximum boat speed and power output.

Needle oars are only 12 feet long (approx 3.66 m); the blade is longer than the Macon but the overall length is less. A standard wooden oar will weigh 9–9½ lbs/4–4.3 kg and costs about £140. A lightweight wooden oar will weigh approximately 8 lbs 12 oz/3.97 kg.

Women's crews often use a slightly smaller oar, a couple of inches shorter in length, which enables them to achieve the same rhythm and momentum as a heavy-weight men's crew without interfering with their technique.

Wooden sculls

A pair of wooden sculls is a true pair, they are actually twins. They are made from three different pieces of spruce which are in turn split in half, one half of each piece going to make each scull. A pair of sculls is always made for the individual sculler who will use them. Height, strength and body weight will be taken into account before their manufacture. An individual scull will weigh from 4 lbs 8 oz to 4 lbs 12 oz (2–2.15 kg). If they are made much lighter they tend to be a little too flexible. A pair of racing sculls will cost around £220.

Construction of composite plastic oars

The development of composite plastic oars and sculls was an inevitable progression following the successful introduction of plastic boats.

Plastic oars require much less maintenance than wooden oars, and through their lighter weight and lighter rigidity give minimal energy loss during the stroke.

Composite plastic blades are made in the component parts from a mixture of graphite and fibreglass, assembled and glued. The whole process taking five days from the receipt of an order to the finished product.

When an order is placed the shaft is moulded to the required stiffness. Stiffness is measured in terms of the deflection in the oar when a 10 kg weight is hung from the neck as illustrated in Fig. 2:1.

The spoon of the blade is moulded into contour and then cut to shape by computerized equipment.

The hollow tubular shaft and spoon are bonded together, and the wooden handle inserted and glued in position. The length of the blade is determined by its constituent parts.

The sleeve of the loom is located and bonded and the pitch is set. The pitch on the blade is usually zero or two degrees positive pitch, however any amount of pitch can be incorporated if ordered.

On completion of assembly each blade is subject to a final inspection and a flexion test.

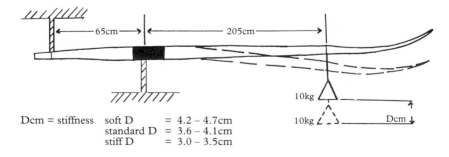

Dcm = stiffness   soft D   = 4.2 – 4.7cm
                   standard D = 3.6 – 4.1cm
                   stiff D   = 3.0 – 3.5cm

Fig. 2:1. Testing the stiffness of a rowing oar. A similar test is used for sculls.

3

STARTING OUT

Rowing in the 1990s is still a sport that very few schools can offer as part of their physical education curriculum. Consequently, it is not a sport you are forced to have a go at, but one that you *choose* to try, perhaps tempted by watching crews on the river or by the glamour of television coverage of races such as the annual Oxford/Cambridge University Boat Race from Putney to Mortlake in London. Once smitten it is a very addictive sport, within a short space of time you will find yourself wanting to train more and more, for ever chasing the glory of victory!

Rowing is a sport that you can learn at virtually any age, able bodied or disabled, the only prerequisite is that you can swim 50 metres fully clothed. When you enrol with a rowing club they will require evidence that you can swim, be this a certificate of competence or a test conducted by an official of the club at a nearby pool. Having decided you would like to learn to row, make contact with the captain of your nearest rowing club. If you do not know where the nearest club is, the Amateur Rowing Association, whose address and telephone number can be found in the appendix of this book, will help you to locate it.

Over the past five years the number of people taking up rowing has increased rapidly, most clubs have been inundated with requests from beginners to learn – do not be put off if you are told that you will have to be placed on a waiting list until a place in a beginners' class becomes available.

As a beginner you will learn the basics of rowing technique in a small group of two or three beginners and a coach. Once

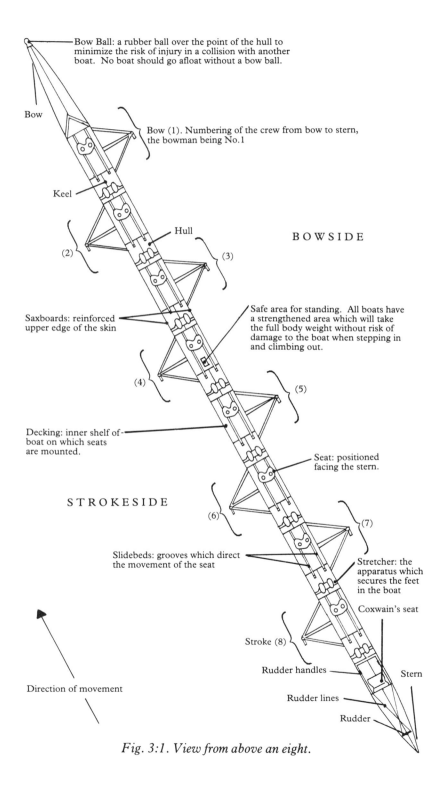

Bow Ball: a rubber ball over the point of the hull to minimize the risk of injury in a collision with another boat. No boat should go afloat without a bow ball.

Bow

Bow (1). Numbering of the crew from bow to stern, the bowman being No.1

Keel

Hull

BOWSIDE

(2)

(3)

Safe area for standing. All boats have a strengthened area which will take the full body weight without risk of damage to the boat when stepping in and climbing out.

Saxboards: reinforced upper edge of the skin

(4)

(5)

Decking: inner shelf of boat on which seats are mounted.

Seat: positioned facing the stern.

STROKESIDE

(6)

(7)

Slidebeds: grooves which direct the movement of the seat

Stretcher: the apparatus which secures the feet in the boat

Coxwain's seat

Stroke (8)

Rudder handles

Stern

Direction of movement

Rudder lines

Rudder

Fig. 3:1. View from above an eight.

beginners start to develop confidence in a boat and have grasped the basic stroke, several groups of beginners will be amalgamated to form a novice group. A novice in rowing is someone who has never won a race at a regatta. The aim of the novice group is to prepare a crew to race.

The cost of taking up rowing as a sport is not prohibitive. There is, of course, a subscription fee to become a member of the rowing club which entitles you to the use of equipment on and off the water (i.e. boats and gym equipment). The subscription fee is set by the individual rowing club and is determined by the cost of running the club and purchasing and maintaining the equipment. There is no need to purchase trendy kit in which to learn to row, any loose-fitting trousers that allow you to touch your toes whilst sitting are suitable, worn with a T-shirt or sweatshirt – depending on the weather – and a pair of training shoes. In cold weather it is always better to wear several layers of clothes rather than a single thick layer as, inevitably, the body will warm up whatever the weather once exercise has started, and you will find yourself wanting to take off clothing to cool down.

At first learning to row will be like learning a new language. There is a rowing vocabulary which you need to become familiar with, Figs 3:1, 3:2 & 3:3 should serve as an illustrated dictionary.

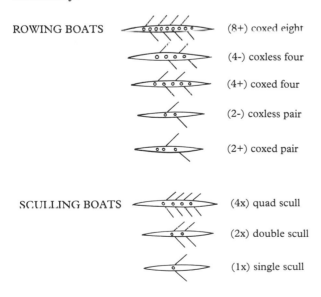

ROWING BOATS   (8+) coxed eight

(4-) coxless four

(4+) coxed four

(2-) coxless pair

(2+) coxed pair

SCULLING BOATS   (4x) quad scull

(2x) double scull

(1x) single scull

Fig. 3:2. Boat categories.

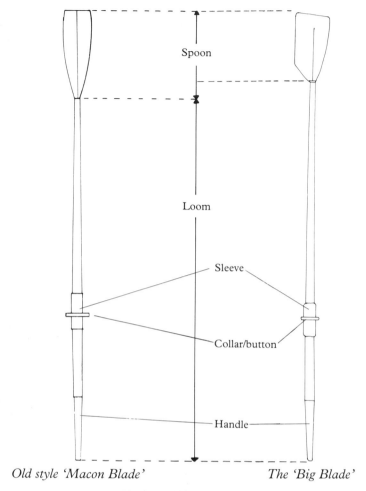

Old style 'Macon Blade'   The 'Big Blade'

Fig. 3:3. The rowing blades.

Handling and carrying a boat

When you first begin to row, more experienced oarsmen/
women will remove the boat from the rack and place it on the
trestles, but you will be expected to help carry the boat to the
water. To do this, with the boat on trestles the right way up,
stand *beside* your rigger. In preparation for lifting place one
hand over the edge of the saxboard and the other on a secure
part of the decking – this is particularly important when lifting
a wooden boat in which some of the internal structure is very
vulnerable to breakage.

The whole crew, on the coxswain's command, lifts the boat
off the trestles. The coxswain will then ask the crew to 'roll the

boat,' and calls for the direction in which the boat needs to roll. For example, 'Bowside riggers up,' or 'Strokeside riggers up'. Alternatively the coxswain may call, 'Towards the boathouse,' or 'Away from the boathouse'. The crew should respond by raising the riggers on one side of the boat, dropping the riggers on the other and gently rolling the boat over until it is upside-down.

When the boat is upside-down hook the fingers of both hands under the edge of the saxboards to support it.

NB. By standing beside your rigger when the boat is the right way up on trestles, you will be standing opposite your rigger when the boat has been rolled upside-down.

To carry the boat to the landing-stage for boating, turn to face the direction in which you are to walk. The coxswain walks at the bows of the boat guiding its passage and ensuring the clearance

To carry the boat, stand opposite the position you will be rowing and hook your fingers under the edge of the saxboards. The cox guides the boat.

of obstacles in front. The crew should check the clearance of obstacles at the other end of the boat.

If it becomes necessary to hold the boat for any length of time, either send the coxswain for the trestles so that the boat can be supported or turn to face away from the boat. With your back to the hull of the boat it is easier to support its weight. Keep your back straight, knees slightly bent.

With more experience the boat can be carried on shoulders rather than at arms' length. To do this, stand opposite your rigger with the boat upside-down and lift the boat up so that the saxboards rest on the shoulders of the crew. This method is inappropriate when the crew are of vastly differing heights and the taller people end up taking all the weight.

Placing a boat on the water

Always approach the landing-stage with the bows of the boat pointing upstream (i.e. against the flow of the water). This is important for the safety of the crew for when the boat leaves the landing-stage the bows will be drawn out by the flow of the

Whilst strokeside are bracing the boat, holding a secure part of the decking, bowside move under the boat.

With everybody on the same side of the boat, feel for the edge of the landing-stage with your foot. Hold the boat securely inside with one hand, and with your other hand hold the side of the boat to ensure it doesn't hit the landing-stage as it is lowered into the water.

river, boating against the flow of the river the crew and cox have the necessary control to manoeuvre the boat safely.

Standing on the landing-stage with the bows pointing upstream, the following drill should be carried out, when the command is given by the coxswain:

1. Roll the boat over the right way up.
2. The crew nearest the edge of the landing-stage move under the boat so that all the crew are standing on the same side of the boat.
3. Slowly edge forward feeling for the edge of the landing-stage with a foot.
4. Placing one hand on the hull of the boat, gently lower the boat into the water taking care not to hit the boat on the landing-stage.
5. When lowering the boat make sure that your knees are bent and your back is held as upright as possible.
6. The coxswain holds the boat beside the landing-stage, and the crew fetch their blades.

With more experience a crew can roll the boat and lower it on to the water in one motion. The coxswain will call, 'Throwing the boat, one, two, three, lift.' The boat is lifted from the trestles to above the heads of the crew, maintaining their grip on the boat the crew move underneath the boat and then slowly lower it to waist height, and on down to the water.

Getting into a rowing boat

For ease of explanation consider the boat to be resting on the water beside the landing-stage with the strokeside riggers lying over the edge of the landing-stage (Fig. 3:4).

The strokeside oarsmen – nos. 8, 6, 4, and 2 in an eight – take their oars and place them in the swivels of their riggers. They then hold their riggers firm on to the landing-stage whilst bowside get into the boat. It is important that the riggers are held firm to prevent the boat rolling over when the bowside oarsmen climb into boat.

The bowside oarsmen – nos. 7, 5, 3 and 1 – in an eight lay their oars across the boat at their respective seat positions and then:

1. The coxswain calls, 'Bowside, hands across, one foot in, together now.'

2. On hearing the command bowside place one hand on each saxboard, locate their left feet onto the safe area of the decking in front of the seat and step into the boat.

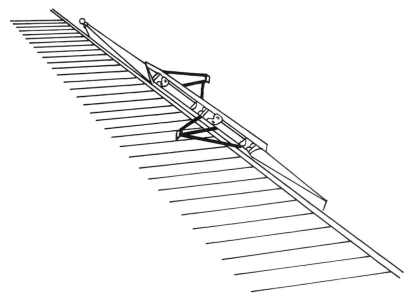

Fig. 3:4. The text assumes a boat resting beside the landing-stage with the strokeside riggers overlapping the edge of the landing-stage.

3. The right foot is then lifted from the landing-stage and placed onto the shoe of the footplate as the oarsman sits down.

4. The oars are placed into the swivels and the gates securely fastened.

Once bowside are in the boat and the gates fastened, the cox in a similar way calls for strokeside to get into the boat. Strokeside follow the same steps 1–4 as bowside.

The crew remove their training shoes, store them in the hull of the boat and fasten their feet into the shoes of the footplates.

With the guidance of the coach the stretcher at each position is moved so that the arc of the blade in the water is correct for each individual and matches that of the other crew members on the same side of the boat (*see* Chapter 4: Rigging, for more detail).

The coxswain calls for the crew to, 'Number off from the bows when ready,' and as each member of the crew is ready with feet secure, blade secure and stretcher adjusted he numbers off. When the whole crew has numbered off the coxswain climbs into his seat.

Again on the coxswain's command, the crew push away from the landing-stage with their hands and then with the tips of the strokeside blades if necessary.

NB. If when the bows are pointing upstream the boat is resting on the landing-stage with the bowside riggers over the edge of the stage, strokeside will be the first to get in followed by bowside.

The correct way to hold the oar

With the oar held squared, i.e. when the spoon is held at right angles to the waterline, the outside hand (the hand furthest away from the rigger) holds the oar at the end of the handle with the fingers rolled over the top and the thumb resting underneath. Using the same grip, the inside hand (the hand nearest the rigger) should be placed on the oar handle with a gap of approximately 10 cm between the hands. The distance between the hands should be a minimum of two hand widths, and a maximum of shoulder width. The knuckles are held in a straight line with the wrist and forearm (Fig. 3:5).

When learning to row you will start to row with the blade squared all the time; only with more experience will turning the oar during the stroke be introduced.

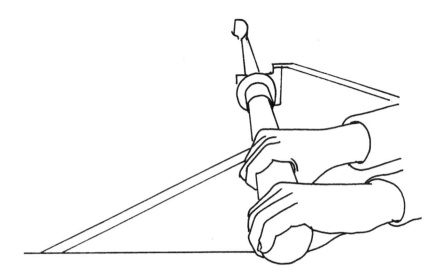

Fig. 3:5. The correct grip of the oar handle when the blade is squared.

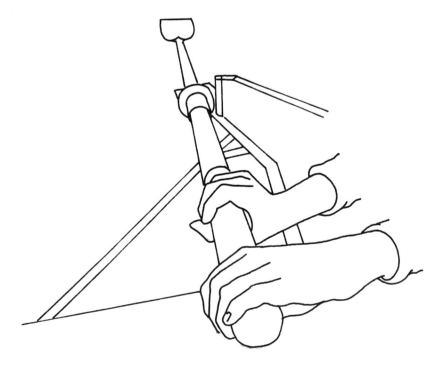

Fig. 3:6. The inside hand rotating the oar on to the feathered position with the outside wrist remaining flat.

Turning the oar on to the feather

Feathering is the term used for turning the oar from the squared position, when the spoon is at right angles to the waterline, to the feathered position when the spoon is parallel to the waterline (Fig. 3:6).

There are three reasons for turning the blade to the feather during the recovery part of the stroke cycle:
1. To give the blade more clearance from the water.
2. To give better balance control.
3. To cause less wind resistance.

Once the blade has been released from the water at the finish of the stroke, the oar is turned from the squared position to the feathered position by dropping the wrist of the inside hand, allowing the oar handle to rotate within the outside hand. As the blade begins to travel forward on the recovery, the inside hand holds the blade more in the fingers, allowing the wrist to rise, thereby providing additional clearance between the oar handle and the thighs. Once the hands have cleared the knees, and the seat is beginning to slide forward, the inside hand turns the oar back to the squared position allowing the oar handle to rotate again within the outside hand. This process is repeated every stroke.

NB. The *inside* hand turns the blade to the squared position and returns it to the feathered position.

Getting out of the rowing boat

At the end of the outing the boat is parked beside the landing-stage by the coxswain with the bows pointing upstream, as before, this is for safety.

The coxswain gets out of the boat first and holds the strokeside rigger firmly to the landing-stage so that the boat cannot drift. The coxswain then gives the command for the crew to disembark.

With the boat resting on the water beside the landing-stage and the strokeside riggers lying over the edge of the landing-stage, strokeside get out of the boat first and then hold the boat whilst bowside get out. The drill for getting out of the boat is as follows:
1. All the crew take their feet out of the shoes of the footplates, and replace their own training shoes.

2. The coxswain calls, 'Strokeside, hands across, one foot out, together. Go.'

3. On hearing the command, strokeside put their hands on the saxboards on either side of the boat and place the left foot on the footrest/safe area of the decking.

4. Putting the weight of the body through the left foot and drawing the body up with the arms it is possible to stand up in the boat on the left leg.

5. Swing the right foot out of the boat onto the landing-stage, and step out of the boat.

6. Strokeside, with their blades still secured in the gates, hold their riggers firmly to the landing-stage.

7. The coxswain calls, 'Bowside out.'

8. Bowside release their oars from the swivels, place them across the boat and close the gates without tightening the locking nuts.

9. Bowside climb out of the boat as described in 3 to 5.

Finally the cox holds the boat while the crew replace the oars on the oar rack.

The boat is lifted from the water using the reverse procedure for putting it on the water, and either placed on trestles or taken back into the boathouse and racked.

Removing and replacing a boat from a rack

In most boathouses there is limited space so the racks are very close together and it is very easy to damage another boat when removing or replacing a boat on a rack if good handling practice is not followed.

To remove a boat from its rack, all of the crew stand alongside the boat in the order that they will sit in the boat, next to or opposite their riggers. The boat is eased gently off the rack, lifting it rather than dragging it towards you. As the boat is moved off the rack half the crew remain in their standing positions and the other half slip under the boat to the other side. As the boat leaves the boathouse the crew are positioned half on either side of the boat opposite to their respective riggers to carry it to the water.

The most common cause of damage to other boats when removing or replacing a boat on its rack, is allowing the riggers of the boat being moved to drag on the hull of another boat.

Rowing boats are very heavy, so make sure that there are enough people moving the boat to cope with its weight. As the boat slides across the rack, it should be tilted slightly to give clearance from the riggers of the boat above and the boat below.

Reverse this process when replacing a boat on to its rack.

Handling and carrying a single sculling boat

One of the problems with carrying the single scull is the awkwardness of its shape, the boat is 9 metres in length and weighs approximately 14–20 kg. It is important to appreciate that the balance point of the single scull is close to the position of the mainstay of the rigger. To lift with ease always position yourself near to this balance point.

As a beginner it is advisable to have help carrying the boat. Position yourself at the beginning of the stern canvas of the boat so that you will take the vast majority of the weight, but are in front of the natural balance point of the boat, and allow someone to hold the end of the bow section for you. The boat may be the right way up, upside-down or on the half turn.

As the boat is taken from the rack, one side of the crew move underneath it, slightly lowering the riggers to ensure no damage to the boat from the riggers above.

The beginner sculler will need help to carry the boat: the helper supports the bow, whilst the sculler supports the boat at the beginning of the stern canvas.

NB. A single scull should *never* be carried with one person standing at the bows and a second person standing at the tip of the stern as this places too much strain through the central part of the boat. If a boat, particularly a wooden boat, is carried repeatedly in this manner it will eventually crack.

When carrying a single scull alone, ease the boat on and off its rack by holding the saxboards on either side of the boat at the balance point. Once the boat has been removed from the rack place it on the half turn with one arm slung around the hull, the seated area leaning against your shoulder. Place your other hand on the uppermost saxboard or rigger for added support. Remember when manoeuvring that there is as much boat behind you as there is in front of you.

The single scull may also be carried upside-down with the seat resting on top of your head, the hands being used to steady the boat by holding the saxboards on either side. A word of caution: carrying the boat by this method may be a problem in very windy conditions.

A sculler carrying the boat on his own should hold the boat at its balance point, with one arm cradled underneath and the other holding the bracing inside.

A more competent way of carrying a sculling boat with the balance point over your head, hands supporting the sides of the boat.

Getting into a sculling boat

Getting into a sculling boat is slightly different to getting into a rowing boat because the boat is much less stable and there are two blades to cope with.

The drill is as follows:

1. Always boat with the bows pointing upstream.
2. Before placing the boat in the water make sure your sculls are near to hand on the landing-stage.
3. Place the boat on the water.
4. Place the sculls into the swivels. With the boat facing upstream and the strokeside rigger on the landing-stage, place and secure the strokeside scull in the swivel. Next, place the bowside scull into its swivel by kneeling down on the landing-stage and leaning across to the bowside swivel. Close the gate and tighten the locking nut.
5. Slip off your shoes.
6. Place the ends of the sculling handles together and using your left hand grip them both together. Keeping the left-hand blade flat on the water and the right-hand blade flat on the landing-stage, place your left foot on the footrest of the decking.
7. Allow the left foot to take the weight of the body, lift and swing the right foot through to the footplate of the stretcher, at the same time lowering your body onto the seat.
8. Place both feet into the shoes of the foot stretcher.
9. Using your right arm push away from the landing-stage.
10. If you have not cleared the landing-stage, use your right-hand scull (strokeside scull) to push completely clear of the stage.
11. You are now ready to scull.

NB. For a beginner it is best for someone to help you get into the boat by holding the rigger firm, keeping the boat stable.

When more confident of getting into the boat it is not necessary to do up the gate on the bowside rigger until seated.

A very confident way of getting into the scull is to push away from the landing-stage with the right foot as the left foot is placed on the footrest of the decking, and then sit down.

Getting out of a sculling boat

Having docked at the landing-stage with the bows pointing upstream against the flow of the river the following drill should be followed:

1. Take your feet out of the shoes.
2. Push the handles forward and place the ends of the scull handles together. Using your left hand grip them both together, keeping the left-hand blade flat on the water and the right-hand blade flat on the landing-stage.
3. Place the left foot on the footrest of the decking, take your bodyweight on your left foot and stand up. Step out of the boat by placing your right foot onto the landing-stage.
4. Lean across to the bowside swivel, release the gate and take the scull out. Release and remove the strokeside scull. Close the gates on the swivels but do not tighten the locking nuts.
5. The boat is now ready to be lifted from the water and returned to its rack.

With practice and time, all these drills become automatic, just like riding a bike.

4

RIGGING

Rigging is an essential step in the preparation of a boat for any crew, indeed good rigging is critical to the development of correct technique; bad rigging encourages the ingraining of technical faults (*see* Chapter 6: Faults).

Rigging is the adjustment of the movable parts of a rigger and blade to achieve maximum mechanical efficiency for a given individual. In an ideal world each rigger would be set for the rower using it at any given time. However, as rigging is very time consuming it becomes impractical to adopt this approach in a busy club where the crew may change for each outing and a standard rigging has to be adopted for each boat.

Rigging charts have been drawn up which give the recommended rigging for heavyweight and lightweight men, heavyweight and lightweight women and in age categories for junior girls and boys for each boat class (*see* Appendix I).

Setting the rig is often looked upon as the coach's job but as an oarsman it is important to learn how to do basic rigging for yourself.

There are five adjustments to be considered: **spread/span, pitch** and **height** which relate to the rigger itself, **stretcher position** which relates to the position of the athlete's feet within the boat, and the **gearing of the blades.**

Spread/span

In a rowing boat the spread is the distance from the centre of the swivel to the centre of the boat, and in a sculling boat the span is the distance from the centre of the swivel of one rigger to the centre of the swivel of the opposite rigger (Figs 4:1 & 4:2). Alterations to the spread/span of a boat change the arc through which the blade travels during the stroke and provides a means for changing the gearing or workload on the athlete (Fig. 4:3). The gearing may also be adjusted on the blade itself (*see* p.57). **NB.** The spread of a rowing boat is often mistakenly referred to as the span, this is incorrect.

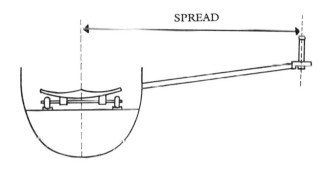

Fig. 4:1. Definition of spread.

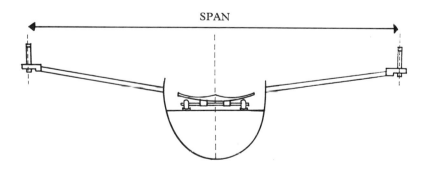

Fig. 4:2. Definition of span.

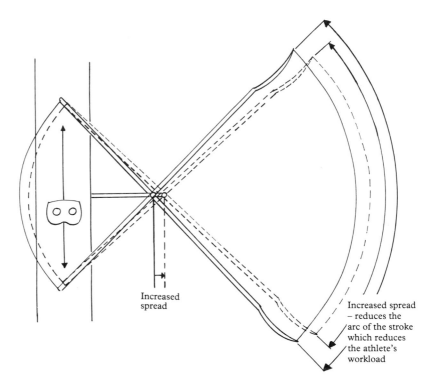

Increased
spread

Increased spread
– reduces the
arc of the stroke
which reduces
the athlete's
workload

Fig. 4:3. The effect of changing the spread of the rigger on the arc of the stroke.

Measuring and adjusting the spread of a rowing boat

Equipment required: tape measure, selection of spanners – usually 10 mm, 13 mm, and 22 mm.

Read from the rigging chart (Appendix I) the recommended spread for the particular boat class being adjusted; then measure the spread to which the rigger has previously been set.

To do this, using Fig. 4:4 as a guide, measure the distance between the saxboards across the boat in line with the pin from A to B. Divide this measurement by two to determine the distance from the saxboard to the centre line (C) of the boat. Holding the tape at measurement C, place it on the edge of the saxboard nearest to the rigger B. Extend the tape in a straight line at right angles to the boat past the pin from B to D. Read off the spread by measuring to the centre of the bottom of the pin E.

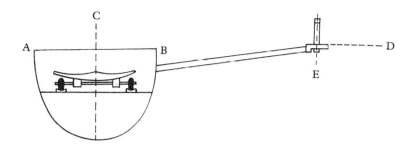

Fig. 4:4. Measuring the spread of a rowing boat.

If the spread needs to be adjusted, i.e. if the recommended spread and that just measured differ, first loosen the backstay of the rigger by undoing the top nut of the rigger. Loosen the securing nuts of the pin, and move the pin in or out to the correct spread as appropriate. Once the spread has been adjusted, reattach the backstay making sure to lengthen/shorten it as appropriate. (The exact method of changing the spread may vary depending on the type of rigger.)

NB. Each rigger throughout the boat needs to have its spread checked to allow for the taper of the boat. It is no good measuring one rigger and adjusting all the riggers on the boat by the same distance.

Measuring and adjusting the span of a sculling boat

Equipment required: tape measure, selection of spanners – usually 10 mm, 13 mm, and 17 mm.

Read from the rigging chart (Appendix I) the recommended span for the class of sculling boat to be adjusted, then measure the span to which the boat has previously been set.

To do this, using Fig. 4:5 as a guide, first check that the gates have been set equidistant from the centre line of the boat by measuring the distance between the saxboards across the boat in line with the pin from A to B. Divide this measurement by two

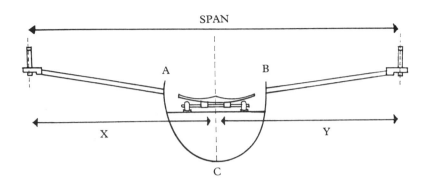

Fig. 4:5. Measuring the span of a sculling boat.

to give the distance from the saxboard to the centre line (C) of the boat. Measure from the centre line to the centre of the bottom of the pin of each rigger. This measurement should be the same for both the bowside and strokeside sculling riggers i.e. x should equal y. If it is not, adjust them until they are equal.

Then measure from the centre of the pin of the gate of one rigger to the centre of the pin of the opposite rigger and adjust if necessary to the recommended span, in a similar way to that used when adjusting a rowing rigger.

The pitch

The pitch is defined as the angulation of the face of the spoon from the vertical when the button is held tight against the swivel and the spoon is in the water. It is measured from the vertical in degrees.

Correct pitch allows the blade to be held through the stroke at the right depth with only the spoon covered. It allows smooth efficient rowing. But *what is correct pitch*?

Experimentation with blade pitch has established that it is more comfortable, in fact almost a necessity, to row with positive pitch effective on the blade, to provide a degree of lateral stability.

In theory, the less the positive pitch exerted on the blade the more efficient the stroke will be, because the greater the pitch

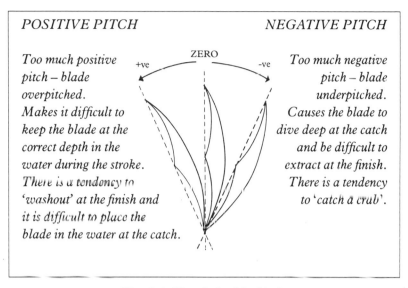

Fig. 4:6. The pitch of the blade.

angle the greater the force lifting the boat from the water. Any force lifting the boat from the water will naturally subtract from the force of forward propulsion.

RECOMMENDED PITCH FOR ROWING:
four degrees positive

RECOMMENDED PITCH FOR SCULLING:
six degrees positive

NB. For beginners there is often a need to give more pitch at the catch to help blade entry.

Factors affecting the pitch

The oar

Oars are manufactured with pitch incorporated into the loom at the sleeve or collar. Usually the blades are set at two degrees of positive pitch or zero degrees.

Wear of the sleeve will cause variations in the pitch set on the blade and the sleeve should therefore be checked regularly, at least once a season and resleeved if necessary.

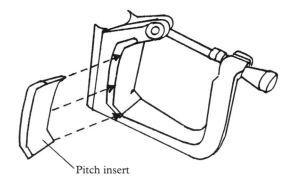

Pitch insert

Fig. 4:7. Changing the pitch of the swivel face by means of pitch inserts which slot into the swivel face. When the blade is held against the back of the swivel, pitch is exerted on to the blade.

The swivel

Swivels are made with four degrees of positive pitch, though most modern swivels are now pitch adjustable by means of inserts either in the face or through the central core of the swivel (Fig. 4:7).

The pin angle

The swivel is mounted onto the pin of the gate. Any angulation of the pin from the vertical changes the plane of rotation of the swivel, which in turn changes the pitch effective on the blade. This angulation may be in an anterior – posterior (AP) – front – back – or lateral – sideways – direction relative to the boat (Fig. 4:8).

Let us consider the effect of lateral pin angulation: for each degree of lateral pin angle the effective pitch of the blade at the catch is increased by half a degree and reduced at the finish by half a degree, i.e., with four degrees of positive pitch effective on the blade, if the lateral pin angulation is zero degrees, the pitch on the blade remains four degrees throughout the stroke, whereas in the presence of a two-degree lateral pin angle there will be five degrees positive pitch at the catch, four degrees positive pitch in the middle of the stroke and three degrees positive pitch at the finish.

It is argued that setting the rigger with a two-degree lateral pin angulation can help a rower to achieve a clean catch, to hold

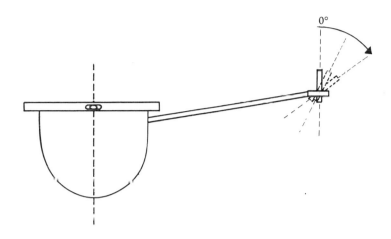

Fig. 4:8. Lateral pin angle: the deviation of the pin from the upright away from the boat.

the blade at the correct depth in the middle of the stroke and to hold the blade in at the finish.

This is true. However, I feel it is wrong to encourage the correction of faults by adjustments of rigging. It is more appropriate to correct the technique, no matter how long this may take, with good rigging.

I recommend that all boats are set with zero lateral pin angle, zero forward and aft pin angle and with an effective blade pitch of four degrees positive – this being a combination of blade pitch and swivel-face pitch.

Checking and adjusting the pitch of a rigger

Applicable to both rowing and sculling boats.

1. Check pitch of blades.
2. Set pin to zero forward and aft pin angle.
3. Set pin to zero lateral pin angle.
4. Set swivel to four degrees positive pitch minus the pitch of the blade, or six degrees for sculling.

Checking the pitch of the blade: blades are usually marked for bowside or strokeside using numbers – odd numbers for bowside and even numbers for strokeside, and/or coloured buttons – green for bowside and red for strokeside. However, it is possible to pick up any blade and assess by inspection alone which side of the boat the blade was made for. Looking down the loom at the face of the spoon, if the left side of the spoon is raised, the blade is a bowside oar, and if the right side of the spoon is raised then the blade is a strokeside oar.

Having assessed whether the blade is strokeside or bowside, the actual pitch on the blade needs to be measured numerically. *Equipment required:* a pitch gauge, a small spirit-level and a flat solid surface of at least 4 cm width.

Centralize the bubble of the pitch gauge on the solid flat surface and adjust the pitch arm to read zero degrees (Fig. 4:9). Place the sleeve of the oar on the solid surface and hold the

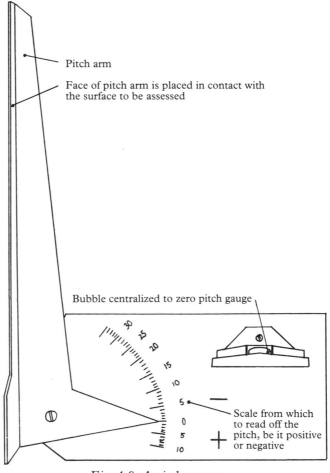

Pitch arm

Face of pitch arm is placed in contact with the surface to be assessed

Bubble centralized to zero pitch gauge

Scale from which to read off the pitch, be it positive or negative

Fig. 4:9. A pitch gauge.

blade steady. Position the pitch gauge on the spoon 5 cm from the tip of the blade. Centralize the bubble of the pitch gauge and read off the pitch present on the blade.

This reading is usually two degrees or zero, but may vary in older blades where the sleeve has been allowed to wear or the blade has warped/twisted. If the blade is found to have negative pitch the blade should be repitched by the manufacturer.

Setting the pin to zero forward and aft pin angle: the boat should be placed firmly on sling trestles, level from stern to bow. This can be checked by placing a small spirit-level on the inwales and keel of a wooden boat, or the top of the saxboards and the keel of a plastic moulded boat. Once level the boat should be braced and not disturbed from this position.

Remove the swivel from the pin. Place the pitch gauge on the keel of the boat and set to zero. Maintaining the pitch gauge parallel to the boat, place the face of the pitch arm on the pin anteriorly and adjust until the bubble of the pitch gauge is centralized. A reading of the pin angle is then taken from the scale on the pitch gauge.

The pin angle can be adjusted if necessary to zero by gently levering a hollow tube placed over the pin. Since most riggers are aluminium this method of adjustment will give three or four degrees of change without damaging the rigger. If more change than this is required the rigger should be returned to the manufacturer for adjustment.

Setting the pin to zero lateral pin angle: for this the boat should be level from side to side. Place the spirit-level on the decking at right angles to the side of the boat and adjust until the boat is level. Secure the boat in this position and do not disturb. Centralize and zero the pitch gauge by placing in a similar position to the spirit-level at right angles to the side of the boat.

Maintain the pitch gauge in this position and place the face of the pitch gauge on the side of the pin. Adjust to read off the lateral pin angle. If necessary lever the pin with the hollow tube to achieve a zero lateral pin angle.

Double check the forward and aft pin angle and replace the swivel.

Setting the swivel pitch: having determined how much pitch is present on the blade, the required swivel pitch can be calculated to give a total of four degrees positive. The necessary pitch on the swivel is then achieved by the use of swivel face or core inserts. Once the insert has been located and secured, double check that the pitch is as expected.

Height

The height of the work is defined as the distance from the waterline to the floor of the swivel (Fig. 4:10).

It is impractical, however, to measure this distance and since the height of the seat above the waterline in a stable boat is constant, the height of the work may be considered to be the distance between the lowest point of the front edge of the seat, when placed at frontstops and the floor of the swivel. (Fig. 4:11).

From the oarsman's point of view the height of the work reflects the space available above the thighs at the end of the draw, in which the hands push the oarhandle down and away at the finish to clear the waterline in preparation for the recovery (Fig. 4:12).

Although, as stated, the height of the work is a very individual adjustment, boats should initially be rigged with a standard height throughout (*see* Appendix I: Rigging Charts) and then changed for the comfort of each oarsman as necessary.

Height, unlike span/spread is easy to change quickly and may be adjusted each time the crew changes.

Adjustments to the height of the work make it possible for a

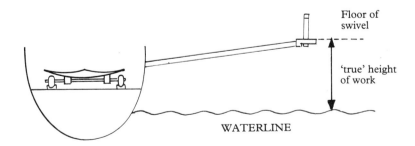

Fig. 4:10. Defining the 'true' height of the work.

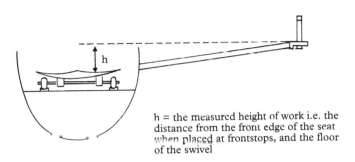

h = the measured height of work i.e. the distance from the front edge of the seat when placed at frontstops, and the floor of the swivel

Fig. 4:11. The height of the work as measured and adjusted.

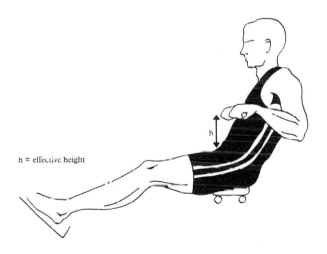

h = effective height

Fig. 4:12. The oarsman's perception of the height of the work is the space available at the finish for the hands to be pushed down.

crew to row in a boat that is too large or too small for them: if overboated (boat too large) the height should be dropped: if underboated (boat too small) the height should be raised.

Measuring and adjusting the height of the work

Equipment required: adjustable spanners, height stick, tape measure.

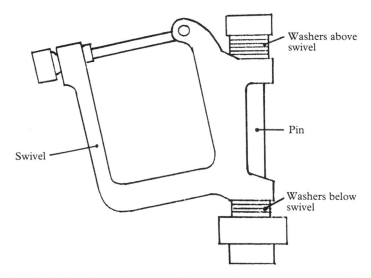

Fig. 4:13. To adjust the height of the work the washers above and below the swivel are rearranged.

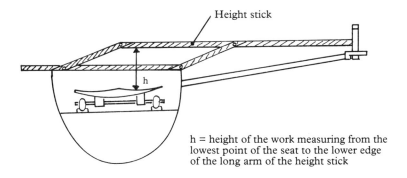

h = height of the work measuring from the lowest point of the seat to the lower edge of the long arm of the height stick

Fig. 4:14. Using a height stick to measure the height of the work. The height stick rests on the saxboards and the floor of the swivel.

The height of the work is adjusted by rearranging the washers above and below the swivel on the pin of the gate (Fig. 4:13).

Stabilize and brace the boat on sling trestles. Place the height stick across the saxboards at right angles to the boat, with the long arm of the height stick resting on the floor of the swivel, the swivel being positioned parallel to the side of the boat. (Fig. 4:14).

Slide the seat underneath the height stick. Using the tape, measure the distance from the lowest point of the front edge of the seat to the lower edge of the long arm of the height stick. i.e., the edge in contact with the floor of the swivel.

To reduce the height of the work, move the swivel to a lower position on the pin by removing some washers from underneath the swivel and replacing them above the swivel until the requisite height of work is attained. To raise the height of the work reverse the process.

NB. In a sculling boat the bowside rigger is set a few milli-metres higher than the strokeside rigger to enable the hands to draw one on top of the other during the propulsive phase of the stroke without upsetting the balance (*see* Chapter 5: Technique).

Stretcher position

The stretcher or footplate is the apparatus used to position the feet in the boat. The stretcher may be adjusted in three ways (Fig 4:15):
a. in a vertical direction;
b. in a horizontal direction;
c. by changing the 'rake' of the stretcher.

Careful adjustment of the stretcher position can optimize the work angles of the knees and ankles to obtain maximum efficiency from the leg drive.

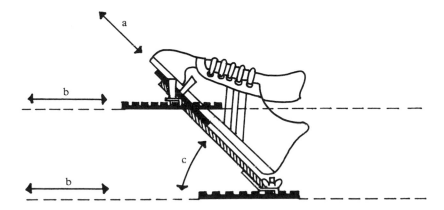

Fig. 4:15. The stretcher can be adjusted in three ways: a. vertically; b. horizontally; and c. by changing the 'rake'.

Adjustment of the stretcher in a vertical direction

This adjustment is referred to as *changing the height of the footplate*. The height of the footplate determines the direction of the leg drive; to provide maximum forward propulsion the leg drive needs to be on a horizontal plane.

The stretcher is at the correct height when the balls of the feet are positioned only slightly lower than the seat. In this position the *heels* of the shoe will be considerably lower than the level of the seat, and in the smaller boats e.g. the coxless pair, this means that the heels of the shoes may only just be clear of the skin of the boat.

Adjusting the height of the stretcher is quite simple. The shoes are attached to the stretcher by two or three wing-nuts on each side of the boat (Fig. 4:16). To raise or lower the shoes simply loosen the wing-nuts, slide the shoes off the bolts and reposition as appropriate on a different line of holes. Replace the wing-nuts tightly to prevent the shoes pulling away from the stretcher when rowing.

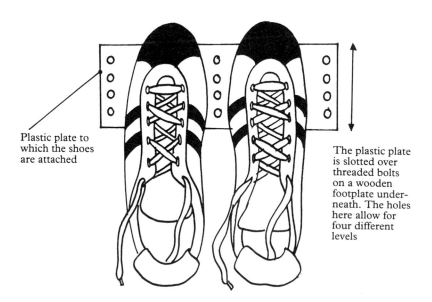

Plastic plate to which the shoes are attached

The plastic plate is slotted over threaded bolts on a wooden footplate underneath. The holes here allow for four different levels

Fig. 4:16. Adjusting the footplate in a vertical direction.

Adjusting the stretcher in a horizontal direction

Adjusting the stretcher in a horizontal direction provides a means of positioning the rower relative to his/her line of work (Fig. 4:17). Horizontal stretcher adjustment allows the arc of the stroke to be predetermined, and to be identical at each position in the boat.

The *stretcher* position is set to obtain the correct *finish angle*, and the slidebeds are adjusted to a *specific frontstops position* to obtain the correct *catch angle* (Fig. 4:18).

The *line of work* is defined as an invisible line projected from the face of the swivel across the boat, perpendicular to the side of the boat (Fig. 4:19).

Setting the stretcher position to achieve a specific finish angle: sit the boat on sling trestles. Using a straight edge mark the line of work across the boat. Read from the rigging chart the *required* distance behind the work. Using the tape, measure from the marked line of work towards the bows of the boat the

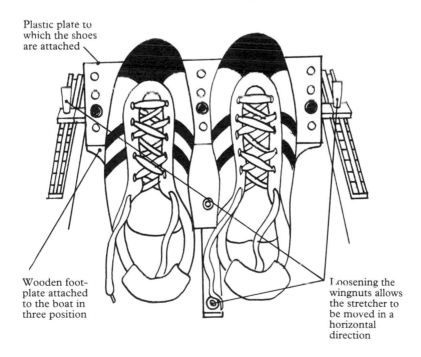

Plastic plate to which the shoes are attached

Wooden foot-plate attached to the boat in three position

Loosening the wingnuts allows the stretcher to be moved in a horizontal direction

Fig. 4:17. Adjusting the stretcher in a horizontal direction.

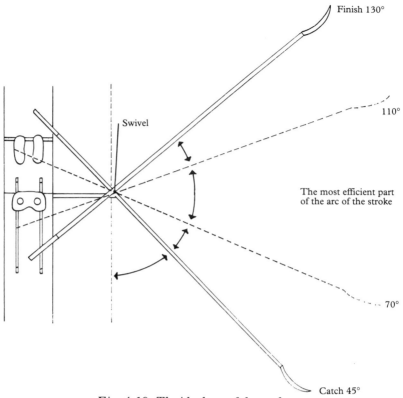

Fig. 4:18. The ideal arc of the stroke.

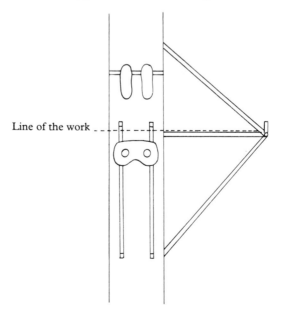

Fig. 4:19. Line of work: an invisible line projected from the face of the swivel across the boat perpendicular to the side of the boat.

required distance. Mark this point on the decking or side of the boat with PVC tape. (Ensure you know which edge of the tape is at the specified distance e.g., use the front edge of the tape.) Repeat this process at each position in the boat.

When the crew have boated, they should adjust their stretcher positions so that when sitting at backstops the furthest point of the back wheel of the seat is in line with the front edge of the tape.

Setting the frontstops position to predetermine the angle of the catch: read from the rigging chart the required distance through the work. Slide the seat to frontstops and measure from the front edge of the seat to the line of work. If the recommended and the actual measurements differ, adjust the frontstops position by moving the slidebeds. The slidebeds are secured by two wing-nuts beneath the decking; to adjust their position simply loosen the wing-nuts and reposition. Once the correct frontstops position has been found giving the recommended distance through the work retighten the wing-nuts.

With the frontstops position predetermined, when the wheels of the seat just touch the frontstops, with the body held in the correct position, the blade will be positioned at the correct angle for the catch.

Changing the rake of the stretcher

The *rake* is defined as the angle of the stretcher from the keel of the boat (Fig. 4:20).

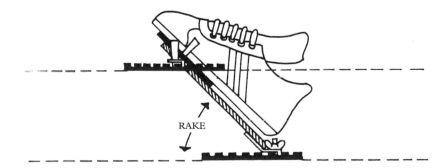

Fig. 4:20. The rake is the angle of the stretcher from the keel of the boat.

The rake in combination with the height of the footplate determines the angles of the knees and ankles at the catch and during the leg drive, and allows ease of movement forward up the slide during the recovery. The rake should be set in the range of forty-one to forty-five degrees from the horizontal. I personally use forty-two degrees. If a rower is very inflexible at the ankles it may be necessary to use less rake, thus flattening the stretcher. However, in the long term this type of person should be encouraged to increase ankle flexibility through specific exercises.

Checking and adjusting the rake of the stretcher: with the boat on trestles, centralize the bubble of the pitch gauge on the level keel and set to zero degrees. Place the face of the gauge on

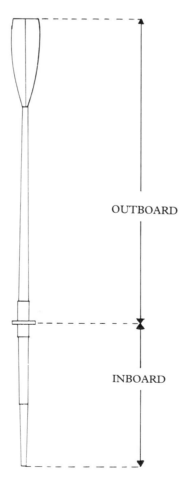

OUTBOARD

INBOARD

Fig. 4:21. The outboard/inboard ratio of the blade.

the stretcher board, centralize the bubble again and read off the rake of the stretcher.

If the rake needs to be adjusted, loosen the stretcher as you would to move its position forward/backward. In addition loosen the central bolt which controls the angulation of the stretcher. By sliding this bolt up or down the angle of the stretcher can be adjusted. Adjust the rake to the required angle and retighten all screws and nuts.

NB. Changing the rake of the stretcher may result in a short period of shin stiffness until the calf muscles adapt to working in a different position.

Gearing of the blades

The gearing is the workload on the athlete, and it can be altered by adjusting the spread/span of the boat and by adjusting the ratio of the inboard:outboard of the blades (Fig. 4:21). The workload that a rower can tolerate is determined by his physique and his endurance strength. (In a crewboat the gearing used should be that which is suitable for the weakest member of the crew.)

Depending on the length of blade the inboard is usually set to be used in combination with a particular span (*see* Appendix 1: Rigging Charts). The length of macon blade recommended for a particular calibre of rower is now well documented. The ideal length of hatchet blade or 'big blade' remains open to debate. It is generally accepted that to achieve equivalent loading the length of the big blade should be shorter than the recommended length of macon blade because the big blade achieves a more efficient pick up at the catch. Even now, three years after the introduction of the big blade, the recommended lengths for each calibre of rower are still reducing. There is no right or wrong – the correct length of blade is that which the rower can use efficiently through the correct arc and repeatedly without failure.

Rigging Charts are not absolute. They give guidance about the starting point for setting up a boat for a given crew. If the crew are having difficulty in achieving or holding a target rate it *may* be that they are overgeared, try lightening the gearing by using shorter blades, a wider span or a combination of the two.

5

TECHNIQUE

I n all sports it is essential to have a good understanding of the basic technique. In rowing it is particularly relevant as there is no significant difference between the technique of a beginner and the technique of an Olympic champion. It is the application of the basic technique and the development of efficiency which differentiates the two.

In some sports there is an inherent instinct to perform the basic skills: everyday you see toddlers of two or three instinctively kicking a ball; submerge them in water and they naturally start to swim. But, put anybody of any age in a rowing boat and they are like a fish out of water! Rowing does not come naturally.

Basic technique is very easy and straightforward in theory, but, in practice, it is very difficult to achieve as it is complicated by the need for the coordinated action of arms, legs and back, with a sense of balance.

The theory of the rowing stroke

The stroke is made up of four phases, which run one after the other in a continuous cycle: the CATCH,

the DRIVE,
the FINISH,
and the RECOVERY.

The way these four phases are put together determines the rhythm of the stroke.

The catch

The catch is the point where the blade enters the water.

The catch body position

At the catch the seat rests momentarily at frontstops. The legs are fully compressed with the shins at ninety degrees to the boat. The eyes are looking directly ahead and not cast downward. The chest is lifted forward and over the knees, which are shoulder width apart. The arms are straight without the elbows being locked (Fig. 5:1). The body follows the arc of the oar handle. The outside arm should be above the gap between the knees. The inside arm should be on the outside of the knee closest to the rigger (Fig. 5:a). The heels naturally lift off the footplate of the stretcher as the body draws towards the knees. The knuckles, wrists and elbows are in a straight line (any bend in this position will cause weakness in the stroke resulting in a loss of power). The fingers grip the handle from above, while the thumbs lie under the handle (Fig. 5:b).

The catch blade position

The blade is held square. Before the point of entry into the water, the spoon of the blade should be approximately 10 cm

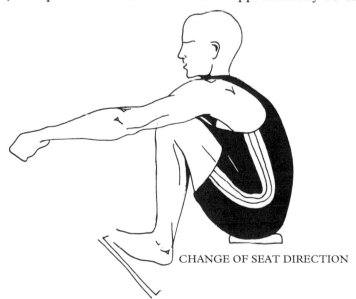

CHANGE OF SEAT DIRECTION

Fig. 5:1. The catch – shins at 90°.

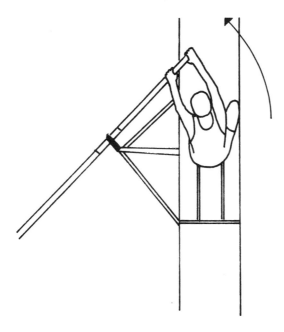

Fig. 5:a. The catch – the body follows the arc of the oar.

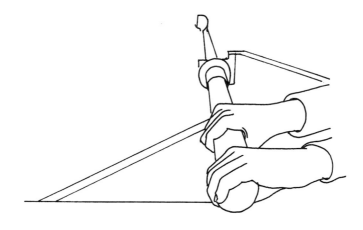

Fig. 5:b. The catch – the grip of the oar handle when the blade is squared.

above the waterline (Fig. 5:i). As the blade descends towards the water it should be travelling forwards towards the stern of the boat (Fig. 5:ii), this prevents backsplashing (*see* Chapter 6: Faults). To effect a clean blade entry into the water, the hands should allow the weight of the oar to raise the handle, and the

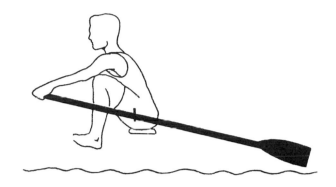

Fig. 5:i. The catch.

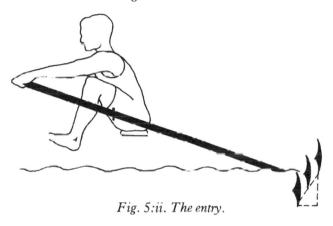

Fig. 5:ii. The entry.

blade should enter at the *same* speed as the boat is travelling. If the blade doesn't enter the water smoothly it will act as a brake thus slowing the forward motion of the boat. A tell-tale sign of this is stern dipping.

No power should be applied to the stretcher until the spoon is covered. If power is applied earlier than this, it will cause the boat to slow because the power being applied to the stretcher is trying to force the boat backwards. Once the spoon is covered then the power applied to the stretcher will be transmitted into moving the boat forwards. By driving too early on the stretcher you lose effective power in the water.

Depth of blade

As the blade enters the water it is important that only the spoon is covered and water is not allowed to come up the loom. If the spoon is allowed to go deep this will result in a number of unwanted effects such as reduction of blade resistance, back watering and reduction in the forward propulsive force created. All these effects will slow the boat.

The drive

The drive is the action which levers the boat past the body.

The drive body position

The body position throughout the drive is split into three parts:

a. the leg drive
b. the back opening
c. the draw

The leg drive: the legs begin to flatten (that is, the knees begin to extend), driving the seat towards the backstop position (Fig. 5:2). At this stage the back should be held firm and not allowed to open. This enables the power of the leg drive to be transmitted to the blade.

Back opening: continuing the leg drive, the body begins to swing backwards from the hips (Fig. 5:3). This opens the body angle through the upright position, enabling the body weight to add to the power of the legs (Fig. 5:4).

The draw: the continuation of the leg drive and the back opening leads into the draw. The hands draw the oar handle towards the nipple line, causing the elbows to bend. The balls of the feet maintain the pressure against the footplate. The

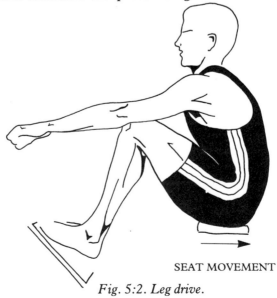

SEAT MOVEMENT

Fig. 5:2. Leg drive.

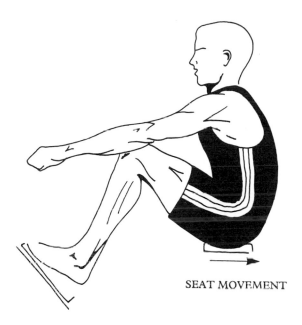

SEAT MOVEMENT

Fig. 5:3. Body angle opening.

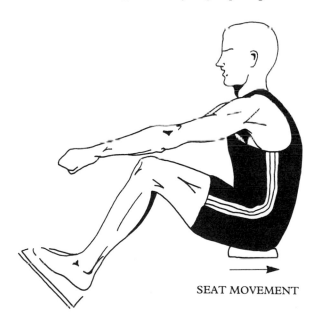

SEAT MOVEMENT

Fig. 5:4. Body angle and legs opening.

power of the upper arms and shoulders is used to sweep around
the rigger to the finish position (Figs 5:5 & 5:6).

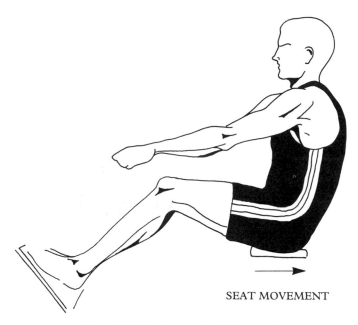

SEAT MOVEMENT

Fig. 5:5. The draw – shoulders moving.

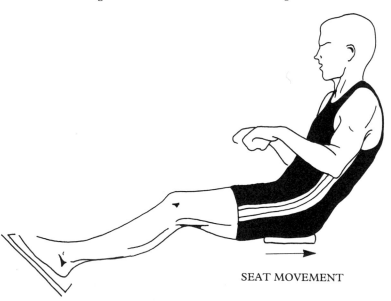

SEAT MOVEMENT

Fig. 5:6. The draw – legs down flat, pulling into chest.

The finish

The finish is the point in the stroke where active forward propulsion of the boat ceases. It is the point at which the blade should be extracted from the water and the seat rests at backstops. The following movements are completed simultaneously. The legs fully extend, the body leans back through the upright position to approximately thirty-five degrees, but still following the arc of the oar handle, the hands and the outside shoulder draw the oar handle close to the lower chest (without touching the body) (Fig. 5:c). The elbows are kept close to the body, with the outside elbow easing back past the

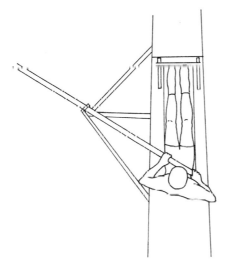

Fig. 5:c. The finish – the body follows the arc of the oar.

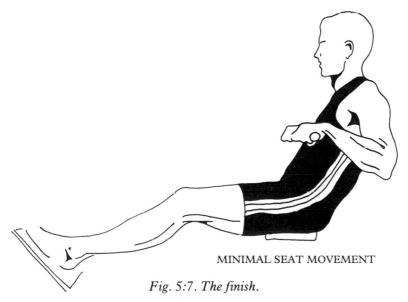

MINIMAL SEAT MOVEMENT

Fig. 5:7. The finish.

body. The head is kept behind the handle of the oar and not allowed to drop forward over it. The eyes remain looking directly ahead (Fig. 5:7).

The drive and the finish blade position

As soon as the blade has bitten the water, ensure that only the spoon is covered (top edge of the spoon level with the water-line). Once the spoon has been covered at the catch, the acceleration of the leg drive carves a hole in the water behind the spoon, and develops a mound of water in front of the spoon (Fig 5:iii). As long as the acceleration of the blade is maintained to the finish this hole and mound will remain. The neater the hole the more efficient the work output.

The blade should be held at the same level throughout the drive and the draw (Fig. 5:iv).

Fig. 5:iii. The drive.

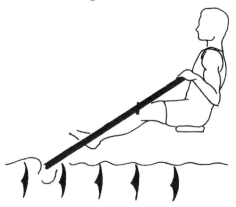

Fig. 5:iv. The finish.

At the finish the blade is extracted cleanly from the carved hole.

The extraction

The extraction is the removal of the blade from the water and is essentially the completion of the finish (Fig. 5:v). The body and leg position are the same as the finish but to effect the release of the blade from the water, the hands push the handle down towards the upper thigh (Fig. 5:8). When the blade has been extracted, the wrists drop, turning the oar to the feathered position. Feathering is achieved by turning the handle with the inside hand thereby letting the wrist drop. Allow the handle in

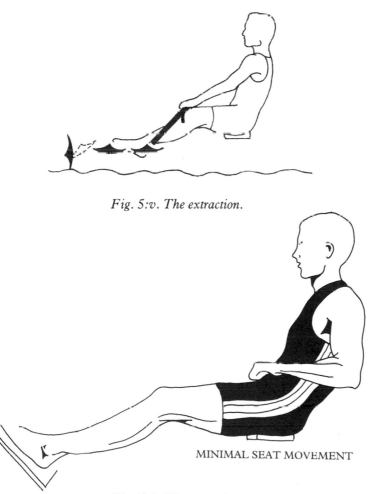

Fig. 5:v. The extraction.

MINIMAL SEAT MOVEMENT

Fig. 5:8. The extraction.

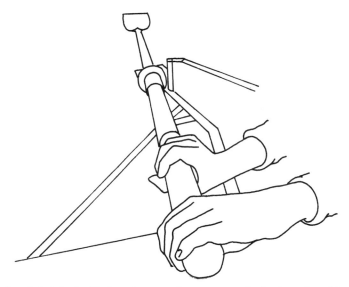

Fig. 5:d. The inside hand rotates the oar on to the feathered position, the outside hand remains flat.

the outside hand to rotate in the fingers, whilst maintaining a flat wrist position (Fig. 5:d)

The recovery

The recovery is the time spent coming forward up the slide from backstops to frontstops between the finish and the catch. Although there is no active propulsion of the boat during the recovery, the boat continues to travel because of the momentum developed in the leg drive phase of the stroke. The key words to remember at this part of the stroke are hands, body, slide. The recovery should be a smooth, flowing action.

The *hands* push the oar handle towards the footplate, keeping the handle parallel to the thighs (Figs 5:9 & 5:10).

The *body* swings forward from the hips, with the arms extended taking the oar handle to the lower shins (Figs 5:11 & 5:12).

The *slide* consists of compressing the legs by allowing the knees to rise, drawing the seat forwards to the frontstops position. Again the heels lift naturally off the footplate. (Figs 5:13, 5:14 & 5:15).

Completing this phase returns you to the catch position. (Fig. 5:16).

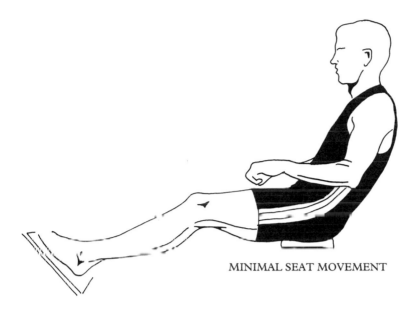

MINIMAL SEAT MOVEMENT

Fig. 5:9. The recovery – legs flat, hands moving away.

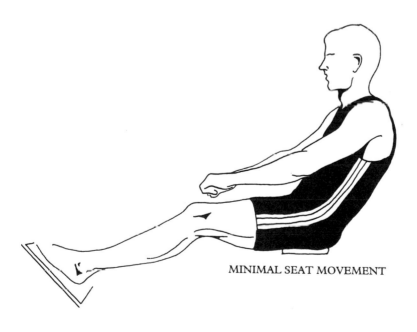

MINIMAL SEAT MOVEMENT

Fig. 5:10. The recovery – legs flat, hands over knees prior to body swing.

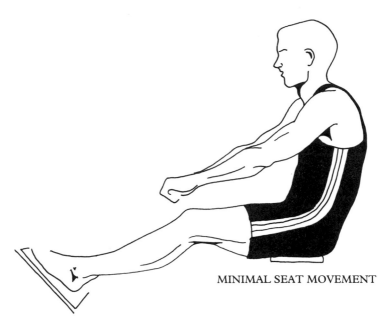

Fig. 5:11. The recovery – hands remain at same height, but now over knees.

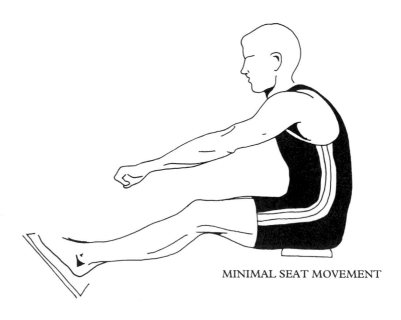

Fig. 5:12. The recovery – body. Body swings, hands remain at same height.

SEAT MOVEMENT

Fig. 5:13. The recovery – slide. Hands rising to the catch, knees breaking.

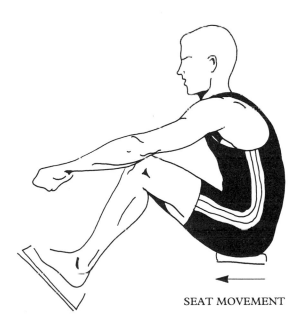

SEAT MOVEMENT

Fig. 5:14. The recovery – slide. Legs compressing.

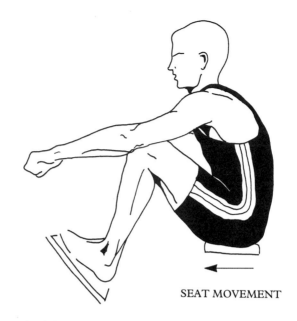

SEAT MOVEMENT

Fig. 5:15. The recovery – slide. Legs continue to compress.

CHANGE OF SEAT DIRECTION

Fig. 5:16. The catch – shins return to 90°.

The recovery blade position

When the blade has left the water it is turned to the feather (Fig. 5:vi). Feathering reduces wind resistance, aids the balance of the boat, and gives more clearance from the water avoiding the blade catching in rough water. As the hands travel parallel to the thighs and down to the knees, the blade has maximum clearance from the water (Fig. 5:vii). Once the handle has passed the knees the blade is turned back to the squared position and the hands rise smoothly returning to the catch position (Fig. 5:viii), blade approximately 10 cm above the waterline.

Fig. 5:vi. The recovery – hands.

Fig. 5:vii. The recovery – body/slide.

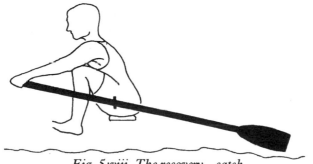

Fig. 5:viii. The recovery – catch.

Sequence shots of the body position through the stroke

Sequence shots of the rowing stroke from behind

Sequence shots of the rowing stroke from the side

The theory of the sculling stroke

In many respects sculling technique is identical to rowing technique, however, there is the added complication of coping with two blades at the same time!

The sculling stroke is made up of the same four phases as the rowing stroke, which run in a continuous cycle:

the CATCH,
the DRIVE,
the FINISH,
and the RECOVERY.

As in rowing, the way these four phases are put together determines the rhythm of the stroke.

The catch

The catch is the point where the blade enters the water.

The catch body position

At the catch the seat rests momentarily on frontstops. The legs are fully compressed, the shins are at ninety degrees to the boat. The eyes are looking directly forward not cast downward. The chest is lifted forward and over the knees, which are shoulder width apart (Fig. 5:1). Each hand holds a sculling oar with the

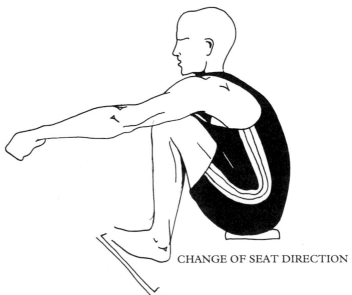

CHANGE OF SEAT DIRECTION

Fig. 5:1. The catch – shins at 90°.

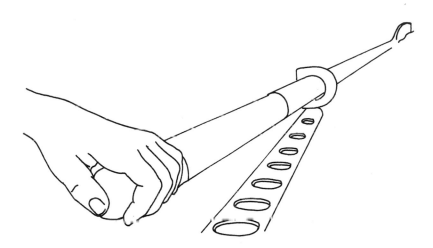

Fig. 5:e. The catch – the grip of the sculling oar.

spoon squared. The fingers are hooked over the sculling handle, with the knuckles, wrists and elbows in a straight line (Fig. 5:e). Any bend in this position will cause weakness, resulting in a loss of power and a loss of control of the sculls. The thumbs sit lightly on the end of the sculling handles, keeping a light lateral pressure pushing the button out against the swivel. The arms

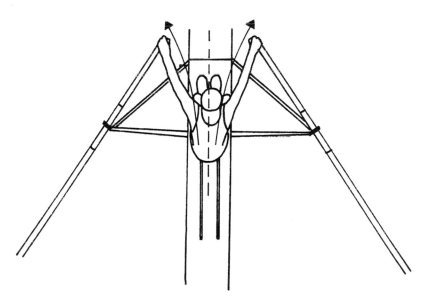

Fig. 5:f. The body remains centre line as the arm follows the arc of the sculls.

are straight and follow the arc around which the sculling oars rotate on the pin of the swivel. The body follows the centre line of the boat (Fig. 5:f). The heels will naturally lift off the footplate of the stretcher as the body draws towards the knees.

The catch blade position

The blade is held square. Before the point of entry into the water, the spoon of the blade should be approximately 8 cm above the waterline (Fig. 5:i). As the blade descends towards the water it should be travelling forwards towards the stern of the boat (Fig. 5:ii), this prevents backsplashing (*see* Chapter 6: Faults). To effect a clean blade entry into the water, the hands should allow the weight of the oar to raise the handles, and the blade should enter at the *same* speed as the boat is travelling. If the blade doesn't enter the water smoothly it will act as a brake, thus slowing the forward motion of the boat. A tell-tale sign of this is stern dipping.

No power should be applied to the stretcher until the spoon is

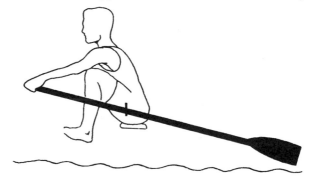

Fig. 5:i. The catch.

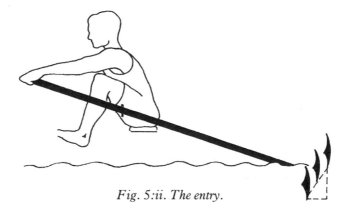

Fig. 5:ii. The entry.

covered. If power is applied earlier than this, it will cause the
boat to slow because the power being applied to the stretcher is
trying to force the boat backwards. Once the spoon is covered
then the power applied to the stretcher will be transmitted into
moving the boat forwards. By driving too early on the stretcher
you will lose effective power in the water.

Depth of blades

As the blades enter the water it is important that only the
spoons are covered, not allowing the water to come up the
looms. If the spoons are allowed to go too deep this will result in
a number of unwanted effects such as reduction of blade
resistance, back watering and reduction in the forward propulsive force created. All these effects will slow the boat.

The drive

The drive is the action which levers the boat past the body from
the catch to the finish.

The drive body position

The body position throughout the drive is split into three parts:
a. the leg drive
b. the back opening
c. the draw
The leg drive: the legs begin to flatten (that is, the knees begin
to extend), driving the seat towards the backstop position (Fig.
5:2). At this stage the back should be held firm and not allowed
to open. This enables the power of the leg drive to be
transmitted to the blades.
Back opening: continuing the leg drive, the body begins to
swing backwards from the hips (Fig. 5:3). This opens the body
angle through the upright position, enabling the body weight to
add to the power of the legs (Fig. 5:4). At this time the hands
and the sculling oar handles will overlap. This overlap is due to
the length of the sculls which is important in determining the
correct leverage for the stroke. The left hand should be above
the right, keeping them as close as possible without touching
(Fig 5:g). To prevent the overlap upsetting the balance, the
bowside gate should be adjusted so that it has slightly more
height than the strokeside gate (*see* Chapter 4: Rigging).

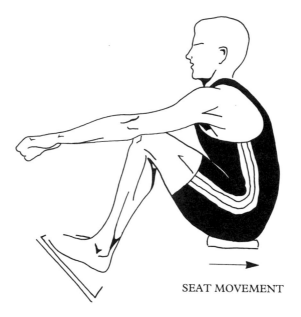

SEAT MOVEMENT

Fig. 5:2. Leg drive.

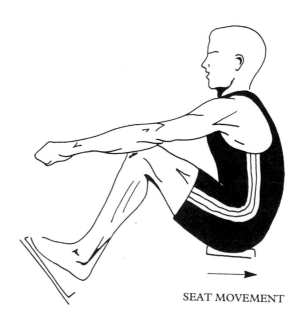

SEAT MOVEMENT

Fig. 5:3. Body angle opening.

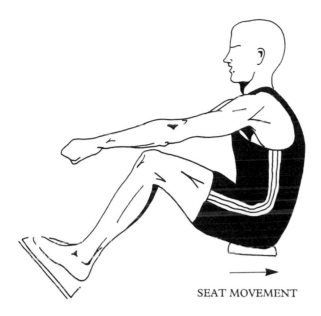

SEAT MOVEMENT

Fig. 5:4. Body angle and legs opening.

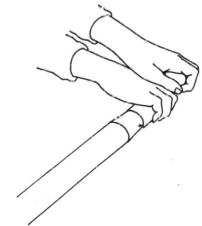

Fig. 5:g. The draw – one hand on top of the other at the overlap of the sculls.

The draw: the continuation of the leg drive and the back opening leads into the draw. The hands draw the sculling handles towards the body, causing the elbows to bend. The balls of the feet maintain the pressure against the footplate. The power of the upper arms and shoulders is used to sweep the sculling handles around the riggers (Figs 5:5 & 5:6).

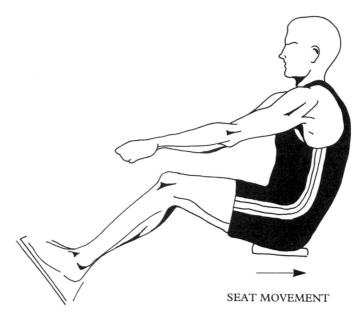

SEAT MOVEMENT

Fig. 5:5. The draw – shoulders moving.

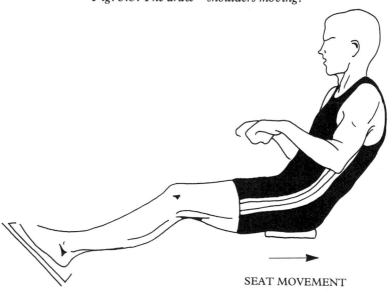

SEAT MOVEMENT

Fig. 5:6. The draw – legs down flat, pulling into chest.

The finish

The finish is the point in the stroke where active forward propulsion of the boat ceases. It is the point at which the blades should be extracted from the water and the seat rests at backstops. The following movements are completed simultaneously. The legs fully extend, the body leans back through the upright position to approximately thirty-five to forty degrees, but still following the centre line of the boat, the hands continue to sweep the sculling oars around the rigger. The hands will come out from the overlap and be drawn towards the outside of the lower chest, holding the elbows in past the body

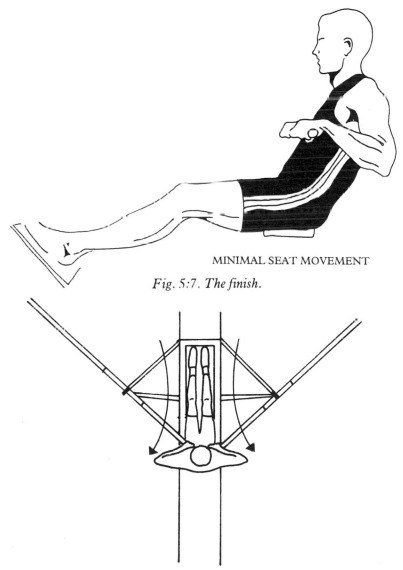

MINIMAL SEAT MOVEMENT

Fig. 5:7. The finish.

Fig. 5:h. The finish – the arms following the arc of the sculls.

(Fig. 5:7). The head is kept behind the handles of the sculls and not allowed to drop forward over them. The eyes remain looking directly ahead (Fig. 5:h).

The drive and the finish blade position

As soon as the blades have bitten the water, ensure that only the spoons are covered (top edge of the spoon level with the waterline). Once the spoons have been covered at the catch, the acceleration of the leg drive carves a hole in the water behind the spoons, and develops a mound of water in front of the spoons (Fig. 5:iii). As long as the acceleration of the blade is maintained to the finish this hole and mound will remain. The neater the hole the more efficient the work output. The blades should be held at the same level throughout the drive and the draw (Fig. 5:iv).

Fig. 5:iii. The drive.

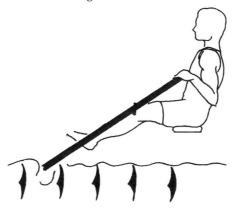

Fig. 5:iv. The finish.

At the finish the blades are extracted cleanly from the carved holes.

The extraction

The extraction is the removal of the blade from the water and is essentially the completion of the finish (Fig. 5:v). The body and leg position are the same as the finish but to effect the release of the blades from the water, the hands push the handles down towards the thighs (Fig. 5:8). When the blades have been extracted, the wrists drop, rolling the sculls on to the feathered position (Fig. 5:i).

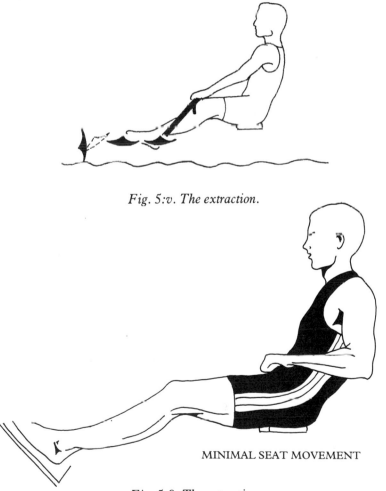

Fig. 5:v. The extraction.

MINIMAL SEAT MOVEMENT

Fig. 5:8. The extraction.

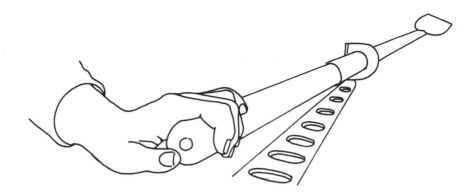

Fig. 5:i. The extraction – grip as the sculling oar is rolled on to the feather.

The recovery

The recovery is the time spent coming forward up the slide from backstops to frontstops between the finish and the catch. Although there is no active propulsion of the boat during the recovery, the boat continues to travel because of the momentum developed in the leg drive phase of the stroke. The key words to remember at this part of the stroke are hands, body, slide. The recovery should be a smooth, flowing action.

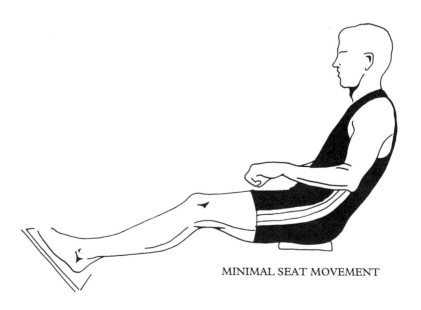

MINIMAL SEAT MOVEMENT

Fig. 5:9. The recovery – legs flat, hands moving away.

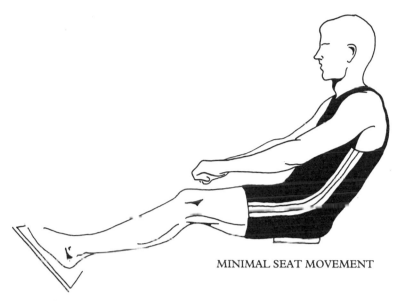

MINIMAL SEAT MOVEMENT

Fig. 5:10. The recovery – legs flat, hands over knees prior to body swing.

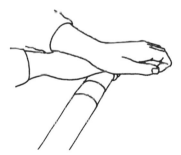

*Fig. 5:j. The recovery – one hand in front of the other at the overlap of the
sculls.*

As the *hands* leave the body, the sculling oar handles are
rolled in the fingers, allowing the wrists to flatten again. The
sculls are pushed down and away towards the footplate, keeping
the handles travelling parallel to the thighs (Figs 5:9 & 5:10).
As the hands travel forward, the oar handles will overlap again.
Keep the handles level by allowing the left scull to lead the right
scull. (Fig. 5:j).

The *body* swings forward from the hips, with the arms
extended, bringing the scull handles to lower shins (Figs 5:11 &
5:12).

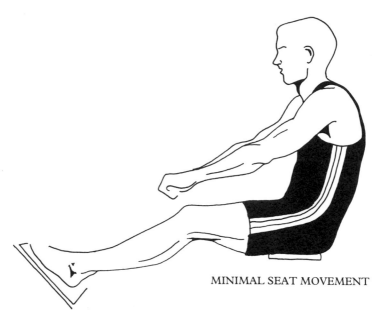

MINIMAL SEAT MOVEMENT

Fig. 5:11. The recovery – hands remain at same height, but now over knees.

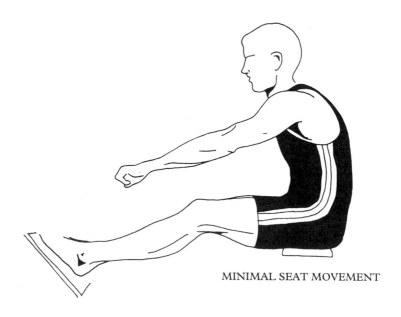

MINIMAL SEAT MOVEMENT

Fig. 5:12. The recovery – body. Body swings, hands remain at same height.

The *slide* consists of compressing the legs by allowing the knees to rise, drawing the seat forwards to the frontstops position. Again the heels lift naturally off the footplate (Figs 5:13, 5:14 & 5:15).

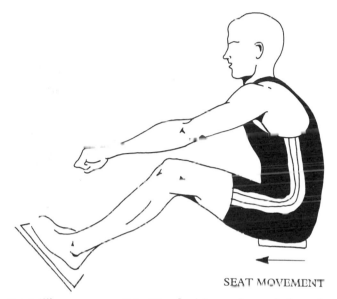

SEAT MOVEMENT

Fig. 5:13. The recovery – slide. Hands rising to the catch, knees breaking.

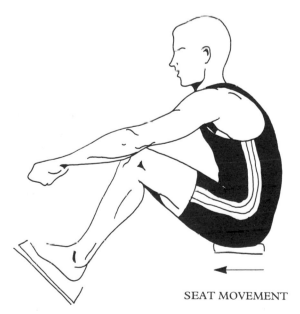

SEAT MOVEMENT

Fig. 5:14. The recovery – slide. Legs compressing.

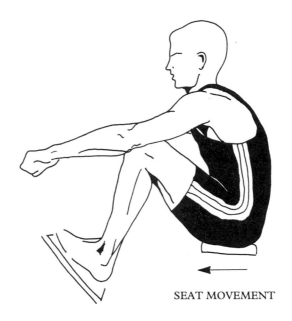

SEAT MOVEMENT

Fig. 5:15. The recovery – slide. Legs continue to compress.

CHANGE OF SEAT DIRECTION

Fig. 5:16. The catch – shins return to 90°.

Completing this phase returns you to the catch position (Fig. 5:16).

The recovery blade position

When the blades have left the water they are turned to the feather (Fig. 5:vi). As the hands travel parallel to the thighs down to the knees, the blades have maximum clearance from the water (Fig. 5:vii). Once the handles have passed the knees the blades are turned back to the squared position and the hands rise smoothly, returning to the catch position (Fig. 5:viii), blades approximately 8 cm above the waterline.

Fig. 5:vi. The recovery – hands.

Fig. 5:vii. The recovery – body/slide.

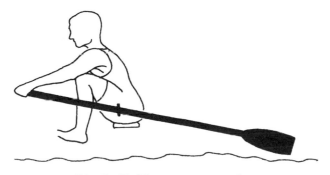

Fig. 5:viii. The recovery – catch.

Sequence shots of the sculling stroke from behind

Sequence shots of the sculling stroke from the side

Rhythm

In rowing the term 'rhythm' is used to describe the ratio between the drive and the recovery, i.e., the ratio between the work phase of the stroke and the relaxation phase of the stroke. Good rhythm enables you to get the optimum run from the boat during each stroke cycle, utilizing maximum power, and to create a space for rest between strokes. It makes rowing look easy, even effortless, and the rate of striking to appear lower than it actually is!

How do you create a rhythm?

When a novice crew first learns to row, the coach enforces a ratio of one to two by asking the crew to count, 'one, two, three' through the stroke. The count of 'one' from the catch to the finish, and 'two, three' for the duration of the recovery. The actual ratio used by any one crew to develop rhythm may vary, but the most common ratio used is one to two.

The coach of a more experienced crew, rather than counting, will often use the expression, 'sting and float' to remind the crew how to develop rhythm. Sting refers to the quick pick-up of the catch, and float to the more relaxed movement during the recovery.

In any crew the rhythm is set by the stroke of the crew and mirrored by the oarsman positioned on bowside directly behind him (No. 7 in an eight, No. 3 in a four and the Bowman in a pair). It is essential that the whole crew rows with the same rhythm and moves as one. This is achieved by each oarsman having identical seat movement and bladework. To achieve identical seat movement you should mirror the seat movement of the oarsman sitting directly in front of you. To achieve identical bladework, follow the bladework of the oarsman ahead who is situated on the same side of the boat as yourself. The rhythm may also be shaped and supported by the commands of the coxswain.

The most common rhythm fault is a breakdown of the ratio, usually failing to take enough time to come forward up the slide on the recovery. Consequently, the ratio becomes one to one, rather than one to two, and there is then no time to rest on the way forward during the recovery. This alteration to the ratio is often referred to as 'rushing up the slide', and causes the crew to tire more quickly.

Balance

Executing a perfect rowing stroke is not an insurmountable ambition for any oarsman, but it is made more difficult to achieve by the *instability* of the rowing boat. This instability is created by the narrow, hydrodynamic shape of the boat which has evolved to minimize the drag (the braking effect of the surface tension of water) and to maximize the speed attainable. Surface tension exists because the surface of any liquid behaves like a stretched elastic membrane. The braking effect exerted by the surface tension of the water, is proportional to the surface area (SA) of the boat in contact with the water. The flatter the bottom of the boat, the greater the surface area in contact with the water, and therefore the greater the braking effect of the surface tension. Thus, a flat-bottomed boat is a stable, but slow boat. The choice, therefore, is speed or stability. Obviously, it is more important for the beginner to have stability and the élite oarsman to have speed, hence, a spectrum of boats of differing stability is usually made available at most rowing clubs.

To overcome the problem of having to cope with the instability of a boat whilst learning basic technique, it is advisable to teach the beginner the basic stroke on a rowing ergometer or in a rowing tank. On a rowing ergometer or in a rowing tank the action of rowing in a boat may be assimilated

A rowing tank in use.

whilst sitting on dry land. They may be used throughout the year in the warmth of indoors and present no balance problems. The tank is the ideal because it is possible to teach both body position and bladework orientated around the actual parts of a boat, using oars that are similar to those which will be used once the basics have been grasped. Unfortunately rowing tanks are few and far between in this country but the ergometer has proved to be a satisfactory substitute as a teaching apparatus. However, the action is more like sculling than rowing, and it is only possible to teach body positions not bladework on the ergometer.

With a good grasp of the basic movements the beginner should be taken afloat in a tub pair. This is a very stable, heavy boat that allows the beginner to practise movements taught in the tank/ergometer whilst experiencing the gentle roll of a boat. In the tub pair confidence drills are practised along with balance drills (*see* Chapter 7: Training). The new rower is introduced to the concept of moving in unison with another person. The tub pair is probably the most important boat for the development of good rowing technique, it is also, sadly, probably the most under-used boat in any club. It should not be an embarrassment for the more experienced oarsman to be seen spending a couple of hours in the tub pair concentrating on basic technique. I am Olympic and World Champion and yet I *still* regularly use a tub pair to correct small technical faults.

Once good technique has been mastered in the tub pair, the oarsman moves into a restricted four or eight and the process starts all over again. These boats introduce a slightly more unstable platform (being less flat bottomed but possessing a small keel) and the need to move in unison with a larger number of people.

The final step is to move into a 'fine' or 'best' boat. These are the least stable and permit the development of considerable speed in favourable weather – if good technique is maintained.

The progression of boat types listed above is used to teach an individual to row, a similar progression of boat stability is found for sculling. The basic movements are again taught in a rowing tank/ergometer and then the beginner is taken afloat in a playboat, a restricted scull, a tracer scull and finally a fine sculling boat.

A balanced boat is necessary if a crew are to achieve maximum efficiency when rowing flat out. To maintain good

An international oarswoman using a playboat to revise her basic technique.

balance the oar handles need to be held at the same height throughout the stroke, the bodies need to remain as central as possible and all movements or changes in weight distribution need to be done as one throughout the crew.

The development of equal hand heights may be helped with the use of drinking straws. Straws are attached to the side of the boat at frontstops marking the length of the stroke and the height of the hands at the catch. With each stroke the crew are encouraged to bring their hands to the height and position of the straws. In addition to the use of straws there are a number of rowing drills which help to develop balance in a crew (for a full explanation of these drills refer to Chapter 7: Training).

Technique for different boat types

Basic technique is identical for all boat types – sculling and rowing, but there needs to be a different emphasis in the stroke to allow for differing boat speeds. In the faster boat the emphasis needs to be on the catch. This is because in the faster boat it is virtually impossible to accelerate the blade to the finish *faster* than the speed at which the boat is travelling. The greatest opportunity to increase boat speed is during the first half metre of the stroke. Conversely, in the slower boat the emphasis needs to be on the finish, as it is possible to accelerate the blade to the finish faster than the speed at which the boat is travelling. The last half metre of the stroke become the most important for developing increased boat speed.

6

FAULTS: CAUSES AND SOLUTIONS

This chapter is designed to provide a quick and easy reference for unravelling problems of technique within a crew. It considers the more common faults, their causes and the possible solutions.

Bladework faults

FAULT
Timing late at the catch.

SYMPTOM
Blade not covered and locked on to the water quick enough at the catch in comparison with the blade of the stroke of the crew.

CAUSE	CAUSE
Rushing up the slide too fast into frontstops with little control.	Lack of co-ordination between arms and legs at the catch.

SOLUTION	SOLUTION
Practise rhythm exercises, establishing a good ratio will establish good slide control.	Concentrate on driving with the arms and legs at the same time, opening out the body angle simultaneously.

FAULT
Skying at the catch.

SYMPTOM
As the blade approaches the catch, instead of being lowered to just above the waterline, it is lifted away from the waterline.

CAUSE
Pushing the hands down towards the toes just before the catch.

SOLUTION
Allow the hands to rise just before the catch. You should feel as though you could stand up on the stretcher as you begin to apply the pressure at the catch. To do this the upper body needs to be raised up over the knees.

CAUSE
Over reaching at the catch.

SOLUTION
Practise body-position exercises, and mark with straws the 'body-over' position from backstops. Once this position is reached following the finish, the body position should be held through to the catch.

CAUSE
Dropping the head over the feet.

SOLUTION
Always look up at the head of the person seated in front of you or at an object in the distance if there is no one in front of you.

CAUSE
Too much height of the work.

SOLUTION
Check the height of the work.

CAUSE
Blade being held too close to the water during the recovery, and therefore raised just before the catch to provide room to square without clipping the water.

SOLUTION
Practise square-blade paddling and blade-control exercises.

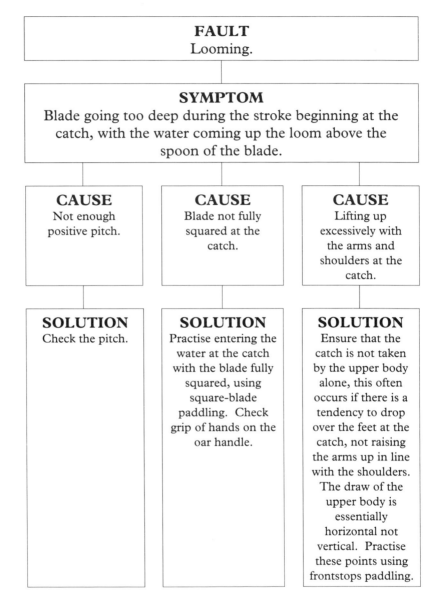

FAULT
Looming.

SYMPTOM
Blade going too deep during the stroke beginning at the catch, with the water coming up the loom above the spoon of the blade.

CAUSE
Not enough positive pitch.

CAUSE
Blade not fully squared at the catch.

CAUSE
Lifting up excessively with the arms and shoulders at the catch.

SOLUTION
Check the pitch.

SOLUTION
Practise entering the water at the catch with the blade fully squared, using square-blade paddling. Check grip of hands on the oar handle.

SOLUTION
Ensure that the catch is not taken by the upper body alone, this often occurs if there is a tendency to drop over the feet at the catch, not raising the arms up in line with the shoulders. The draw of the upper body is essentially horizontal not vertical. Practise these points using frontstops paddling.

FAULT
Backsplash.

SYMPTOM
Water being knocked back towards the bows by the blade at the catch.

CAUSE
Too slow blade entry relative to the speed of the boat.

CAUSE
Incorrect direction of blade entry.

SOLUTION
Increase the speed of connection at the catch by practising frontstops paddling.

SOLUTION
Make sure the blade enters the water travelling towards the stern as well as downwards. Refer to Chapter 5: Technique.

FAULT
The short stroke.

SYMPTOM
Arc of the blade obviously short in comparison with other blades in the boat. The stroke may be short at the finish, the catch or both.

CAUSE
Stretcher positioned too close to the line of work, or the rake of the stretcher is too steep.

CAUSE
Not allowing the body to follow the arc of the blade around the rigger at the catch and the finish.

SOLUTION
Check the stretcher position.

SOLUTION
Ensure that the shoulders remain parallel to the blade throughout the stroke, twisting through the lower rib-cage.

FAULT
The two-part stroke.

SYMPTOM
Blade deceleration in the middle of the stroke. The blade is accelerated from the catch, allowed to slow in the middle of the stroke and again accelerated to the finish.

CAUSE	CAUSE	CAUSE
Overgearing.	Uneven power through the stroke.	Driving with the legs before the blade is locked ('Bum shoving').

SOLUTION	SOLUTION	SOLUTION
Check the spread of the boat and the inboard of the blades and ensure it is appropriate for the type of boat and size of crew in question.	Accelerate the blade evenly through the stroke from the catch to the finish.	Practise blade-control exercises.

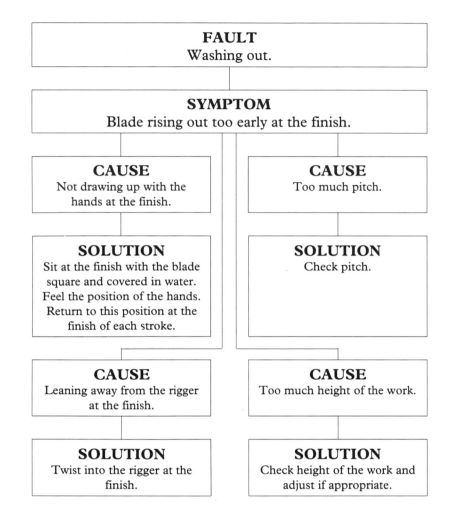

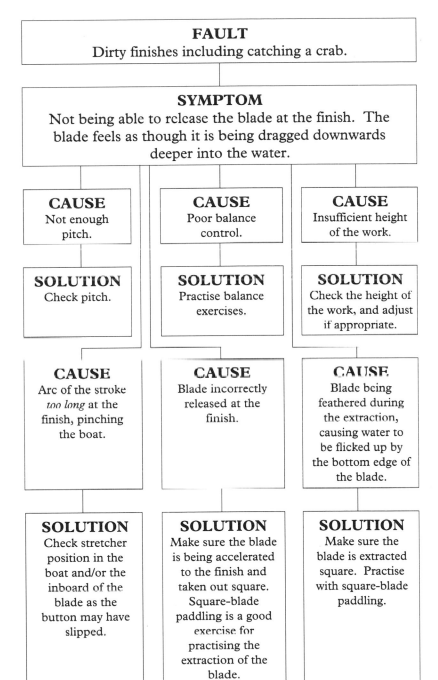

FAULT
Dirty finishes including catching a crab.

SYMPTOM
Not being able to release the blade at the finish. The blade feels as though it is being dragged downwards deeper into the water.

CAUSE
Not enough pitch.

SOLUTION
Check pitch.

CAUSE
Poor balance control.

SOLUTION
Practise balance exercises.

CAUSE
Insufficient height of the work.

SOLUTION
Check the height of the work, and adjust if appropriate.

CAUSE
Arc of the stroke *too long* at the finish, pinching the boat.

SOLUTION
Check stretcher position in the boat and/or the inboard of the blade as the button may have slipped.

CAUSE
Blade incorrectly released at the finish.

SOLUTION
Make sure the blade is being accelerated to the finish and taken out square. Square-blade paddling is a good exercise for practising the extraction of the blade.

CAUSE
Blade being feathered during the extraction, causing water to be flicked up by the bottom edge of the blade.

SOLUTION
Make sure the blade is extracted square. Practise with square-blade paddling.

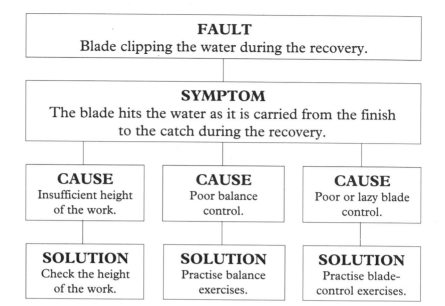

FAULT
Blade clipping the water during the recovery.

SYMPTOM
The blade hits the water as it is carried from the finish
to the catch during the recovery.

CAUSE
Insufficient height
of the work.

CAUSE
Poor balance
control.

CAUSE
Poor or lazy blade
control.

SOLUTION
Check the height
of the work.

SOLUTION
Practise balance
exercises.

SOLUTION
Practise blade-
control exercises.

Body position faults

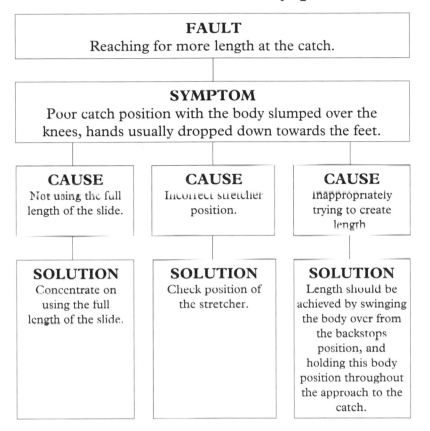

FAULT
Reaching for more length at the catch.

SYMPTOM
Poor catch position with the body slumped over the knees, hands usually dropped down towards the feet.

CAUSE
Not using the full length of the slide.

CAUSE
Incorrect stretcher position.

CAUSE
Inappropriately trying to create length

SOLUTION
Concentrate on using the full length of the slide.

SOLUTION
Check position of the stretcher.

SOLUTION
Length should be achieved by swinging the body over from the backstops position, and holding this body position throughout the approach to the catch.

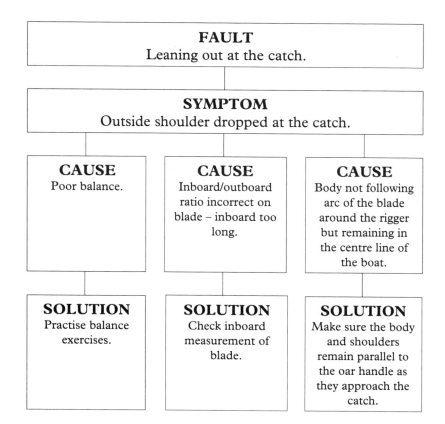

FAULT
Leaning out at the catch.

SYMPTOM
Outside shoulder dropped at the catch.

CAUSE
Poor balance.

CAUSE
Inboard/outboard ratio incorrect on blade – inboard too long.

CAUSE
Body not following arc of the blade around the rigger but remaining in the centre line of the boat.

SOLUTION
Practise balance exercises.

SOLUTION
Check inboard measurement of blade.

SOLUTION
Make sure the body and shoulders remain parallel to the oar handle as they approach the catch.

| **FAULT** |
| The bent arm catch. |

| **SYMPTOM** |
| Arms bent at the moment the blade enters the water. |

| **CAUSE** | **CAUSE** |
| Applying too much pressure with the arms at the catch. | Sliding forward on the recovery with bent arms. |

| **SOLUTION** | **SOLUTION** |
| Relax the grip of the hands on the blade. The hands should be hooked around the blade, and when the legs drive at the catch the hands should feel as though they are momentarily left behind, thus keeping the arms extended, feeling a pull through the shoulders. | Stretch off backstops with straight arms, and maintain this position. Do not allow a lack of slide control to let your seat try to overtake your hands! Remember, 'Hands, body, slide.' |

FAULT
Bum shoving (slide shooting).

SYMPTOM
Driving the seat towards backstops before the spoon of the blade has entered the water at the catch.

CAUSE
The legs being driven faster than the speed at which the blade is being pulled by the hands.

CAUSE
Commencing the leg drive before the blade has entered the water.

SOLUTION
The hands and legs need to have a co-ordinated action. The speed at which the seat travels needs to match that at which the blade is travelling. To help correct this fault try to pull the blade through the shins on the drive.

SOLUTION
Speed up the blade entry at the catch. Useful exercises include backstops paddling, 1/2 slide paddling and frontstops paddling.

CAUSE
Stretching for too much forward length, which places the back in a weak position.

CAUSE
Trunk not strong enough to hold firm during the leg drive.

SOLUTION
Establish position of body over from backstops and mark on the saxboards with a straw, always swing over to this point on all strokes and no further.

SOLUTION
Strengthen the back and stomach muscles by leg raises lying face down, dorsal raises to the horizontal lying over the side of a table with the legs held firm and abdominal crunches.

FAULT
Inside shoulder hunched up.

SYMPTOM
Inside shoulder held high next to the earlobe and never relaxed during the stroke.

CAUSE	CAUSE	CAUSE
Pulling too hard with the inside arm, common in people changing sides.	Hands too close together.	Grip of the inside hand too far over the oar handle.

SOLUTION	SOLUTION	SOLUTION
Establish that the inside hand controls feathering and squaring, and the outside hand draws the blade. Emphasized by the exercises: a. Paddling with the outside hand off the blade, b. Paddling with the inside hand down the loom.	Check the position of the hands they should be a minimum of two hand widths apart, but no more than shoulder width apart. A good method of establishing the correct position of the hands is to row with the outside hand off allowing the inside hand to find a position of comfortable draw, then replacing the outside hand close to the end of the oar handle.	Check the position of the grip, wrists and arms in a straight line during the draw (*see* Fig. 5:5 in Chapter 5: Technique).

FAULT
Lack of slide control.

SYMPTOM
Usually recognized by a feeling of being rushed, constantly chasing the next stroke. The rating always feels and appears to be higher than it actually is. E.g., a rating of 28 may look and feel like a rating of 36.

CAUSE
Poor rhythm.

SOLUTION
Establish good rhythm as described in Chapter 5: Technique by counting through the stroke.

FAULT
Legs not driving evenly through the stroke.

SYMPTOM
Knees failing to reach the flattened position at the end of the stroke together.

CAUSE
Unequal pressure of the legs on the stretcher during the drive.

CAUSE
Poor balance.

SOLUTION
Concentrate on pushing evenly with both legs. There may be a discrepancy in the strength of the quadriceps of the two legs which will produce an unequal drive. In this case strengthen the weaker leg by static quadriceps exercises. Check for an underlying leg length difference and/or low-back problems which may be the cause of strength discrepancy between the legs.

SOLUTION
Practise balance exercises.

FAULT
Drawing the body up on to the oar handle at the finish.

SYMPTOM
At the finish the shoulders and head are held above or in front of the oar handle instead of behind it, and the body has not passed back through the vertical but is held at the vertical or slightly hunched forward.

CAUSE	CAUSE	CAUSE
Not maintaining the pressure on the stretcher in the later part of the stroke.	Failure to use the power of the shoulders at the finish.	Using the arms to pull too early during the stroke.

SOLUTION	SOLUTION	SOLUTION
Do not allow the feet to lose their grip on the stretcher during the stroke, especially the last third of the stroke.	Ensure that the outside shoulder is being drawn around the rigger parallel to the oar handle and that the shoulders are opened out at the finish. Imagine that you are trying to get your shoulder blades to touch each other as you approach the finish. Practise the draw while paddling with the inside arm down the loom.	The arms should act as tight ropes linking the oar handle to the trunk until the body has reached at least the vertical. Once the body is at the vertical the arm draw should commence. With the arm draw the elbows begin to bend.

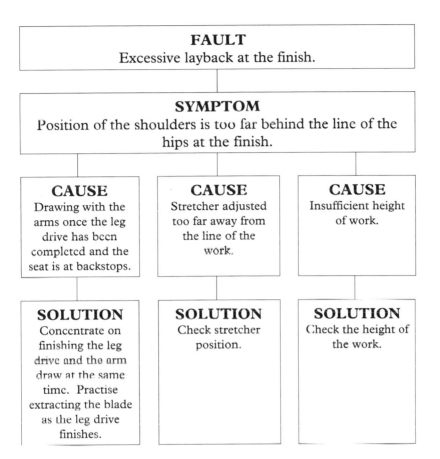

FAULT
Excessive layback at the finish.

SYMPTOM
Position of the shoulders is too far behind the line of the hips at the finish.

CAUSE
Drawing with the arms once the leg drive has been completed and the seat is at backstops.

CAUSE
Stretcher adjusted too far away from the line of the work.

CAUSE
Insufficient height of work.

SOLUTION
Concentrate on finishing the leg drive and the arm draw at the same time. Practise extracting the blade as the leg drive finishes.

SOLUTION
Check stretcher position.

SOLUTION
Check the height of the work.

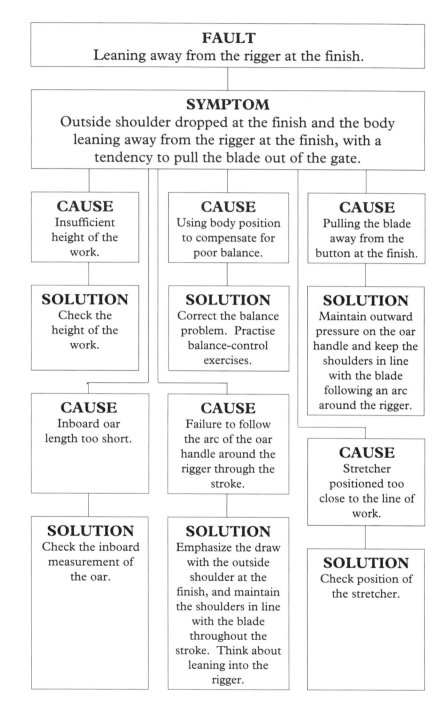

FAULT
Leaning away from the rigger at the finish.

SYMPTOM
Outside shoulder dropped at the finish and the body leaning away from the rigger at the finish, with a tendency to pull the blade out of the gate.

CAUSE
Insufficient height of the work.

CAUSE
Using body position to compensate for poor balance.

CAUSE
Pulling the blade away from the button at the finish.

SOLUTION
Check the height of the work.

SOLUTION
Correct the balance problem. Practise balance-control exercises.

SOLUTION
Maintain outward pressure on the oar handle and keep the shoulders in line with the blade following an arc around the rigger.

CAUSE
Inboard oar length too short.

CAUSE
Failure to follow the arc of the oar handle around the rigger through the stroke.

CAUSE
Stretcher positioned too close to the line of work.

SOLUTION
Check the inboard measurement of the oar.

SOLUTION
Emphasize the draw with the outside shoulder at the finish, and maintain the shoulders in line with the blade throughout the stroke. Think about leaning into the rigger.

SOLUTION
Check position of the stretcher.

Hand faults

FAULT
Using the outside hand to square at the catch and feather at the finish.

SYMPTOM
The wrist of the outside arm instead of remaining flat through the stroke is raised above the oar handle at the catch and dropped below the oar handle at the finish.

CAUSE
Gripping the oar handle too tightly especially with the outside hand. This prevents the oar handle being rotated within the outside hand by the inside hand.

SOLUTION
Ensure that the inside hand is responsible for squaring/feathering the blade at both the catch and the finish. Useful exercises to practise this are: a. Outside hand off. b. Inside hand down the loom.

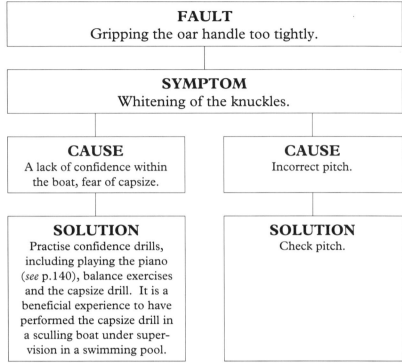

FAULT
Gripping the oar handle too tightly.

SYMPTOM
Whitening of the knuckles.

CAUSE
A lack of confidence within the boat, fear of capsize.

CAUSE
Incorrect pitch.

SOLUTION
Practise confidence drills, including playing the piano (*see* p.140), balance exercises and the capsize drill. It is a beneficial experience to have performed the capsize drill in a sculling boat under super-vision in a swimming pool.

SOLUTION
Check pitch.

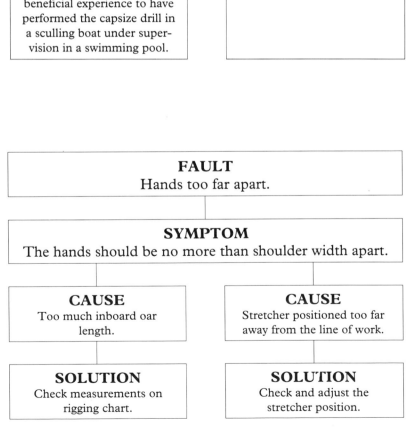

FAULT
Hands too far apart.

SYMPTOM
The hands should be no more than shoulder width apart.

CAUSE
Too much inboard oar length.

CAUSE
Stretcher positioned too far away from the line of work.

SOLUTION
Check measurements on rigging chart.

SOLUTION
Check and adjust the stretcher position.

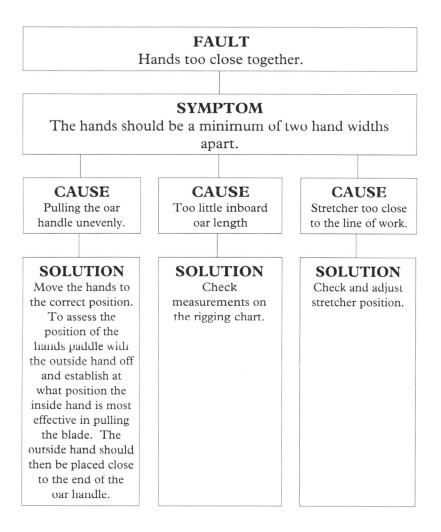

Crews who do not have the luxury of a personal coach should be able to coach themselves by the critical appraisal of a training/racing video together with the information provided.

7

TRAINING

Anyone who has rowed at any level will have experienced the misery of winter training – running in the rain, rowing on rough water created by adverse wind conditions, fingers turning blue as the temperature drops. If winter training is so unpleasant why do so many people continue to do it year after year?

Without a doubt the answer is: to improve the next season's performance.

But does the training you do really benefit you in the way that you want? Every crew has its own failings, every individual his own weaknesses determined by his physiology, and training to improve performance should be directed specifically at these weak parameters.

The aim of training

Figure 7:1: The aim of training is an attempt to break down and analyse the aims of a training programme. It identifies three methods of achieving an improvement in performance, each on their own would provide a means for progress, but if used together the effect is amplified.

The three methods identified are:

1. Increase muscle efficiency by increasing strength and lactate tolerance; exactly how will be examined further in this chapter.

2. Improve mental skills. This aspect of sports training is rapidly being recognized as an important prerequisite for success. It is essential to develop skills that allow a realistic development of self-belief, and a way of controlling the body's

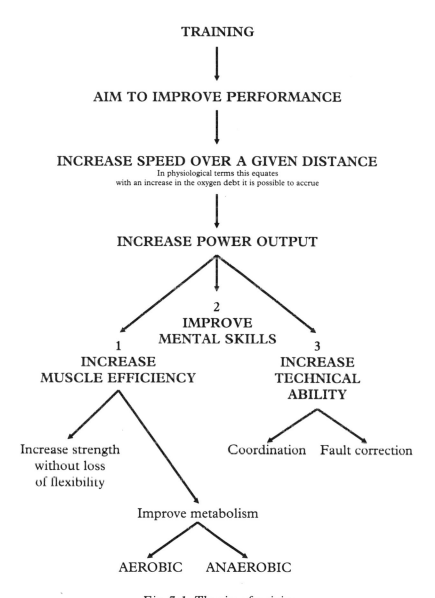

Fig. 7:1. The aim of training.

response to stress. A competition is perceived by the body as a threat and produces the 'fight or flight' reaction that we all recognize – increased heart rate, sweaty palms, butterflies in the stomach, nausea etc., etc. This response is only natural but can lead to a disappointing performance.

An introduction to training the mind is given in Chapter 9: Racing: preparation and strategy.

3. Increase technical ability. Watching crews race at domestic regattas I am amazed at the poor technical ability of even the 'top' crews. Boat speed is achieved by brute force and is made very much more strenuous through technical errors. Time spent developing good basic technique will make a crew more efficient at developing boat speed.

NB. Some useful exercises are listed later in this chapter for use during technical outings and warm-up routines. (Refer also to Chapter 5: Technique.)

Muscle

Before examining the principles of training, let's spend some time considering muscle itself.

Muscle is a contractile tissue by which movement is effected. Muscles which exert their influence across joints are referred to as skeletal muscles, and account for 40–50 per cent of the total body weight. Skeletal muscle is the largest organ of the human body.

When a muscle contracts the muscle belly is visibly shortened, initiating movement. The detail of how the muscle shortens is not relevant here, but it is important to appreciate that for a muscle to contract *energy* is consumed. Failure in the supply of energy prevents the muscle from contracting and is a recognized cause of fatigue in training or competition.

Metabolism of glycogen within the muscle cell provides the main source of energy for contraction. Glycogen is derived from the diet as explained in Chapter 12. The metabolism can be aerobic, in which oxygen is required, or anaerobic, which is able to occur in the absence of oxygen.

Aerobic metabolism of glycogen

$$\textbf{GLYCOGEN + OXYGEN} \rightarrow$$
$$\textit{Energy + Carbon Dioxide + Water}$$

The aerobic metabolism of glycogen produces thirteen times more energy than the anaerobic metabolism, and is thus the preferred metabolic pathway for any form of endurance exercise. The body has sufficient stores of glycogen in the muscles and liver to supply energy through aerobic metabolism for two hours of continuous intense exercise.

A further advantage of aerobic metabolism is that the waste products of carbon dioxide and water are easily eliminated from the body by respiration.

In an event that lasts less than two hours the contribution of this metabolic pathway is limited by the supply of oxygen to the muscle cells. Training to improve both cardiovascular and respiratory function improves the body's ability to supply oxygen to the muscle during exercise and maximizes the aerobic component of exercise.

Anaerobic metabolism of glycogen

> ## GLYCOGEN →
> ### *Energy + Lactic Acid*

During intensive bursts of exercise the body is unable to deliver oxygen to the muscle cell quick enough to maintain aerobic production of energy. For muscle contraction to be possible the muscle is forced to derive energy by a less efficient pathway – anaerobically.

Metabolism of glycogen by this method produces lactic acid as a waste product. This is not easily disposed of and accumulates within the muscle cell. Accumulation of lactic acid causes muscle soreness to develop and prevents continuation of exercise at the same intensity.

It is the accumulation of lactic acid that limits the contribution of this metabolic pathway during exercise. The level of intensity of exercise at which the lactic acid begins to accumulate can be altered through training. If the intensity of exercise is dropped and the supply of oxygen to the muscle reestablished, lactic acid itself may be metabolized aerobically to provide a source of energy. This means that an athlete can push for short periods at higher intensity during an endurance event.

A further source of energy is provided by the anaerobic metabolism of creatine phosphate, a substance that is stored in the muscle. Anaerobic metabolism of this substance does not produce lactic acid which is an obvious advantage. The stores of creatine phosphate are rapidly depleted however and can only provide sufficient energy for the 'start up' of exercise.

During exercise the body is able to use both aerobic and anaerobic pathways to provide energy. The two pathways are not alternatives, but are used simultaneously, the contribution of each being determined by the duration and intensity of the exercise. It is possible to train specifically for either anaerobic development or for aerobic development. Short intense periods of exercise tend to develop the anaerobic pathway whilst prolonged training at a lower intensity tends to develop the aerobic pathway.

During a 2,000 metres rowing event, 80 per cent of the energy for muscular contraction is derived aerobically and 20 per cent anaerobically.

Skeletal muscle can be classified by the type of contraction it undergoes:

a. Fast twitch (FT): fibres which contract very rapidly, fatigue rapidly and use predominantly anaerobic metabolism of glycogen as a source of fuel. These fibres are responsible for high speed movements of small duration.

b. Slow twitch (ST): fibres which contract more slowly, are more resistant to fatigue and are able to use the aerobic metabolism of glycogen and fat as a source of fuel. These fibres are responsible for a more sustained lower level of effort.

The distribution of FT:ST fibres in an individual is partly inherited, but it is possible to alter the distribution by stressing the muscle specifically in training.

Fast twitch fibres may be trained to change to slow twitch fibres by endurance work, and vice versa by interval work. It is easier to change FT to ST.

The muscular involvement of the rowing stroke

At the catch the opening of the body angle is effected by the contraction of the buttock muscles. The leg drive is created by contraction of the quadricep muscles of the anterior thigh flattening the bent knees, and contraction of the calf muscles – gastronemius and soleus – which open out the angle of the ankle joint. For the leg drive to be effectively transmitted through to the oar the trunk needs to be held firm. This is achieved by contraction of the muscular corset formed by the lumbar erector spinae (back) muscles and the abdominal muscles (Fig. 7:2).

The arms are held straight throughout the draw by the contraction of the tricep muscle on the back of the upper arm, the height of the arm being adjusted by muscles that act around the shoulder joint, in particular, pectoralis major, deltoid and latissimus dorsi.

As the finish is approached the oar handle is drawn into the body using biceps, brachioradialis and brachialis, the muscles of the anterior upper arm. The extraction of the blade is completed by turning the wrists effected by contraction of the forearm muscles.

During the recovery, the body is pulled forward over the knees by the momentum created by the passage of the oar handle and by activity of the abdominal muscles. Contraction of the hamstrings in the posterior thigh bends the knees and draws the body towards the feet which are fixed in the shoes of the footplate (Fig. 7:3).

Principles of training

As demonstrated a large muscle mass is used in rowing, and the

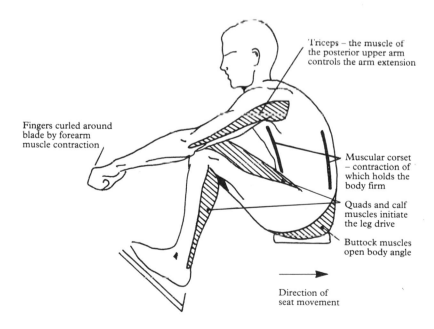

Triceps – the muscle of the posterior upper arm controls the arm extension

Fingers curled around blade by forearm muscle contraction

Muscular corset – contraction of which holds the body firm

Quads and calf muscles initiate the leg drive

Buttock muscles open body angle

Direction of seat movement

Fig. 7:2. Muscular effort at catch and initiation of the leg drive.

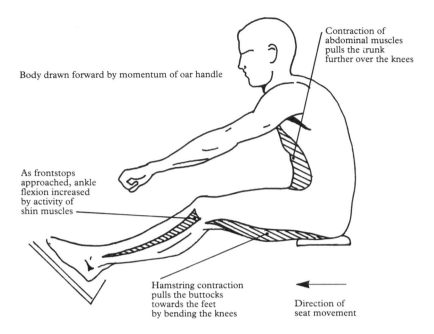

Contraction of
abdominal muscles
pulls the trunk
further over the knees

Body drawn forward by momentum of oar handle

As frontstops
approached, ankle
flexion increased
by activity of
shin muscles

Hamstring contraction
pulls the buttocks
towards the feet
by bending the knees

Direction of
seat movement

Fig. 7:3. Muscular effort during the recovery of the stroke.

duration of the exercise lends itself to the use of predominantly aerobic power.

Training for rowing should therefore be directed at developing the strength and the aerobic capacity of the skeletal muscle mass. To do this the *intensity of training* needs to be just below the anaerobic threshold of the individual.

The anaerobic threshold (AT)

The anaerobic threshold (AT) or onset of blood lactate accumulation (OBLA) is defined as the point during exercise when the cardiovascular and respiratory systems fail to supply the exercising muscle with adequate oxygen for the metabolism of glycogen to continue aerobically, and anaerobic metabolism starts to dominate.

There are several methods of assessing the AT of an athlete, but only one is really possible without sophisticated laboratory equipment. This involves a step-up workload on an ergometer whilst reading heart rates from a heart-rate monitor, and gives an approximation of the AT which is good enough to establish the intensity of training for an individual.

Assessing AT with step-up ergometer
work and heart rates

This method requires the use of a Concept II ergometer and a heart-rate monitor, consisting of a chest band and a digital wrist display, measuring beat per minute (bpm).

Before commencing the workout, do a thorough warm up and stretch routine. The procedure for the test is very simple, every 2 minutes the 500-metres' split time is reduced and at 10–15 second intervals the heart rate is recorded. The step-ups are continued until the athlete is unable to maintain the power for the full 2 minutes. As soon as the power starts to fall the test is over.

Men	Women
155	210
150	205
145	200
142	157
139	154
136	151
133	148
133 etc.	145 etc.

Fig. 7:4. Step-ups – 500-metres' split time

Plot the heart rate against the power as in Figure 7:5. The steep incline of the heart rate corresponds to the heart rate of the anaerobic threshold.

Having established the heart rate of the AT, aerobic training is most effective at a heart rate just below, i.e. if the heart rate of the AT is 175 bpm, training for aerobic improvement should be at a heart rate of 155–170 bpm.

Adequacy of the training load

The load of training must always be a challenge to an athlete's present physical condition, and the load needs to be adjusted on a cyclical basis for continued improvement to be maintained. It is recognized that a given stress to the body will result in a period of fatigue when the body first experiences the load, followed by recovery and then overcompensation. (Fig. 7:6).

Once the body has adapted itself to a given load no further

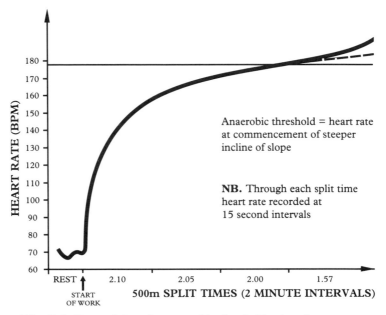

Anaerobic threshold = heart rate at commencement of steeper incline of slope

NB. Through each split time heart rate recorded at 15 second intervals

Fig. 7:5. Determining the anaerobic threshold using the ergometer step-up test.

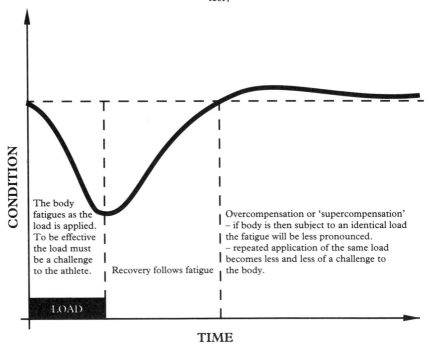

The body fatigues as the load is applied. To be effective the load must be a challenge to the athlete.

Recovery follows fatigue

Overcompensation or 'supercompensation' – if body is then subject to an identical load the fatigue will be less pronounced. – repeated application of the same load becomes less and less of a challenge to the body.

Fig. 7:6. The effect of a given training load on the body providing the load is a challenge to the physical fitness of the athlete.

improvement can be made unless a training load of higher quality or quantity is used to force the body into further adaptation.

This scenario is probably one with which you are all familiar. A training programme always feels harder for the first few sessions, but with repetition the body adapts to the load and the training begins to feel easier – at this point the load is always raised.

Rest and recovery are also important parts of the training load, as it is during this time, rather than whilst the load is being applied, that the body actually adapts.

The wrong combination of frequency and loading of training leads to a chronic fatigue state, with failure to adapt and failure to perform. Looking at the human function curve (Fig. 7:7), further stress at this time only pushes an individual towards ill health. This situation in an athlete is referred to as overtraining syndrome – or burnout.

It is important for any athlete to realize that everyday life is a stress to the body; exercise is added stress. The body is only able to tolerate a given quantity of stress at any one time. For this reason events outside the training programme need to be taken into consideration, and, if necessary, the load reduced to

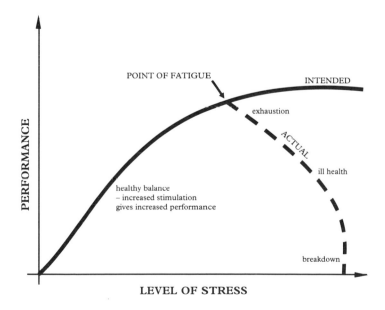

Fig. 7:7. The human function curve (P. G. F. Nixon 1984).

prevent the development of overtraining/overstress syndrome. The first thing that should cross an athlete's or coach's mind when recurrent injury or illness occurs is whether the total load is too high.

Wave principle of training

The training cycle is a limited period of training usually between four to eight weeks, during which time the programme is directed towards a specific goal.

Training cycles follow the wave principle by varying the load in different training sessions. The best results are achieved if the load is increased over three consecutive days followed by a lighter day or a day of rest.

The same principle applies to the changing load of the whole cycle – week by week, day by day.

Specificity of training

Finally each training session needs to be specific, the body responds in a specific way to a particular type of training.

So what training should you do?

It is not possible to draw up one training programme which would suit everyone because each person is different and the load and intensity should vary depending on individual circumstances and needs. The equipment available also varies.

However, it is possible to illustrate the type of exercise both within the boat and on dry land that encourages aerobic and anaerobic development.

Using this information in combination with the basic principles of training, and an understanding of muscle itself, you should be able to draw up a training programme for yourself.

Talking to the top coaches within the sport, it is evident that although they are all equipped with the same basic knowledge, they have vastly differing ideas about how to make a crew move a boat. Experience obviously plays a large part in judging the load of a training programme, experience which sometimes can only be gained by learning from mistakes.

A training programme needs to be as varied as possible to prevent the development of boredom and mental fatigue, especially during the winter when races are few and far between.

The current opinion about the type of training necessary is that during the winter (September to March) 90 per cent of the workload should be aerobic exercise, with only 10 per cent anaerobic workload. During the summer months (March to September) this changes to 70 per cent aerobic workload and 30 per cent anaerobic workload.

Aerobic training methods

A. Water work

1. Steady state: a continuous piece of work at constant speed using firm pressure and low rating. Duration of session: 60–100 minutes. Rating 18–22. Heart rate (HR): 140–160 bpm (assuming a maximum HR of 190–200 bpm and an AT of 175 bpm).

2. Alternate work: a continuous piece of work alternating the speed of the boat at four-minute intervals by changing the rate of striking and the working pulse rate. Duration of session: 60 minutes. Rating: 20 alternating with rating 18/19. Heart Rate: 160–170 bpm alternating with 140–150 bpm.

3. Set-distance work on a background of steady state: a continuous piece of steady-state work. Heart rate: 120 bpm into which set-distance pieces are incorporated. Set-distance work involves rowing a distance of, for example, 2,000 metres in which at every 500-metres' point the rate is increased. At the end of the set distance the work continues but settles back into the steady-state work. Duration: 60–90 minutes.

As the season progresses, the rates used in the set-distance work increase, only ever reaching Race Pace (RP) during the last 500 metres.

Rates for winter set-distance work: 18–22
Rates for summer set-distance work: 26–30 (28–34 over 1,000 metres)

B. Land training

1. Cycle at constant heart rate of 15–20 bpm below the anaerobic threshold.

2. Run at constant heart rate of 15–20 bpm below the anaerobic threshold.

3. Ergometer work at constant heart rate of 15–20 bpm below

the anaerobic threshold. Always trying to achieve increased power for the same heart rate.

Anaerobic training methods

A. Water work

1. Anaerobic work on an aerobic base: used during the winter on a background of steady-state heart rate of 140 bpm: This consists of twelve to fifteen strokes in which the power is built to a maximum, the boat speed is built to a maximum and the rate is built up above race pace. The short burst of high-intensity exercise produces lactic acid which is then cleared by the continuing steady state.

Up to eight repetitions of fifteen strokes is possible during a steady-state workout of 60 minutes' duration, with long intervals of steady work in between.

2. Set-distance pieces: during the summer set-distance pieces are used alone for speed work, developing the anaerobic pathways. Distances of 500 metres, 1,000 metres and 1,500 metres are used, varying the rates every 500 metres through the distance. Usually two 1,500-metre pieces will be done in an outing or three 1,000-metre pieces or three to four 500-metre pieces. The rating is always race pace or above, for example: 2 × 1,500 metres = 500 metres race pace – 500 metres above race pace – 500 metres race pace – repeat.

3. Maximum speed work: a series of sets of twenty firm-pressure strokes with ten light-pressure strokes in between each set of twenty. The number of sets is determined by the target rate of striking (R), e.g. R36 = five sets, R38 = four sets and R40 = three sets. Building the rate of striking over the first ten strokes and holding the target rate for the second ten strokes.

To increase the training load, the number of light strokes between each set of twenty is reduced to five, and to reduce the load the number of light strokes is increased to twenty.

NB. It is important that anaerobic speed work is all done in the boat. As so little time is dedicated to speed training, it is critical to practise maintaining technique at the higher rates – this can only be done on the water.

B. Land Training

1. Circuit training with weights: there is always debate about

the relevance of using weights to train for rowing. My own opinion is that the use of weights predominantly in a muscular-endurance circuit can be very beneficial. I do feel, however, that lifting heavy weights to develop absolute muscle power is relevant and can make one prone to injury.

A muscular-endurance circuit is a continuous circuit of twelve to fifteen exercise stations, that lasts for up to one and a half hours. Each exercise should be of good quality, the circuit is done at a consistent pace without rest between exercises.

This is a more intense form of endurance training than steady-state boat work as you tend to work much closer to your anaerobic threshold.

The weights used during the circuit are only 40–50 per cent of maximum (a maximum weight being that possible for one lift without loss of range or technique).

The following are examples of the type of exercises to use in a muscular endurance circuit using weights:

i. Bench pulls: 40 repetitions.

ii. Squat jumps: 30 repetitions, jumping from a squat position with the fingers touching the floor to touch an object 12 inches above your outstretched arm when standing.

iii. Press ups: 20 repetitions.

iv. Upright rowing with a weight in each hand: 25 repetitions.

v. Sit-ups twisting to the opposite knee: 20 repetitions.

vi. Power strokes on the ergometer: 15 strokes.

vii. Bench press: 30 repetitions.

viii. Bench pull (greater weight than station i): 25 repetitions.

ix. Dorsal rises: 10 repetitions.

x. Angels, raising one arm with a weight of 2.5 kg and the opposite leg simultaneously whilst lying face down. Lift and hold: 20 repetitions.

xi. Abdominal crunches: 20 repetitions.

Rowing drills

1. Confidence drills

i. Standing up in the boat.

ii. Rotating the oar in the swivel during the recovery.

iii. Pushing the boat down to bowside by raising the strokeside blades.

iv. Pushing the boat down to strokeside by raising the bowside blades.

2. Finger relaxation exercise – piano playing

This exercise involves releasing the grip of each hand in turn, stretching the fingers out straight, and curling them back around the blade handle one at a time. It is a good exercise for releasing the grip on the oar handle whilst paddling at different pressures.

3. Rowing in pairs or fours through the boat

A useful exercise for the beginning of an outing as it develops good timing within the crew. Begin with bow pair or stern pair and work through the boat, then if appropriate work up into bow four and then stern four, and finally whole crew together.

4. Rhythm exercises

Paddling at different pressures, focusing on the speed of travel of the wheels of the seat during the float forwards on the recovery phase of each stroke. The wheels should move slower and slower as they approach frontstops but should never actually stop moving. Practising rhythm control with the eyes closed helps to develop this aspect of the stroke. This is a good exercise for learning to move as one in the boat and to move with the boat rather than upsetting its run.

5. Outside hand off

In this exercise the outside hand is removed from the blade; blade control is purely by the inside hand. It is usually done as a series of ten strokes followed by ten strokes at full pressure when the outside hand is replaced. This exercise reminds even the élite oarsman that the inside hand is principally for feathering and squaring the blade. When the outside hand is removed the inside hand often slips towards the end of the blade handle to be in a stronger position. If this occurs the hand positioning on the blade should be checked and adjusted if necessary. A good exercise for developing the use of the inside hand.

6. Inside hand down the loom

The inside hand is moved down the loom towards the spoon. As with the previous exercise this position is used for ten strokes, the hands are replaced in their normal position and ten strokes firm follow on. This exercise emphasizes the use of the outside arm in the draw. A good exercise for developing the use of the outside arm.

7. Single-stroke exercises

Single-stroke exercises are for balance practice. To balance a boat every person in the boat needs to move as one; moving identically so that the boat will sit level.

The exercise commences once the boat is running with the crew at half pressure. Single strokes are performed stopping at different positions through the stroke, e.g. hands away; body over; quarter slide; half slide; three-quarter slide.

Once the crew seem able to hold the boat level for each single stroke, try five strokes and then ten strokes. A good exercise for establishing good balance, slide control and reiterating movement as one within the boat.

8. Square-blade paddling

Rowing with the blade squared throughout the stroke is useful for several reasons. It reduces the clearance of the blade above the waterline, which in turn means that the blade control has to be more precise to maintain good even balance. It demonstrates the importance of accelerating the blade through to the finish, for in this exercise blade extraction is much more difficult if the blade is not accelerated. A good exercise for balance control and clean extraction of the blade at the finish.

9. Rowing with the feet out of the shoes

This exercise demonstrates the importance of co-ordinating the leg drive and the draw as one smooth action finishing at the same time. Drawing with the arms after the leg drive is complete takes the weight off the balls of the feet, the feet lift off the shoes and the rower is thrown backwards.

10. Extraction of the blade at the finish as the legs complete the drive

In this exercise the blade is purposely extracted from the water at the point when the legs are fully straightened. At first it will feel as though the blade handle is a long way from the body at the extraction. The object of the exercise is to pace the leg drive through the stroke. A good exercise for preventing the development of a two-part stroke.

11. Short-slide rowing

This exercise is performed at varying slide lengths: fixed seat no body swing; fixed seat with body swing; ¼ slide; ½ slide; ¾ slide; and full slide. The object of the exercise is to achieve quick catches and co-ordination of the body opening with the leg drive. The blades enter the water at a fast point in the stroke and have to move quickly to achieve grip on the water. Since the stroke is short, the quickness has to be emphasized because the sooner the blade grips the water the longer the stroke will be and therefore the more effective it can be. A good exercise for developing the connection at the catch and the application of the leg drive.

12. Light-pressure catch followed by firm finish

This exercise emphasizes the acceleration of the blade through the stroke to the finish.

13. Firm catch followed by light-pressure finish

This exercise emphasizes the pick up at the catch.

14. Half slide – full slide

Rowing firm for ten strokes using only half slide on the recovery, followed by rowing firm for ten strokes using full slide. This exercise emphasizes a quick catch and develops a strong connection between the leg drive and the pick up.

15. Air shots

In this exercise a normal stroke is taken followed by a stroke in which the blade is not placed in the water at the catch. The resistance felt as the leg drive is applied is so much less during the air shot that to be able to row an air shot without disturbing the run of the boat requires good blade and slide control.

8

STEERING AND COXING

Steering

If all rowing was done in perfect weather conditions on still water, with the blades on both sides of the boat pulling an identical force on a straight course with no obstacles, there would be no need to have a mechanism to steer.

A steering mechanism is a necessity to avoid obstacles, to counteract cross winds or currents, to follow the meandering course of the river and to compensate for the inequality of the 'pull' of the less experienced oarsman. It is a means of escape from potentially dangerous situations.

Broadly speaking there are two methods of steering a rowing boat:

a. With a rudder
b. Without a rudder

A rudder is defined in *Chambers's Twentieth Century Dictionary* as 'a flat structure hinged to the stern of a boat for steering' (Fig 8:1). Although this describes the type of rudder now only found on the older wooden rowing boats, in essence the idea is correct. More commonly today the rudder is a square- or oblong-shaped piece of metal or plastic attached to the end of a metal rod. This rod is threaded through a tube in the stern of the boat, and connected by a yoke to a system of wires which enable the steersman or coxswain to manoeuvre the boat. When the rudder is moved out of parallel with the boat, changes in the flow of water around the boat hull lead to a change in the direction the boat is travelling.

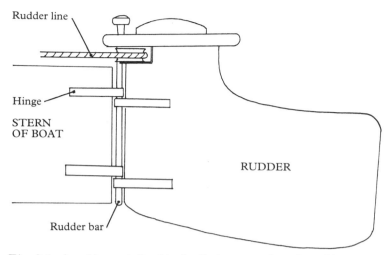

Fig. 8:1. A rudder as defined in the dictionary and used on older wooden boats.

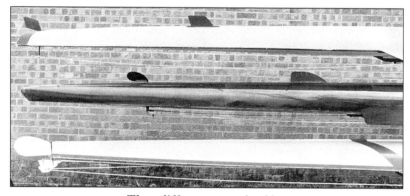

Three different types of rudder.

Steering without a rudder

With the exception of the single scull and the double scull, all types of rowing boat are steered with a rudder. Steering, in the absence of a rudder, is achieved by applying different pressures to the strokeside or bowside blade(s) during the propulsive phase of the stroke cycle. Although this method of steering is generally accepted, the way in which the pressure on the blade is increased remains a controversial issue. Commonly, a sculler is taught to accelerate the blade harder into the finish to change direction. I believe that with the body weight in the bows, and the lack of leverage at the finish position, the boat is less responsive at this point in the stroke and steering by this method becomes energy consuming and ineffective.

The most efficient way of steering is to apply a little more power at the commencement of the leg drive, with the opposite leg to the direction in which you wish to move. This in turn makes the catch slightly sharper on that side and changes the direction of the boat smoothly. If it is necessary to change direction more quickly to avoid the river bank or after being warned by an umpire for example, the same steering method as above is used, but in addition the power transmitted to the spoon of the blade is 'let off' on the side to which you wish to travel. When changing direction abruptly, it is often necessary to readjust your course to prevent oversteering.

Good steering is dependent on good visibility and a prior knowledge of the course being navigated. Sculling does not lend itself to good visibility as positioned in the boat your back faces the direction in which the boat travels. To check the boat is on course it is necessary to use both the senses of hearing and sight. By glancing, with gentle head and neck movements only, when halfway up the slide on the recovery, the boat course may be checked with minimal disturbance of rhythm or balance. Frequent brief glances rather than a long stare are sufficient to maintain a good course. In theory the shoulder over which to glance can be of personal preference, however, in practice it is safer to look over the shoulder closest to the river bank when travelling upstream i.e. the left shoulder.

In a double scull it is the bowman's job to steer in the same way as in a single scull. If the bowman has difficulty maintaining the desired course, he should ask the strokeman to help in an appropriate way. The strokeman of a double scull must have confidence in the steering ability of his bowman and should resist the temptation to correct the course of the boat until asked by the bowman.

Remember to anticipate a change in direction if at all possible and change direction gradually. Steering comes with practice and experience. Mistakes will be made on the way but these should be learnt from, not ridiculed.

Steering with a rudder

Steering by means of a rudder may be done by a coxswain or by a member of the crew acting as steersman, controlling the steering with the use of his foot.

The rudder is always positioned in the stern of the boat. It is

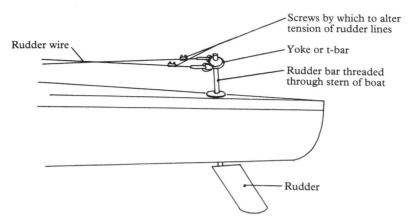

Fig. 8:2. A typical modern rudder.

attached to a rudder bar which slots into a tube running from
the bottom of the hull through to the stern canvas. Attached to
the top of the rudder bar is a yoke (or T-bar). Rudder wire, a
flexible metal cable, is attached to each side of the yoke by
means of a pulley which stops the wear from friction on the
rudder wires (Fig. 8:2).

In a coxless boat the rudder line passes from the left-hand
pulley, through eyelets along the inside of the right-hand
saxboard, across the boat and through eyelets along the inside
of the left-hand saxboard to attach to the right-hand pulley of
the yoke. As the rudder line crosses the boat it is attached to the
steersman's footplate. In a non-steering position, the soles of
the oarsman's shoes are fixed to the footplate by four screws.
One of the steersman's shoes is fixed in the normal way, and the
other is attached to his footplate by means of an extended
aluminium plate which allows the shoe to swivel from side to
side, permitting the rudder to be moved right and left. At the
top of the aluminium toe extension there is a wing-nut holding a
small clamp. The rudder line is attached to this clamp (Fig.
8:3).

The rudder, rudder bar and yoke are of similar construction
in a coxed boat. The rudder lines may be crossed as in the
coxless boat, or uncrossed. If they are uncrossed the wire
attached to the right-hand side of the yoke passes down
the right-hand side of the boat and similarly for the left. As the
rudder line crosses the boat it is attached to a handle which
the coxswain adjusts by hand to steer the boat. In some boats
there is no handle but loops in each side of the wire (Fig 8:4).

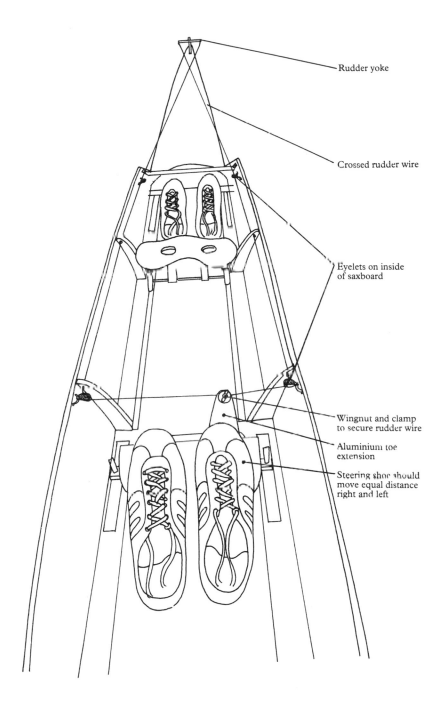

Rudder yoke

Crossed rudder wire

Eyelets on inside of saxboard

Wingnut and clamp to secure rudder wire

Aluminium toe extension

Steering shoe should move equal distance right and left

Fig. 8:3. Steering mechanism of a coxless pair.

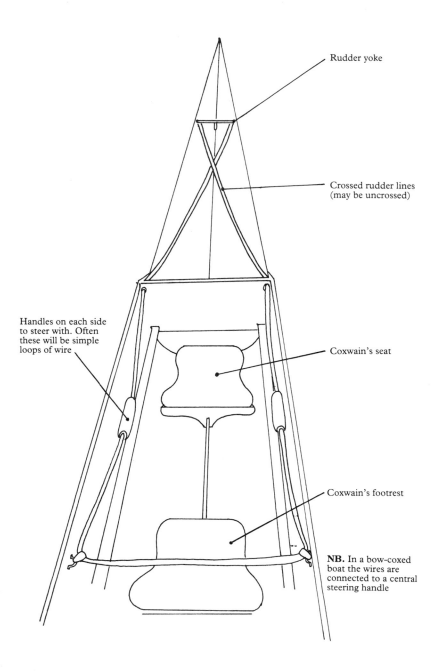

Rudder yoke

Crossed rudder lines
(may be uncrossed)

Handles on each side
to steer with. Often
these will be simple
loops of wire

Coxwain's seat

Coxwain's footrest

NB. In a bow-coxed
boat the wires are
connected to a central
steering handle

*Fig. 8:4. The steering mechanism of a stern coxed rowing boat with crossed
rudder lines.*

With the rudder lines *crossed* the footplate/steering handle is moved in the direction in which the boat needs to travel, i.e., if the boat needs to travel to the right the footplate/steering handle is turned to the right. In the absence of a steering handle the right-hand wire is pushed forward.

If the rudder lines are *not crossed* as in some coxed boats, to steer the boat to the right the coxswain has to push the left hand forward and vice versa.

In both coxed and coxless boats the rudder line should be adjusted oo that the wires are responsive but not too tight. This is done by loosening two tiny screws close to the yoke and pulling the wires to the correct tension, then retightening the screws.

In the coxless boat the wire tension is also affected by the position of the footstretcher. When using a boat for the first time the oarsman should adjust his footstretcher so that he is sitting at the correct position on backstops, and then adjust the tension of the rudder line.

To avoid oversteering it is useful to place a piece of tape around the rudder line above the steering foot, and another piece on the stretcher. The pieces of tape line up when the rudder is set straight or 'off'. When steering the foot is moved away from this point and back to minimize the drag that occurs when the rudder is out of parallel with the boat.

The steersman, with no exceptions, must be able to swivel the steering foot an equal distance to the right of neutral and to the left of neutral *in comfort*. Before leaving the bank/landing-stage for an outing he must make sure he can do this and if he can't, he should adjust the steering shoe on the rudder wire until confident that steering in both directions is not compromised. Adjusting the steering shoe is best done whilst sitting in the boat with the legs fully extended. Detach the rudder wire from the steering shoe by releasing the wing-nut on the toe extension. With a fellow oarsman holding the rudder at neutral, move the steering foot to the correct position and reattach the wire.

NB. It is wrong to compensate for the uneven pull of strokeside or bowside by adjusting the steering shoe with a bias against the stronger side.

In a coxless boat, be it a pair, a four or a quadruple scull, the boat is steered by a member of the crew. The steersman can be

A Russian coxless pair steering over the buoys during an international regatta.

in any position in the boat. Traditionally it is done by the oarsman sitting in the bow seat, as in this position the steersman has the clearest view of the course. However, it may be that the best steersman in the crew is actually sitting at another position in the boat, maybe at No. 2 or No. 3 in a coxless four, and there is no reason why this person cannot steer although their view will be impaired by the bodies behind them. It may be easier on a straight buoyed course for the stroke of the crew to steer, looking at the buoys behind as they are passed.

In a coxless boat the steersman has to become *the coxswain as well as a rower*. It is his job to ensure the safety of the boat and crew. For this reason all that follows about coxing is also relevant to *the steersman* of a coxless boat.

Coxing

What makes a good coxswain?

In many ways, a coxswain and a horse jockey are very similar. Both must be relatively small and light individuals; both are responsible for steering their vehicles and for extracting from them their best possible performances; both must work closely with the coach/trainer prior to the event best to prepare their vehicles for competition, and lastly, but just as important, both are responsible for the well-being and safety of their vehicles, before, during and after competition.

Obviously, when choosing a suitable coxswain the coach or crew must consider the individual's size, but this should not be the only selection criterion. As with the jockey, a feel and love for the sport is also important, for without these natural traits, the novice cox is unlikely to master the required skills. It takes years to develop a top-level oarsperson, and the aspiring coxswain must also be willing to devote him or herself to many years of training. The basics of coxing can be learned in a relatively short period of time, but mastery requires a long-term commitment.

It is important that the coxswain learns all aspects of his sport, for he is the link between coach and crew. In both training and racing situations, the cox must be prepared to assist the coach as mechanic (rigging, cleaning and repair of equipment), trainer, technical consultant, general organizer and race tactician. For the rowers, the cox should be a friend and confidant, as well as a leader and motivator, and, at the required times, must be in complete charge of his boat and crew.

An individual who is alert, bright and keen – and light in weight as well – has the makings of a good coxswain. Beyond that, the ability to cox well comes from a mixture of natural talent, helpful instruction and constructive criticism (by both coaches and rowers), self-motivation and hard work. For the developing coxswain, the best teacher is experience. The more kilometres steered, and the more opportunities given to experience various training/racing situations, the better prepared the cox will be to contribute to his crew.

The new coxswain will make mistakes in his steering, commands, etc., just as the oarsperson makes mistakes in his bladework. However, unlike the oarsperson, who is constructively criticized (i.e. coached) to correct his faults, the cox is often subjected to ridicule, even chastisement, for committing a single error. Coaches and rowers alike should understand that good coxing takes time to learn just as good rowing does. Firm instruction is important for the novice cox, but so, too, is encouragement and patience.

A positive way to teach or correct the faults of an inexperienced coxswain is for the coach to refrain from criticizing too heavily on the water, and to spend a short period of time after the training session going over those faults with the cox. This approach should help to encourage a healthy working relationship between the coach and the cox, which is sure to benefit future crews. Similarly, it is usually best for a rower to discuss coxing technique after the outing, when everyone is more relaxed and more open to suggestion. Indeed, a good coxswain will invite constructive criticism from his rowers.

Position within the boat

As a coxswain, you will be spending many hours either sitting or lying in a boat. To make this experience as comfortable as possible, you should wedge yourself firmly in, so as to prevent being thrown about and thus adversely affecting the balance of the boat. To accomplish this in the sitting position, you should push your feet against the footplate so that there is pressure on your feet and lower back at all times (use of a back pad will help reduce the risk of back damage). Unnecessary hand and upper body movements can be prevented by grasping the sides of the shell, while controlling the rudder lines.

If lying in the bow of the boat, position yourself centrally. To prevent movement, pack yourself in, preferably with a material that will not wrap around your feet and hinder your escape if an emergency occurs.

Frontloader: steering a coxed pair from a lying position in the bows.

Traditional coxing position in the stern. Note the warm clothing for cold weather.

Clothing

Clothing is of primary importance in the winter. Good quality waterproofs and thermals are necessities in cold, wet weather conditions. To insulate yourself, wear many thin layers rather than one heavy layer. In general, keep the hands, feet and head dry and protected from the wind to prevent wind-chill. Hats are important, as a great amount of body heat is lost through the head. Boots (wellies) are often necessary for boating and landing, but these should be removed while on the water for safety reasons, so be sure to wear two to three layers of socks (both cotton and wool). Basically, for your own health and comfort, which has an effect on your coxing performance, stay warm and dry!

In the summer, the use of sunglasses and/or hats with visors is recommended to lessen the effect of glare off the water. Use of sunblock creams/lotions is also a good idea. When travelling to regattas, whatever the season, always be prepared for variable weather conditions.

General responsibilities

Now that you are comfortable in the boat, what are your basic jobs? You should be in charge of the boat from the time it leaves the rack until it returns. Your commands to the crew should be clear and sharp and confident. Rowers do not respond well to a hesitant, wishy-washy coxswain, so be decisive. Most of the time, common sense will dictate your course of action, but don't be afraid to make a mistake. Just make sure you learn from your mistake, and try not to repeat it. Again, experience is all-important, and your confidence and competence as a coxswain will grow with it. Take it upon yourself to gain feedback from the coach and rowers – such feedback is not often forthcoming, so you have to ask for it – and learn to monitor yourself, with the aim of improving your performance each time you go out.

You will probably learn to boat and land in one environment (i.e. at your own school or club), so be sure when you are training or racing away from home that you take the time to look around the unfamiliar docking area; observe what the locals do. Stillwater boating is fairly straightforward, but with streams, the general rule is: boat and land with your bow pointed *against* the current. When boating from crowded areas, especially at races, you will be required to clear the area quickly, so before taking the boat from the rack, make sure that the oars have been placed near the dock.

Dealing with environmental factors is an important responsibility of the coxswain. Immediately upon arrival at the training/race course, make a mental note of all relevant factors: wind and water conditions (on tidal waters this includes which way the stream is running), docking and storage facilities, boat traffic, and any obstacles or potential hazards to look out for when on the water.

Another job of the coxswain is to be the 'in-boat coach'. In order to do this job well, you must learn good rowing technique yourself. Listen carefully to your coach during the training sessions, and begin to recognize the common technical faults and how to correct them. Try not to be talking while the coach is speaking, so that neither you nor your crew misses what is being said. When you are coaching, try to phrase your commands in a *positive* rather than negative way, and be encouraging to your crew without being patronizing.

In addition to the above responsibilities, the coxswain may also be required to help with the basic maintenance of his crew's equipment: checking the *blades* (inboard lengths, tight/clean collars, no cracks/weaknesses in spoon or shaft); checking the *boat* (tight rigger bolts, clean gates, clean seats/slides, no cracks/weaknesses in shell or fittings, alignment/operation of steering mechanism); recharging the *coxbox* between outings, and maintenance of the *speaker system* in the boat.

Steering

The shortest distance between two points is a straight line, and this should be the coxswain's guiding rule when steering. Of course it is not always possible to follow a straight line, especially on rivers, but it is the job of the coxswain to keep steering to a minimum.

In addition to simply causing the boat to have to travel further, the act of steering will also cause it to *slow down* by increasing the drag on it. This increase in drag occurs because of an increase in the water pressure on the boat when the boat is turned. Without going into too much detail about hydrodynamics and the physical properties of rowing shells, it should be explained that rowing boats do not instantaneously change course when turned – there is a 'transition period' (the length of which depends on the length of the boat and the degree of the turn), during which the boat shifts to its new course. During this transition, the 'cutting point' (i.e. bow) moves off the original course, and the whole of one side of the boat, still moving forward on the original course, experiences increased water pressure against it, until the new course becomes established. This process occurs each time the boat is turned, and it is for this reason that steering must be kept to a minimum.

One of the worst offences a coxswain can commit is wandering: allowing the boat to drift or be pushed off course. Whether due to sloppy ruddering or to outside forces, wandering will result in increased drag on the boat, as described above, and will slow the boat down. Although wandering may be caused by water conditions or crosswinds, or even one side of the crew outpulling the other, it is still the coxswain's fault, and is generally caused by a lack of concentration. It is possible, and desirable, to *anticipate* outside turning forces, and to offset their effect by proper use of steering. Two of the most common disruptive forces are strong cross-head winds and, in the more inexperienced crews, unequal pulling pressures. In strong cross-head winds, you can keep the boat going fairly straight by using the rudder gently and repeatedly to offset the wind's turning force on the boat. In general, you don't actually want to tack into the wind, because this will cause your boat to run slightly askew of its course, and will therefore increase the drag on it. Instead, stay on course by making *small* turns: the wind pushes you one way, you counteract by steering gently back against it, and so on. Similarly, for unequal crew pressures, try to react *before* the imbalance has too greatly affected the course of the boat, and, if necessary, compensate for the imbalance by applying the rudder gently and repeatedly against the strong side. If the disruptive force occurs unexpectedly, be sure to react immediately. By reacting sooner rather than later, you can get back on course with just a little rudder, and thus keep the negative effect of the rudder to a minimum.

Remember, the rudder is your friend, but it can also be your enemy. A rudder will act as a brake, especially if used heavily. However, a small amount of ruddering will steer the boat and not brake it. Never hold the rudder in the 'on' position – always apply the rudder: on/off, on/off, etc., until it has the desired effect. It is always best to use a little rudder at a time, rather than just to slam it on.

When getting in a boat for the first time, note how the rudder lines are attached to the rudder post: crossed or uncrossed. This determines which way each line pulls the boat. Make sure that the *tension* of your rudder lines is properly adjusted: not too tight (so that the rudder is too sensitive) nor too slack (so that there is not enough rudder effect).

Set up your course well in advance, so that you can anticipate what steering will be necessary; in general, try to sight at least 500 metres ahead, noting the positions of all moving and stationary objects. This technique will also help you to avoid the problem of over-steering, that is, going too far one way, and then having to come back again, causing a zig-zagging effect – most annoying to a crew! You probably won't be commended for steering a straight course, but you can be sure you'll get an earful if your course is an erratic one! Rowers hate to see their precious energy being wasted on unnecessary turns.

The following list includes additional guidelines for steering:

1. As coxswain, it is *your* responsibility to know the specific rules of the river or body of water on which you are steering. Generally, on *tidal* waters: when rowing *against* the tide, keep to a shore (be careful not to steer so close to the shore that you risk hitting the bank, or objects submerged in the shallows such as rocks, plants or supermarket trolleys); when rowing *with* the tide, stay in the middle. Be especially careful when the tide is on the turn, that is, when the tidal stream has stopped running one way and is about to start running the other way – it is at this time that there may be confusion, and the risk of colliding with another crew is at its greatest. On still water, such as lakes or man-made courses, there will be set traffic patterns for you to follow.

2. If you are steering against a fast-flowing stream, it will try to push your bow out towards the middle of the river. Be aware that you need to keep the bow pointed slightly in towards the near bank.

3. When turning a bend, once again the key is anticipation. Plan ahead so that you can make a gradual turn, with only gentle ruddering. Depending on the length and sharpness of the bend, you may have to start steering before you actually reach the bend.

4. The braking effect of the rudder will also destabilize the boat. By applying the rudder when the blades are locked in the water, the boat will be less likely to fall over.

5. When turning the boat around, especially on tidal waters or rivers with a strong current, allow plenty of space to clear any obstacles. If in doubt, don't turn. Move to a point where it is safe, and then make your turn. Always respect the force of tides and streams.

6. While the boat is stopped, you are still responsible for its position on the water. Wind and stream will still have an effect on the boat, so be alert. If sitting against the stream, do not allow the boat to be pushed out, keep the bow pointed in towards the near shore. Be aware of other boats still moving, and, as a courtesy, move out of their way.

7. When docking or landing your boat, do so at a safe (i.e., *slow*) speed. Use the wind whenever possible to blow you on to the dock/bank. On rivers and tideways, always boat/land with your bow pointed *into* (against) the stream – this gives you greater control of the boat.

8. When steering alongside other crews (especially in race situations), you should keep yourself informed as to their positions relative to you by occasional glances – do not just stare at them, for this will tend to draw you into them.

The basic steering rules are the same for all categories of boat, whether eight, four or pair. However, you must bear in mind that differences in the speed and length of shells (and indeed, in the strength and experience of different crews), will affect the timing of your steering and how much space to allow when making a turn. In the smaller boats, where stability (balance) is more delicate, it is especially important that you keep your body still and use the rudder gently and as little as possible.

The technique of steering is actually quite simple, and just takes a little practice. As already discussed, course changes should be accomplished by applying the rudder a little at a time – no strong, jerky movements – and, whenever possible, should be anticipated well in advance. More specific instruction on steering and manoeuvring would require a larger work than this. It should be noted, however, that every waterway and every racecourse is different, and each will require different handling in terms of boat manoeuvring. In general, always be aware of your surroundings and what is going on around you, and be extra cautious when steering in an unfamiliar environment.

Commands for the beginner

The following set of verbal examples is presented to give the novice coxswain an idea of the basic commands, or types of commands, that are required to conduct a typical rowing session. As coxswain, your two primary aims when manoeuvring your boat, whether on land or water, are safety and efficiency. In order to fulfil this responsibility, you must be able to communicate with your crew effectively. Make your commands simple and direct, and remember to speak clearly and loudly enough for your crew to hear you. Remember also that when it comes to manoeuvring the boat, you alone are in charge.

In the boathouse (taking the boat out)

'Hands on the boat.

'Ready . . . LIFT!'

Always precede lifting commands with 'Ready . . .' to prepare crew for the command and to prevent them from injuring themselves by lifting out of synch.

'Strokeside (or bowside) holding the boat – bowside (or strokeside) move under – GO.' After the boat has been lifted from the rack, half of the rowers will move under the boat to support the other side. The general rule when carrying the boat is for the rowers to be positioned opposite (the other side of) their riggers, so this determines which side you command to move.

'To shoulders – Ready . . . UP!' The crew carries the boat out on their shoulders. If there is not enough space in the boathouse to carry the boat this way, then command the crew to carry the boat 'on the half-turn,' i.e., rotate the boat 90 degrees – one side of the riggers is straight up, the other side straight down – and carry the boat like this until clear, then re-rotate and lift to shoulders to carry the remainder of the way.

'Forward – GO.' Watch your boat carefully as it is being carried down – especially the bow and stern – to avoid hitting any obstacles in its path. The rowers carrying the boat cannot see very well what is around them, so you must guide them.

Boating (at the water's edge)

If boating on a river or tideway, make sure you position your boat so that the bow is pointed *against* the stream. This gives you greater control when manoeuvring away from the boating area.

'Lifting over your heads – Ready . . . LIFT!' The rowers push the boat straight up over their heads.

'One hand in [to grasp hand-hold], and . . . LOWER!' The rowers lower the boat *away* from themselves and into the water. Watch that the fin/rudder doesn't hit the dock or bank as the boat is being lowered.

Or,

'Lowering boat to waist – Ready . . . DOWN!' The rowers lower the boat off their shoulders and down to their waists. The boat is then rolled right-side up, and, while the shoreside rowers hold the boat, the waterside rowers move under, and the whole crew lowers the boat into the water. This technique is especially useful for inexperienced crews.

'Bowside (or strokeside) holding the boat, strokeside (or bowside) get the blades.' The side whose riggers are closest to the dock/bank holds the boat, while the other side gets the blades and puts theirs in first.

Make sure all oars are secured in their oarlocks and pushed out before commanding the crew to get in the boat. Decide whether the whole crew gets in the boat together, or whether one side gets in first and then the other. For inexperienced crews, it is usually best for the shoreside rowers to continue holding the boat, while the waterside rowers get in first. Once seated, they can stabilize the boat by holding on to their oar handles (blade spoons *flat* on the water), making it easier for the other side to get in.

'Whole crew – one foot in and down,' (to sit in the boat).

Or,

'Whole crew – one foot in. Ready to push off—' (with the other foot), 'And . . . PUSH!' (to push the boat away from the dock/bank before sitting down.)

Or (if one side getting in first),

'Bowside (or strokeside) holding the boat, strokeside (or bowside) in and down . . . hold on to your blades. Now bowside (strokeside) – one foot in, and push off — GO.'

Sometimes you must move the boat away from the dock or bank immediately, especially in a strong stream or wind, or when the area is crowded with other crews trying to boat or land. Command all or part of your crew to take the necessary strokes to get you clear, even if they're not tied in yet.

On the water

Precede all major commands with 'Ready . . .' or 'Next stroke
. . .' etc., to prepare the crew for your command so that they
make the change in unison. For example,
'Moving up two pips to rate 32. Ready . . . UP!'
Or,
'Ready for ten-stroke burst. Next stroke . . . GO!'
Be consistent in the *timing* of your calls: the main command
(i.e., 'UP!' or 'GO!') should be called either at the catch or
finish of the stroke. This way the crew will learn to anticipate
your commands, and can effect the change on the very next
stroke cycle without confusion or hesitation.

By using the preceding examples as a general guide, you should
be able to conduct your boat and crew safely out of the
boathouse and on to the water, and you should have an idea of
how to deliver your rowing commands. When landing and
taking the boat in, your commands will basically be the reverse
of those described above for taking the boat out. Remember to
land the boat at a safe speed.

Control and tone of voice

Rowers learn that in order to be most effective in the boat, they
must not waste their energy – good technique means that all the
rower's energy is transferred through the oar to the forward
movement of the boat. It is also important that the coxswain
does not waste his voice. The cox's words have one primary
purpose: to co-ordinate the energy output of the individual
rowers, and to drive the crew to attain its best possible
performance, whether in training or in race situations.

Before the age of speaker systems in the boat, coxswains had
to learn to project their voices, in much the same way a stage
actor learns to project to his audience. The coxswain had to
achieve a high volume (loud enough for the bowperson of an
eight to hear) without losing voice control, that is, without
becoming high-pitched or screechy. In the old days, it was said
that the best way to train a loud, husky voice was to drink
plenty of cheap whiskey and smoke a packet of cigarettes a day!
This technique, while effective, is neither healthy, nor recommended! However, the idea that your voice must be trained is
an important one. You must practise voice control, both in the

boat and on your own. Learn to project your voice from your diaphragm, not your throat, and to enunciate clearly and forcefully. Again, do not waste words – it takes energy to cox well, and you, as much as the rowers, must be able to last the training session or the race. Even with the benefit of a speaker system, which alleviates the problem of volume, you should be conscious of using your voice wisely. You never know when your system might break down – it could be in the middle of the final!

As the coxswain, you must use your own judgement, based on common sense and experience, as to how much or how little communication your crew requires. A good cox is distinguished not by the *amount* of verbalizing he does, but by the *quality* of what he says. In fact, the actual words you choose are less important than the *tone* and *timing* of those words. Learn to use the rhythm of your voice to encourage a good rhythm in the boat. Your voice should reflect the action of the oar: sharp at the catch, strong at the finish, relaxed on the recovery.

Some coxswains make the mistake of confusing forcefulness with aggressiveness in the boat. While aggressiveness with your crew can sometimes be effective, it should be used with discretion, and never allowed to become brutal or personally insulting. There may be times when you become frustrated by seeing the same mistake being made over and over again by one of your rowers, and it is up to you to decide whether strong criticism will be productive or just make things worse. Part of the art of coxing is knowing how hard to push an individual or crew. Again, we return to the analogy of the jockey. The jockey uses his whip to push his horse, and the strength of the blow conveys urgency to the horse, and will affect the horse's performance. But the jockey's whip is wrapped, so it doesn't actually hurt or do damage to the horse. Use your voice in the same way: regulate your tone to convey urgency, but don't allow your words to be unnecessarily hurtful.

Courtesy vs. aggressiveness

Having touched upon the subject of aggressive coxing within the boat, what about aggressiveness outside the boat, or towards other crews on the water? Here, the inexperienced cox may confuse competitiveness with aggessiveness. As coxswain it is your job to look after the interests of your crew, and to do your best to make sure that outside factors do not disrupt the performance of your boat. But again, you must use discretion. In training situations, be courteous to other crews using the same waterway. If you are stopped or just paddling, move your boat to make way for another crew doing a work piece. If you are training with another crew, do not try to slow them down by cutting in front of them and making them row in your puddles. You should be determined at all times to steer the best course for your crew, but in training, it is better, and sáfer, to steer a little bit off rather than to cause a collision with the other boat, or cause the other boat to crash into an obstacle.

In racing situations, your role as coxswain is more single-minded: to get your boat to cover the course in the fastest possible time, to compete to win. However, this attitude does not require that you be rude and aggressive to everyone outside your crew. You should be especially courteous to and respectful of the organizers and officials at a race – often they are volunteers who are donating their time and energy to provide the race in which you are participating.

On the racecourse itself, again, be respectful of the officials. The same officials tend to be at many of the races and regattas throughout the year; it is not wise to create for yourself the reputation of being a trouble-maker. It is in the best interest of your crew to work well with the race officials.

On buoyed courses, collisions with other crews should not be a problem, but always be aware of what is around you, and be especially careful when going on to or coming off of a buoyed course. On all courses, whether buoyed or not, be defensive in order to avoid other cox's mistakes. Your first responsibility is to get your boat and crew onto the starting line, safely and intact.

In head-style races, contact with other boats is sometimes unavoidable, but you must always determine the cost vs. benefit of your action. When racing on tidal waters or rivers, staying in the fastest-moving part of the stream is of obvious importance to your crew, and if you have to crowd out another crew to get there, then so be it. It may mean that blades will clash, but don't go looking for such collisions. A good cox will not allow clashing to occur if his boat would be less-impeded by his steering a little bit further to get around the other boat and into better water. Kamikaze coxswains, besides being dangerous to themselves and others, do not win many races. Again, your job is to use your head to help your boat to attain its fastest possible time.

Race day

Once you have a basic command of steering and manoeuvring your boat, the next step is learning to race. Actually, the most important component of racing cannot be learned: competitiveness. To be effective, the coxswain must be every bit as competitive as his rowers. But instead of moving the boat by physically pulling on an oar, the coxswain contributes to boat speed by using his sensory and communication skills.

The coxswain in the race will be the eyes, ears and coach of the crew, and this job starts on land. Whether racing head-style or on a short course, it is your responsibility to learn the course: ask locals, walk the course, and make sure you know where the marshalling/warm-up areas are located *before* you get on the water. It is also essential that you be well-versed in the rules and regulations published by the governing body overseeing the event, and that you be aware of any additional rules which may be in effect at a particular race venue.

Your coxing responsibilities on race day are really no different from on any training day – you just have to get everything right! The rowers will attempt to row perfectly in the race, and you must attempt to cox perfectly. Concentration should be at its highest level.

You will be getting nervous before the race, just as your rowers will be, but it is important that you remain calm and in control. Don't let your nerves affect your voice control – keep your cool in front of your crew, and your opposition!

The following is a general checklist for you to follow on race day:

1. Check your equipment: boat, blades, speaker system.
2. Synchronize your watch to *official time*. Make sure your crew is aware of when and where they need to be, so you don't have to go chasing after anybody at the last minute (allow time for them to stretch, go to the loo, etc.).
3. Get yourself officially weighed-in as soon as allowed, so you can get back to your crew and not hold things up.
4. If necessary, pick up your boat's bow number (which designates your lane number or starting position), and any pin-on numbers to be worn by yourself/bowperson.
5. Make sure you have all the relevant information about the

race: *rules, regulations, start time* (for your race as well as for that of one or two races before yours, so you can check when you get to the starting area whether the regatta is running to schedule), your *lane* or *starting position*, and the *course circulation pattern* (i.e., the traffic pattern for getting on to/off the course, and for the warming-up and marshalling areas).

6. Get your crew well warmed-up; when boating, allow enough time before your start time to go through the planned warm-up without having to rush it (know beforehand exactly how long your planned warm-up will take).

7. Keep your crew switched on: eyes in the boat, thinking about their own race. Concentrate on the warm-up.

8. If racing is delayed, keep your crew moving, don't let them cool down too much. Stay in the vicinity of the starting area, so that you will know when the officials call your race.

9. Manoeuvre into your starting position at the designated time (usually 2–3 minutes before your start time). Do not get there too early (so that your crew just sits there getting cold), nor too late (so that the officials assess you a false start).

Dieting

Ideally, your natural weight will be close to your race weight (the international minimum weights being 50 kg for men's events, 45 kg for women's events), so that drastic dieting is not necessary for you. If, however, you are a big coxswain and must resort to dieting to reduce your bodyweight, be smart about it. You will be no good to your crew if dieting decreases your ability to function properly. Try to plan your weight loss in advance, so that you can reduce gradually, rather than crashing down at the last minute. Also, be careful not to become seriously dehydrated. In short, if you have to lose so much weight that you start to lose some of your faculties, not to mention your health, then you really should not be coxing. It is particularly unwise for juniors to be put on weight-loss diets, as they need sufficient energy to grow properly. If you are a junior who has grown too big to cox, then you might want to consider rowing. Rowers who have had coxing experience in their youth tend to make proficient oarspersons.

Conclusion

It is really not possible to explain or demonstrate good coxing technique in the same way that a coach would teach good bladework to an oarsperson. This is because so much of the job of coxing has to do with dealing with outside factors, and these are too numerous and varied to be exactly defined. The purpose of this chapter, therefore, has been to present basic guidelines for the beginner to follow, and to introduce certain concepts which each individual coxswain must develop for him or herself.

One concept that has not yet been addressed is that of your own enjoyment of the sport. You can be a serious and competent coxswain, and still be seen to be having fun. In fact, it is important that the cox helps to create a happy working atmosphere, especially at those times when the weather is bad, or when the rowers are becoming bad-tempered due to training fatigue or pre-race tension. That's not to say that you can't be bad-tempered yourself every now and again, but be aware of the effect you have on your crew's morale. And for your own sake, the sport should give you pleasure, otherwise, why do it?

The key to good coxing, at whatever level, club to international, is to use your head, and to ask yourself: What can I do to make my boat go faster today? You can be an invaluable asset to your crew, but you have to work at it. In the end, it is up to you to justify your added weight in the boat, and to earn the respect of your crew. The best coxswains don't just steer the boat, they help to *move* the boat.

A coxman celebrating his crew's success.

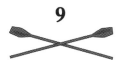

9

RACING: PREPARATION
AND STRATEGY

R owing is practised throughout the full twelve months of
the year. As an outdoor activity, it is almost unique in
this respect.

The racing calendar has two phases. From mid-September to
the end of March races are processional over distances of 2,000
plus metres, the crews essentially pitching themselves against
the clock. From April to September the races are shorter, over
distances of 500–2,000 metres, the crews racing side by side.

The rules of racing

Each country publishes its own rules for competition, laid down
by the rowing association of that country. The rules of racing in
Great Britain are laid down by the Amateur Rowing Association
(ARA), and printed each year in the *British Rowing Almanack*.
These rules are based on those for international rowing races
laid down by FISA, the International Rowing Federation.

Status categories

All races in Great Britain are run with 'status categories' for
each boat type. This provides a wide range of competition for
all age groups and all abilities.

Until 1987 the status categories were: Novice; Senior C;
Senior B; Senior A; and Elite. The status of a rower was
determined by the number of wins that he had attained during
his rowing career as follows:

Rowing status	No. of wins
Novice	0
Senior C	1
Senior C	2
Senior B	3
Senior B	4
Senior B	5
Senior A	6
Elite	More than 4 wins in *one* season

The status of a crew entering a race was that of the crew member with the highest individual status. For example, consider the status of two coxed Fours,

Position in boat		Individual status
Crew A	Bow	Senior B (4 wins)
	2	Senior C (2 wins)
	3	Novice (0 wins)
	Stroke	Senior B (5 wins)

The overall status of Crew A is Senior B.

Crew B	Bow	Novice (0 wins)
	2	Novice (0 wins)
	3	Novice (0 wins)
	Stroke	Senior B (5 wins)

The overall status of Crew B is Senior B.

This particular status ruling encouraged individuals of the same status to row in crews, it prevented a large number of people from racing. Rowing at club level, particularly in the smaller rowing clubs, often necessitates that crews are of mixed ability – in 1988 the status rules changed to enable such crews to be able to race at a standard compatible to their mixed ability. A points system was introduced in which the aggregate number of qualifying wins of the members of a crew determines the racing status of the crew.

With the introduction of the points system the status categories were also changed to: Novice; Senior III; Senior II; Senior I; and open.

SCULLING	Sc	2Sc	4Sc	ROWING	2+ 2-	4+ 4-	8+
Senior Open		Unlimited		Senior Open		Unlimited	
Senior I	10	20	40	Senior I	20	40	80
Senior II	5	10	20	Senior II	10	20	.40
Senior III	2	5	10	Senior III	5	10	20

Fig. 9:1. Status chart.

In essence, a rower is awarded a point for a win, up to a maximum of twelve points. The status of a crew is determined by adding together the crew members' points and translating the total into a status by reading from the Status Chart found in the *Rowing Almanack* and shown in Fig. 9:1.

Consider Crews A and B referred to above. With the status ruling prior to 1988 these crews would have had to race in the same category. Under the new status rules, Crew A has a total of eleven points and is therefore Senior II in status, whereas Crew B has only five points and is Senior III in status.

Crew A and Crew B would not be expected to race against each other.

Setting goals

It is important to recognize whether rowing is recreational or competitive for you as an individual. What purpose does it serve in your life? Is it for the release of stress or are you trying to prove something to yourself? What do you gain by rowing? What do you want to gain from rowing? Sit back and ponder for a while.

Putting rowing into perspective in your life will enable you to set long- and short-term goals. Goal setting provides direction for training and racing. It provides *drive*, but it should be realistic not fantasy.

For example, maybe your long-term aim is to compete at the Olympic Games. To do this, the standard of your rowing needs to develop until you are competent technically and fit enough to be selected for the senior international team. Knowing that your long-term aim is to make Olympic selection, your short-term goals should provide stepping stones *en route* to your long-term goal.

Once you have learnt to row, the goal for the first year should be to gain racing experience and wins at domestic races; for the second year, to win at the National Championships; for the third year, to win at Henley Royal Regatta; and so on.

Each year at the commencement of winter training, review your personal achievements during the previous year and set yourself a target for the next year. It is a good idea to keep a performance record, noting all training that has been done and the outcome of racing. This allows you to look back and realistically assess, possibly with the help of a third party (a sports scientist, your coach or perhaps your crew), the changes that need to be made to keep you on target for your long-term goal.

Having set a short-term goal for the current training year, plan a programme of races. Try to race at intervals of at least two weeks so there is time between races to recover and to perform effective training, gaining from the experience of the race, learning by mistakes that have been made and continuing to improve your ability to row.

The different types of race

Head of the river races

A Head race is a long-distance event usually held in the autumn and winter. Head racing is processional with an interval of 10–15 seconds between crews, the higher-ranked crews starting first, or the starting positions being determined by the finishing order of the previous year's race.

Long-distance races were introduced to encourage crews to train through the early part of the year, thereby increasing their chances in the summer regatta season. The most well-known long-distance race is the Tideway Head of the River Race. Introduced in 1926, to date, it is only open to male competitors (women coxes being tolerated!) and attracts competitors from all over Europe.

The *tactics* for a Head race are very simple, the idea is to get from start to finish as fast as possible; the race is essentially a time trial. The start of the race is a running start, the timing commencing as the crew passes the start line. It is important, therefore, that the whole crew knows where the timing lines are positioned on the course in order to maximize boat speed as timing begins. Approximately 45–60 seconds after the start, the crews settle into a strong consistent pace, consolidating this pace during the first half of the race. It is a misconception that a crew should repeatedly 'push' during a Head race: this may give a short-lived advantage over another crew, but the cost in energy terms is too high. During the second half of the race the crews concentrate on improving boat speed and efficiency: as the finish draws closer they start to push above the maintained pace by letting the rate of striking come up, but without allowing the quality of the bladework to diminish.

Helpful tips

It is important before racing to ascertain the strongest consistent pace that your crew may maintain. The pace of a crew may be determined in training by using either repeated set-timed pieces, noting the distance covered at different rates, or repeated set-distance pieces noting the time taken to cover the distance at different rates. Obviously the distance or time being considered must correlate to the length of the race being prepared for.

Using this information a performance graph may be plotted

Mike Spracklen monitoring the performance of his crews from a coaching launch.

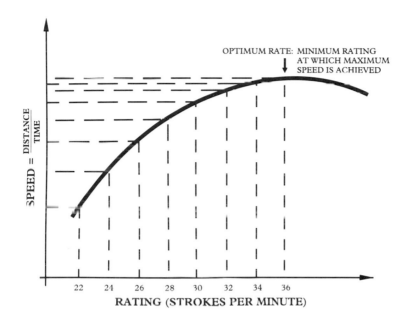

Fig. 9:2. Performance curve used to determine optimum rate.

and the optimum rating for the distance/time considered read
from the graph (Fig. 9:2).

Having calculated the optimum rate of the crew, the preparation for a Head race is essentially over-distance work, i.e.
work of longer duration than the race being aimed for.

Practise the start, going off hard and settling into pace.

Practise the build to the finish.

Specialized Head races

These are races which are essentially long-distance events like
Head races, but special conditions or restrictions are imposed.
As such they do not conform to the format laid out for a Head
race.

Examples:

i. *Armada Cup* This race is held in Bern, Switzerland, in
October each year. It is a 9-kilometre race against the clock, for
approximately 100 plus single scullers starting from a mass
start.

ii. *The Wingfield Sculls* This race is held in London on the River Thames usually in April/May each year, the actual date of the race is decided by the previous year's winner. The race is from a free-floating start, with the tide, from Putney to Mortlake, a distance of 7 kilometres. The winner of this race gains the title of Amateur Champion of the Thames and Great Britain. It is open to the top British Single Scullers, with a start of no more than six in the final, eliminators being held two days earlier if necessary.

iii. *The Boat Race* Held in London from Putney to Mortlake (7 kilometres) in March/April each year. The race is between male students of Oxford University and Cambridge University racing in Eights, from a stakeboat start with the tide.

A women's boat race of 2 kilometres is held one week earlier at Henley-on-Thames.

Domestic regatta racing

A regatta is a race in which boats contend for prizes.

There are over 150 domestic regattas on the British mainland between the end of March and September each year. The majority of domestic regattas are organized by the local clubs to raise some revenue, and are held over stretches of open flowing rivers, distances varying from 1,000 metres to 2,000 metres.

The races are run both with and against the stream, depending on the local obstacles, e.g. weirs, lock channels, etc. Since the races are on the open river it is important to understand the advantages and disadvantages of the meandering contours – knowing where to capitalize on a bend and where to hold off crews in places of disadvantage.

Domestic regattas are side-by-side races with heats, semi-finals and finals being held over the course of a day – with a large entry you can expect to race up to four or five times.

The start may be free standing or from stakeboats. On a free-standing start the crew must be very alert to ensure that they start level with the opposition, whereas with stakeboat starts the stakeboats have usually been located to allow for the advantages of the contours on one side of the river. This may mean that there is quite a stagger between the two stakeboats at the start.

Suggested tactics

Regatta races may be considered to be shortened versions of

Head races – that is, a crew needs to be strong off the start, settle into pace and build into the finish. The difference between the two types of race is the higher pace that can be maintained over the shorter course. In some respects this higher pace is more energy demanding.

The pace for a regatta race can be calculated as for a Head race using times/distances applicable to regatta racing.

Because the races are side by side and often need repeating with minimal rest, if the opposition is easily beaten in the early stages of a race, a crew is advised to settle the pace and conserve energy whenever possible, thereby effectively saving themselves for later in the day when the racing is likely to be closer. Beware, however, that on settling the pace you do not get caught out by a crew with a fast finish pushing you into panic when in fact you could have won easily.

Helpful tips

The start is the most important part of the race psychologically. If a crew is dumped at the start it is very difficult to come back on terms with the opposition. Practise standing starts to work out how to leave the start as quickly as possible without using too much energy and without pushing the boat backwards on the first stroke.

The *first stroke* must be squeezed and not 'whacked', because as the boat is not moving prior to this stroke a sudden application of power on the stretcher will push the boat backwards until the power is transferred to the spoon of the oar when the boat will begin to move forwards.

The *second stroke* can be a short 'jabby' stroke to increase the speed of the forward-moving boat.

Do not use body swing during the first few strokes of the start, as for these shortened strokes the legs are the only useful source of propulsive power.

The start should only last for the number of strokes required to overcome the inertia of the stationary boat and bring it to maximum speed.

Multi-lane racing

Domestic regattas on multi-lane courses are few due to the sparsity of courses available. In the UK there are 2,000-metre multi-lane courses at Nottingham and Strathclyde, and a 1,000-

metre course at Peterborough. All international regattas are multi-lane with usually four to six crews racing side by side.

Sprint racing

A sprint race is a side-by-side race over 500 metres or fewer. It is wrong to believe that you can *blast* for the duration of a sprint race – the same rules apply as in both Head races and regatta races, i.e. start, settle, build. It is important to find a pace that takes you from start to finish as fast as possible without fading in the last few strokes, as in a close sprint race the winner is only decided in the last ten to fifteen strokes.

Helpful tips

The best method for preparing for sprint races is high-intensity short-duration bursts, using explosive energy for very short time periods. This gives the crew the ability to continue rowing despite lactate accumulation in the muscles from anaerobic activity (*see* Chapter 7: Training, for an explanation of these terms).

Stroke ratings may vary from high 30s to high 40s depending on the boat type.

Preparing to race

Once the racing programme for the year has been set, make one member of the crew responsible for entering the races. Entries should be submitted, together with the correct entry fee, on an official entry form giving full details of the crew composition, dates of birth where relevant for Junior/Veterans and ARA registration numbers for each competitor. The entry should reach the race organizers *before* the specified closing date.

Generally speaking the closing date for most races is one to two weeks before the actual race. Telephone entries are sometimes accepted, but this should not be necessary if a predetermined programme of racing is being adhered to.

Registration numbers were introduced by the ARA several years ago. To race each member of a crew *must* have a valid registration number or purchase a day registration on the day of the race. If you are caught racing without a valid registration number or a day ticket the penalties for your club are high. At present the only race that will not accept day registration is the Tideway Head of the River Race.

During the week preceding the race the organizing race committee will send the 'race draw' to your club, together with a map of the course and any relevant local rules and regulations. On receiving the draw, check the time of your race and read the accompanying information carefully – it is for your own safety that this information is provided.

Plan your travel arrangements to the race, book accommodation if necessary, arrange the loading of the boats and equipment and organize a driver to tow the trailer to the race.

The race plan

Basically, a race plan is how the crew foresees the race proceeding. It is the setting of predetermined tactics. The crew has, after all, trained in preparation for the race with the aim to win. Good opposition may mean that to win the race you will need to work close to your known limits and, therefore, a wrong choice of tactics might mean the development of excessive fatigue too soon in the race, resulting in defeat.

Try to obtain as much information as possible about the crews you are going to race against:

What are their usual race methods?

When do they push?

Do they have a particular fade pattern?

What is their weakness?

The race plan is an imagined line of the course that the race will take. It should not be looked upon as a scheme of bursts, for with anticipated bursts the tendency is to soften off prior to the burst – and there is no overall gain in speed.

Race plans are designed to guide the crew through an expected situation, but the cox and/or stroke may have to take the initiative to alter the race plan if the opposition appraisals have been incorrect. It is essential to remain flexible.

The race plan should be discussed by the crew and coach two to three days before the race so that the crew has time for the plan to register mentally and to provide time for visualization. Discuss all eventualities and the possible changes that may have to be made. Stay alert in the race and respond quickly and appropriately. A race may be won or lost by the 'race intellect' of the crew.

Above all else, keep the race plan *simple* but *positive*, be *confident* in your own abilities but *be realistic*.

Race nerves

As the day of the race approaches it is only natural to begin to feel nervous. With experience and the help of psychological training this nervous energy can be put to good use, but in the early days racing as a Novice, nervous energy will exhaust you and is likely to detract from your performance.

It is well recognized that learning to control your nerves is all part of improving your performance. Psychological training is now recognized as an important aspect of race preparation.

The key to consistent performance

Winning races is about successfully performing your skill at a specified time and place during a race. You may spend hours daily on the river producing fast times and finely tuning your technique, but in the end the goal is one of performing to your best ability in a race situation. At the highest level of competition – the World or Olympic Championships – it has been proven time and time again that there is little difference in the physiology, skill levels or the biomechanics of equipment used by the top competitors. However, there is measurable difference in the psychological preparation and readiness of these competitors. Evidence has shown that psychological variables are more important for discriminating final qualifiers and non-qualifiers than any other variable. This evidence alone should convince you that it is worth spending just a little time learning how to prepare yourself mentally before entering a race.

There are many differences between racing and training which will affect your performance if you are not prepared for them:

1. In a race you are more highly motivated to perform well than in training because winning depends upon your best performance.

2. You will usually be in a strange environment, so there will be lots of distractions – people watching, a crowded river, things of interest on the bank, regulations to follow.

3. You are dependent upon feeling good at a specified time, whereas if in training you feel below par you may choose to cut the work.

4. You may be under considerable pressure to perform, because, for example, you want to prove to yourself you have

improved, or you want to impress the selectors as you are trying to make a team.

5. You may be racing someone who you know is good and who other people think and often tell you, you can't beat.

6. The water conditions may be bad or unfair.

7. The race may be delayed, or you may have problems with your equipment.

These are just a few examples of the distractions you are likely to find in competition. You may start out with the best intentions, knowing and feeling positive about the race, but if you are not prepared to deal with these issues, they are likely to affect your performance and consequently undermine your confidence in your ability and your confidence in your training and preparation. Coping with all the distractions is about being prepared so that there are few surprises, and being confident that if there are some distractions or unavoidable problems you will be able to cast them aside and concentrate on the job in hand.

Visualization

There is no magic to being properly mentally prepared. Just as with other components of your training there are a few specific skills which you should learn, develop and practise alongside your daily physical training. These skills will ensure that you can put yourself in the right frame of mind for racing. By learning to control your thoughts you can free your brain to deal with the immense demand you place upon it every time you race. You should practise being in control of what you are thinking and directing your attention to where it is needed in the same way that you practise your rowing stroke. The more you practise the correct action the easier it becomes.

Your body, mind and emotions act as a unit; they operate together. What you think affects how you feel and move; what you feel affects how you move and think; and how you use your body affects how you think and feel. So, if you spend a long time thinking about why you can't get your finishes out clean, what you are actually doing is reinforcing the movement pattern of dragging your finishes out. What you should be thinking about is the action of cleanly extracting the blade. Whilst seeing yourself performing a movement in your mind's eye you are actually moving the muscle groups involved in that action on a subliminal level and thus training the nerve's pathways to perform in this way. This is called visualization.

Visualization is an important skill for any athlete. It can be used to help an athlete learn new skills and perform existing skills more effectively. In a race visualization skills can be used in three ways.

1. Before a race you can use visualization to help eradicate any distractions or anxieties you may have using a technique called dissociation.
2. You can use visualization to prepare yourself to race, focusing on what you are going to do by going over your race plan and seeing the race as you are going to perform it. This is known as mental rehearsal.
3. Visualization can be used during a race to focus (or refocus) on a particular technical aspect, i.e. if the cox calls a push on the catch, being able to see yourself performing the perfect catch will help you to trigger the correct nerve's pathways to execute the required movement effectively and you will be rewarded for your effort by an increase in boat speed.

It is quite likely that you use visualization already, but that what you see and more importantly, when you see it, is not under your direct control. For example, you may have imagined yourself winning races, or have spent ages pondering over yesterday's outing. This is visualization in its crudest form. To gain advantage from what your mind sees, you need to be able to summon the correct images at will.

Visualization training

Before you start visualizing think of something you wish to practise. Start with something simple like part of your race plan, or even part of your stroke (whilst it is fun to imagine you are Steven Redgrave winning your third Olympic gold medal it will do your own performance little good). Imagine yourself performing at a high level of proficiency but one which you know you can reach. To start with you should write down the salient features or cues which will help you to perform that action or race plan. What you write should be cue words to help you feel the right thing in the race. For example, if you are to have a push on the finishes after 500 metres, you might write:

500 METRES – PUSH FINISHES
(draw shoulders, push on footboard).

When the 500-metres push comes you will visualize the combination of drawing the shoulders and the push of your feet against the footboard, this will send the boat off the finishes. Visualizing the action and not 'push off the finish', will make sure that the push happens and the boat speed is increased.

Now you are ready to start.

To visualize successfully you should be completely relaxed but alert and concentrated (i.e. the state you want to be in when you race). Concentration will make the images clearer and send stronger signals to your muscles.

Find a comfortable place and sit down with your eyes closed. It is better to sit rather than lie (lying down may encourage you to go to sleep). There are a variety of patterns of relaxation but the method I find most useful is called Progressive Muscle Relaxation (PMR). PMR is simply thinking through each of the major muscles in your body one by one. As you think of each muscle in turn take a deep breath, then as you exhale feel all the tension drain out of that muscle. Take your time to go through each muscle, until you feel relaxed. How much time you spend relaxing will vary depending on how tense you are feeling and what sort of a person you are. Some people find simply sitting down and exhaling deeply is enough to release any muscle tension and clear their mind, whilst others need to spend more time relaxing each muscle in turn. Certainly the more you practise the PMR technique the quicker you will be able to respond to a deep exhalation being the cue to relaxation.

Once you feel completely relaxed you are ready to watch yourself. Go straight to the task you set yourself before we began and see yourself perform as if you were actually in a race or rowing a stroke. You must visualize as if you are doing it *now*. You are only interested in this moment, the present.

Some people see themselves as if on video, others see what they would see if they were actually in the boat; either is fine, but the ability to do both is better. Now that you are performing, carry out the whole action or race. Never stop in mid-race (or stroke) unless you start to do something wrong. Always visualize the correct way to execute your race plan or stroke. *Remember*, when visualizing you are training your nerves' pathways so don't train yourself to make mistakes, or to lose.

At times you will go through your race plan, or a new movement and things will go wrong, if this happens, go back and replay the image in your mind until it looks and feels right. When you have completed your task, be satisfied and end the session. Don't be tempted to go on to something you haven't planned because you won't have the available cues in your mind to perform the task correctly. As you get more practised you will find that sometimes you are able to complete your goal quickly, while at other times you may have to keep replaying a part of the plan before you have a clear, fixed image in your mind.

NB: When you first start visualization it will help to have your coach or a friend to lead you through the relaxation and visualization. He should act as a guide to keep your thoughts focused on the tasks you have agreed to go through. However, it won't take long for you to become sufficiently practised to be able to go through the sessions on your own.

Once you are practised at visualization you will be able to use it to help you learn new skills in training, to rehearse your race plan and execution of the race, but more importantly you will find it easy to summon up correct and positive images during a race. To get to this stage just requires a bit of practice.

Visualization for racing

During your race preparation you should use your visualization skills to explore your reactions to different race situations. For example, visualize yourself two lengths in the lead, in a close race, or two lengths down. How do you react? Where is your focus? What do you think at that time? Imagine the worst scenarios that could occur – your boat being broken just as you are warming up, a race being delayed by an hour because of the weather. You will never manage to explore all the possibilities but by placing yourself in as many situations as possible you will stretch your ability to accept different distractions and will be able to react to them by returning your focus to your own race plan, your own actions.

Dissociation

On race day you may find yourself not feeling good and unready for racing – maybe you are worried about something outside rowing, or maybe you are not feeling one hundred per cent. If this is the case you should give yourself a moment to accept what is bothering you. Decide whether you are going to race or not, and if you are, act to remove the worry from your mind. Some people like to imagine writing down the source of the worry, then placing it in a black box. After racing they go back to the box, take out the paper and deal with the problem. By writing down your worry you can remove it from your immediate focus so that your mind is clear to concentrate on the race. If you use this method, do go back to the box after racing, take out the problem and spend some time sorting it out. If you don't you will have broken a promise to yourself and next time you try to use the black box it may not be successful.

Maintaining the best focus

During a race or an ergometer test do you have memories of thoughts or words which come in to your head? Take a moment to think back to your last race or competitive training piece. Did you talk or think to yourself and if you did, what exactly did you say or think. For example, are the thoughts mostly negative e.g. 'I can't pull any harder', 'I've STILL got 750 metres to go'? Are they encouraging, e.g. 'Keep going, that's good', or 'Good catches, we moved forward then'? Are they instructive, e.g. 'Stay sharp, quick catches', 'Clean finishes'? Or are they about what you're trying to do, 'I'm not going to win now, I'm a length down', 'Only a length down we can still win'?

Your answers are probably varied, your thoughts will be either positive or negative depending on how well you are doing, or how you feel at the time. Sometimes you may talk to yourself a lot, sometimes not at all. If this is the case you need to train yourself to be in control of your thoughts as you have trained yourself to be in control of your images. Research has shown that athletes perform considerably better when their thoughts are directed to a pre-formulated race plan. When they are left to the 'normal thoughts' which flit through their mind during a race or ergometer test the result is more likely to follow a pattern of grim determination, followed by a lowering in performance as fatigue sets in. Once fatigue sets in you are likely to see an inconsistency in boat/ergometer speed as the oarsman fights to overcome these feelings of fatigue. This is because your thoughts at any one moment will be generated by how you feel or how well you are doing, so as your muscles fatigue your body will be feeding back this information through your mind, and unless redirected these thoughts will have a negative effect on your performance. What you want to be thinking about is what you are doing and what you must do next to keep your performance at its best. So you must instruct yourself about what to do now and what to do next. You must focus your thoughts on the *present* and not on feelings generated from a sensory feedback loop of what you have already done.

In the same way as you planned your visualization exercise you must prepare a race plan. You and your coach should build up a race plan to suit you (or the crew). The plan should have actions to cope with your weaknesses and actions to maximize your strengths. Once you have formed your plan you should use visualization to rehearse it mentally and pin-point the cue words which will help you execute your race plan during the race. How you talk yourself through that plan is important. Your internal voice should be talking to you about the execution of that plan and about nothing else. If this happens you will be focused on what you are doing *now* and not on memories of what has happened in the past, or whether you are winning or losing. Your interest or focus is your execution of this race, each stroke, each metre of the course.

To do this write down cue words or short phrases for each step. You will use these words and phrases to focus yourself on achieving each step of the race. Don't think about the result of your actions. For example, to focus on a quick catch, you should be thinking about key words which will make you start lifting your hands quicker whilst simultaneously driving off the foot stretcher, e.g. think '*catch and drive*', not just '*faster catches*'.

Your capacity to perform will be enhanced by using these positive statements because you will be engaged in a process of performing an action, assessing its merits, then performing another action. You will be focused only on what you are doing and aware of the information your body is giving you about how you are doing. Because you are engaged in a process of focus, perform, assess, refocus, perform, assess, inevitably some negative thoughts will enter your head. Exhaustion may lead to a negative voice, 'I'll never be able to do it', 'I can't keep going', or your senses may tell you that your technique is failing e.g. you are shortening up or beginning to rush. Take time to listen to these voices and sensations. The sensations you feel and the information your internal voice gives you will be accurate but that is not important; what is important is how you react to it. Be *aware* of how much influence you have over yourself. You will probably be shocked. If you lose a length during a race and start to wonder why, acknowledge the presence of this negative thought, then get back on task. Refocus on the task in hand, use your cue words to instruct yourself of the action required. The more fatigued you become the harder you will find it to keep focused on your plan and the more negative thoughts are likely to come in to your head. Be aware of this. Using a race plan that demands more attention as you go on helps, as does thinking your thoughts 'louder' as more effort is required. Both these strategies employ an ever-increasing conscious effort to maintain mental control. Your race plan is your basic strategy and if anything distracts your concentration or if something goes wrong, you will set it right by refocusing on your strategy; going straight to your race plan. With this sort of mental control you will stay focused and aware, giving yourself maximum chance to perform well.

It is good to be nervous

Sportspeople are affected by varying degrees of nervousness or anxiety. To use it to your advantage during a race it is important to understand that anxiety is a necessary component of arousal. Without it you are unlikely to perform to your best ability. The physical changes in your body which accompany nervousness include an increased heart rate, heightened awareness and increased muscle tension. All of these factors, if not extreme, will be useful to you prior to and during a competition. The feelings which accompany being nervous are feelings of lethargy, shakiness and the inability to concentrate. These are often unpleasant, but when not extreme are normal reactions to excitement and stress.

Recognizing when you are too nervous to perform – when you are in a state of over-arousal prior to or during a competition – is important. This state may affect your performance adversely. In this state you will be overcome with worrying thoughts and will be wasting precious energy. However, once you or your coach have acknowledged your over-anxiety, there are a variety of ways of dealing with it.

Nerves during a competition

When you feel over-anxious and out of control, take a moment to reassure yourself that it is normal and *good* to feel nervous. It shows your body is preparing to race. Now, focus your mind on the present: anxiety is the gap between now and the future. You are over-anxious about a race before you have even stepped into the boat. There are many things that you must do before you get in the boat; focusing on the present and the immediate things you must do is often sufficient to overcome your over-anxious state. Take a deep breath and slowly exhale to help you ease the tension from your muscles and to help you make the step towards your warm up. Focus on your warm-up routine and you will have no need to feel anxious about the start of the race. You can control your anxiety by taking one step at a time.

Changing anxiety into excitement

The physical manifestations of anxiety and excitement are very similar. It is worth allowing yourself a moment to feel the excitement of the event, focusing on the feelings within your body, this may well be enough to relieve your anxiety.

Prior to a big competition

You may find yourself overly anxious in the days preceding a big race. If this occurs you may find it useful to go through a relaxation routine such as Progressive Muscle Relaxation before you go out for your practice. You don't need to sit or lie down, just close your eyes and exhale deeply, use your visualization to see all the tension drain from your muscles and then focus on the present – what you must do now, i.e. your outing and how you are going to achieve your goal for that outing. If no goal has been set, set one for yourself. If your anxiety is such that it is preventing your being able to sleep use PMR prior to going to bed, and steer your mind away from tomorrow's worries.

Good mental preparation goes hand in hand with good physical preparation. Developing your ability to control what you think and how you see yourself, and rehearsing focusing and refocusing away from distractions is part of preparing for competition and will help you to perform consistently and achieve your goals.

Check list

1. Arrive at a race well rehearsed, mentally and physically.
2. What happens to you is nowhere near as important as how you react to what happens to you.
3. Always visualize things going right. If at any point something goes wrong then rewind in your mind until you can see it right.
4. It is good to be nervous.
5. Stay alert and in control of your thoughts.
6. You can't make another competitor perform badly – you can only make yourself perform well.
7. Never concentrate on winning but what you must do to win.

Race day

On the day of the race make sure you arrive at the venue at least two hours before your first race. The last thing you need on race day is to be flustered by a lack of time. With pre-race nerves it is a good idea to write down a checklist of what you will need to be doing when you arrive at the race venue before you are ready to race. Here are some guidelines for your checklist:
1. Locate trailer.
2. Meet up with other crew members. When all the crew have arrived check in and declare any crew substitutions.
3. Collect the crew number – there is usually a number for the boat and a number that needs to be pinned to the back of the bowman.
4. Rig the boat and check all the moving parts.
5. Walk the course, or if time allows, paddle the course noting relevant landmarks, e.g. the halfway point, 100 metres from the finish etc., so that during the race you are not lost. Note where the finish line is.
6. Conserve energy by *sitting* in the shade on a hot day or in the warm on a cold day.
7. Do not eat too close to the race time. It is a good idea not to eat for one and a half hours before you race. Eating too close to racing will only make you feel sick whilst racing and will lead to the development of stomach cramps as the blood is diverted away from the stomach to the muscles of the arms and legs during exercise.
8. Keep drinking fluid continually in small quantities. Water is preferable. Avoid fizzy drinks and alcohol.

9. Coxes and lightweights should weigh in and obtain a weight certificate at least one hour before racing. The minimum weight of a coxwain is 50 kilograms for a senior men's crew and 40 kilograms for a senior women's crew or a junior crew.

The weight restrictions for lightweights are, for men a maximum weight per person of 72.5 kilograms, with a crew average of 70 kilograms. And for women a maximum weight per person of 59 kilograms and a crew average of 57 kilograms.

10. Crew pep talk.

11. Forty-five minutes before the race commence stretching (*see* Chapter 10: Flexibility and Stretching) and do a land warm up.

12. Thirty minutes before race time go afloat and warm up in the boat.

13. RACE.

After each race eat some simple carbohydrate e.g., a jam sandwich, and take plenty of fluids. Discuss what happened and whether the race plan was effective. If necessary change the tactics for the next race.

At the end of the day de-rig the boat and load the trailer. Check that all the equipment is securely tied to the trailer before going home. Unload the trailer either the same day or at least within twenty-four hours.

The race post-mortem

At the next training session when emotions have settled, hold a post-mortem to analyse the race/races of the weekend. This is important whether you won or lost. Calculate the split times for the race – the aim always being to bring these splits as close to the ideal as possible (Fig. 9:3). Look at your race profile and concentrate in training on the apparent weaknesses of the crew.

Do not assign blame to anyone if the result was disappointing. The crew is responsible as a whole for its own destiny. Enjoy the challenge of competition.

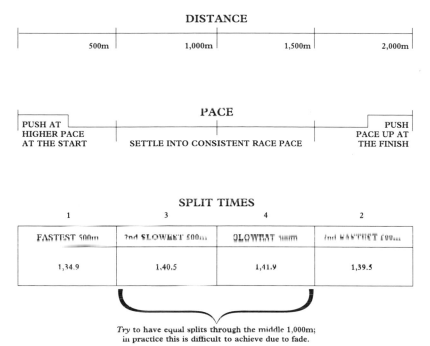

Fig. 9:3. 500-metres' split-time analysis using the times of the GBR coxless pair in the Olympics final 1988.

10

FLEXIBILITY AND
STRETCHING

Flexibility is probably the most neglected and undervalued aspect of all training programmes. A lack of flexibility is the underlying cause of many injuries and is a contributory factor in under performance.

The fundamental basic element of rowing is the performance of a repetitive limited pattern. This encourages the development of reduced spinal mobility particularly through the rib-cage and lower back. Reduced spinal mobility is reflected in reduced flexibility which as stated predisposes the individual to injury. The maintenance of good flexibility using a flexibility training programme can minimize injury.

Historically rowing training has concentrated on the development of power i.e. *Strength*. Muscular strength is increased by weight training. Poor lifting technique predisposes the individual to unnecessary injury, as a result, endless time is dedicated to the teachng and learning of good lifting technique.

The fact, however, that increasing strength by weight training increases the tension in the muscle and shortens the effective muscle fibre length is totally overlooked. The shortened fibre length indirectly reduces the range of movement of the joint across which the muscle is acting, limiting flexibility. At the extreme the body becomes 'muscle bound'.

Furthermore the power developed by weight training is 'trapped' by the shortening of the fibres that occurs – 'Starlings Law' predicts that the power of contraction of a muscle fibre is proportional to the length of the muscle fibre before contraction; shortening the effective fibre length, for instance following weight training, only reduces the power of contraction achieved!

Stretching following weight training returns the muscle fibre to its normal length, reduces post-training muscle soreness/stiffness and allows the power developed through weight training to be used effectively.

Flexibility

Flexibility is defined as the ability of a joint to move. For all joints there is a theoretical normal range of movement that is inherent in the structure of the joint.

The direction of movement in any joint is determined by the shape of the articular surfaces of the joint.

The end point of movement in any joint is determined by the stretchability of:

the muscles that work across the joint;

the capsule that encloses the joint;

the ligaments that hold the joint together.

The freedom of movement of a joint is determined by the tone and strength of the muscles working around the joint and the degree of degenerative change within the joint.

In addition when considering the flexibility of the spinal joints the state of health of the intervertebral discs is all important in determining the freedom of movement.

Joint mobility is notably less in cold conditions, early in the morning and in the presence of physical or mental fatigue.

The athlete is unable to change the anatomy of the joint, but he does have the ability to influence joint mobility by maintaining the surrounding muscles and ligaments in as good a condition as possible, thus maintaining the vitality of the tissues and enabling them to regenerate following exercise. This influence is possible through regular stretching.

Flexibility training consists of a programme of stretching exercises which, if used regularly, attempt to slow the natural deterioration of flexibility that occurs with age. This natural deterioration is accelerated by physical exertion.

Stretching

Stretching can be either dynamic, using momentum or static.

Dynamic stretching is what most athletes think of when asked about stretching. It consists of taking the muscle into a stretched position and bouncing at the limit of stretch. The bouncing however, provokes a stretch reflex which causes the muscle to contract, counteracting any stretch that has been achieved.

Stretching by this method has a tendency to cause muscle soreness and microscopic tears of the muscle fibres. It is not advisable to stretch by this method.

Static stretching is more effective than dynamic stretching for increasing flexibility. A static stretch consists of assuming a stretch position, and then stretching the muscle further by a small change of resistance. This change in resistance may be achieved using gravity, a muscular contraction (be it the muscle being stretched or its antagonist, i.e. the muscle opposing the action of the muscle being stretched), a partner or another piece of apparatus. The slower stretch of the muscle during static stretching prevents the stretch reflex being provoked.

When taking the muscle into the stretch position, it is important that the stretch is felt as a slight pull only, not as pain. Pain is a warning that the stretch is too strong and is probably causing damage to the muscle.

The stretch phase of static stretching should be maintained for 15–30 seconds, and repeated two or three times.

Static stretching if used properly is an effective way to increase flexibility, and may also be used before and after training sessions to eliminate muscle soreness and facilitate the recovery of soft-tissue injuries.

When to stretch

Muscles should be stretched both before and after exercise. Warm-up stretching eases the muscles into action, whereas warm-down stretching returns the fatigued muscle to its normal relaxed length, enabling recovery from exercise.

Stretching should also be incorporated into the training schedule two to three times per week to increase overall flexibility.

How to stretch

There are three types of static stretch that can be incorporated in a flexibility programme:

1. Passive static stretching (Fig. 10:1)

For a particular muscle group a position of stretch is assumed. The position of stretch is slowly changed by movement thereby increasing the stretch. This position is maintained for 15–30 seconds. The stretch is repeated two or three times.

Fig. 10:1. Passive static stretch of the hamstrings: assume position illustrated until sensation of pulling felt in posterior thigh. Hold, relax and repeat.

2. Contract – Relax – Stretch (Fig. 10.2)

For a particular muscle group a position of stretch is assumed. The muscle being stretched is then contracted for 3–7 seconds against resistance. The muscle is relaxed and stretched further for 10 seconds. The process is repeated two or three times.

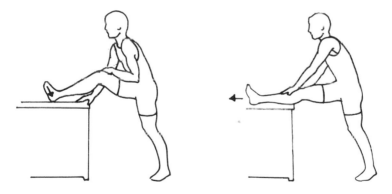

1. Contract – 2. Relax – 3. Stretch

Fig. 10:2. Contract – Relax – Stretch routine for hamstrings (posterior thigh muscles). 1. With knees bent, push ankle down actively contracting the hamstrings for a count of twenty. 2. Relax. 3. Stretch hamstrings by straightening the leg and leaning the body forward, hold for a count of twenty.

3. Active static stretching (Fig. 10:3)

For a particular muscle group a position of stretch is assumed. The antagonist muscle, to that being stretched, is contracted actively increasing the stretch of the muscle. The contraction is maintained for 10–20 seconds and repeated two or three times.

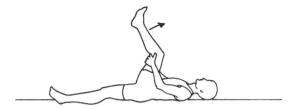

Fig. 10:3. Active static stretch of the hamstrings: lying on back, grasp the leg with both hands behind the bent knee. Straighten leg and hold for 20 seconds. Relax and repeat.

Flexibility assessment

Prior to commencing a flexibility programme the flexibility of an individual should be assessed objectively and documented. The assessment should then be repeated every four to six weeks and any change in flexibility can be plotted by comparing the measurements. The tests should be conducted each time under similar conditions so that any change in flexibility is measured accurately. A simple but useful assessment of flexibility from *Fitness for Sport* by Rex Hazeldine follows:

i) *Stretch and reach*

Sitting with the legs straight, toes pointing vertically upwards. Stretch forwards to try to touch the toes. Measure the distance from the finger tips to the toes. The score is a minus score if the toes cannot be reached and a positive score if the fingers reach beyond the toes.

ii) *Forward flexion*

Sitting with the legs spread apart. Lean forward to place the forearms on the floor, one fist on top of the other. Measure the distance from the forehead to the top of the fists. The score is negative if the forehead is above the fists and positive if the forehead is below the fists.

iii) *Shoulder extension*

In the standing position place one arm over the shoulder and the other arm behind the back. Move the hands towards each other and attempt to overlap them. The score is the measurement of the overlap – negative if no overlap, positive if overlap achieved.

iv) *Sideways – backward movement of the arms*

Stand with your back against a wall and raise arms to the horizontal with the palms forward. Keeping the arms horizontal and the little finger of each hand in contact with the wall, move away from the wall as far as possible. Measure the distance from the wall to the back at the level of the arms.

v) *Trunk extension*

Lying face down on the floor, clasp the hands behind the back, in the small of the back. Lift the chest off the floor as high as possible. Measure the distance from the top of the breastbone to the floor.

The stretches

1. *Shoulder girdle*

Standing, bend right arm at the elbow and bring across the body to hold on to a ledge. Step forward on right leg, pushing the upper body forward. Hold, relax and repeat. Repeat stretch for other side.

2. *Posterior upper arms*

Standing, with arm bent over as shown, elbow resting against a wall, move the trunk forward. Hold, relax and repeat. Repeat stretch for other side.

3. *Anterior upper arms*

Stand, back to wall, holding on to a wall bar behind at shoulder height, move the trunk downwards and forwards by bending the knees. Hold, relax and repeat.

4. *Forearms*

Kneel down, arms straight, palms resting on the floor, move trunk backwards and feel the stretch through the forearms. Hold, relax and repeat. The placing of the hands may be varied for the comfort of the wrists, but the stretch is maximal with the hands pointing backwards.

5. *Pectoral muscle*

Stand side on to wall, arm against wall as shown. Step forward with the leg of the side being stretched and push the shoulder forward. Hold, relax and repeat. Repeat stretch for other side.

6. *Lateral trunk*

Kneel on the floor, right leg out to the side. resting on left arm, raise the right arm over the head. Stretch along the length of the body. Ensure that all the body is in the same plane. Hold, relax and repeat. Repeat stretch for other side.

7. *Spinal mobility (cat stretch)*

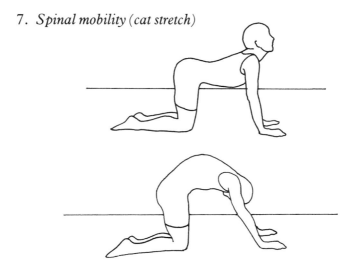

Kneel on all fours, head up. Hold for count of ten. Arch back, lowering head and tightening abdominal muscles. Hold for count of ten. Continue to alternate positions for ten repetitions.

8. *Spinal mobility*

Lying on back, draw both knees up to the chest with hands until pull can be felt in lower back. Hold, relax and repeat.

9. *Extension exercise*

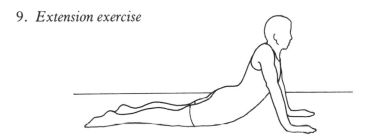

Lying on stomach, legs apart, place hands slightly in front of shoulders, palms downwards. Push up with the arms keeping hips in contact with the floor. Hold, relax and repeat.

10. *Posterior hip muscle*

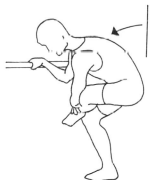

Standing upright, hold support with one hand and with the other grasp the leg on the same side, bending the other knee. Bend forward from the waist to position shown. Hold, relax and repeat. Repeat stretch for other side.

11. *Anterior hip muscle*

With one knee on the floor, the other bent as shown, place hands on knee and lunge forward to feel stretch in anterior muscle of back leg. Hold, relax and repeat. Repeat stretch for other side. NB. The feet should be straight and not turned inward or outward.

12. *Medial hip muscle*

Stand, feet facing forward. Take right leg out to side and bend left knee taking the weight on this side to stretch the inner aspect of the hip on the opposite side. Repeat stretch for other side.

13. *Posterior thigh muscle*

Sitting on the floor, bend one leg to rest sole of foot against knee of extended leg. Bend forward and grasp foot of straight leg to feel pulling in the posterior thigh. Hold, relax and repeat. Repeat stretch for other side.

14. *Anterior thigh*

Standing upright place top of foot on secure surface behind. Lower torso down by flexion of front knee until the stretch is felt through the anterior thigh of the other leg. Hold relax and repeat. Repeat stretch for other side.

15. *Posterior calf muscle*

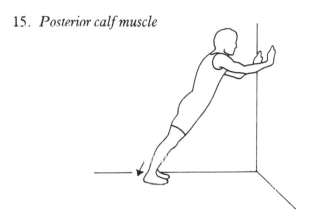

Stand a few feet from a wall, legs shoulder width apart. Place hands against wall with body leaning forwards arms straight. Bend the elbows, lowering body towards the wall. Hold then push off. This stretch may be increased by placing a telephone directory under the front of the feet.

16. *Anterior lower leg/shin*

From kneeling position, hands placed behind, raise the knees slightly. Hold, relax and repeat. NB. There is no need to take the knees more than a few inches off the floor.

NB. It is always advisable to obtain the approval and recommendations of your doctor before beginning this, or any other, exercise programme.

11

INJURIES:
PREVENTION/CURE

With all sports there are injuries. It almost seems to have become accepted as the inevitable, just part of the sporting experience. This, I believe, is a fallacy, as the majority of injuries are probably avoidable if the athlete is prepared to seek help at the first hint that something is wrong, rather than waiting until the symptoms are so severe that continuing the sport becomes an impossibility without treatment.

With most significant injuries, there are usually warning signs for some time prior to the onset of the injury. Treatment at this earlier stage may well prevent losing valuable training time.

Injuries within any sport are specific to that sport, the nature of the injury being dictated by the biomechanics of the actions involved.

Within the sport of rowing a large proportion of injuries occur whilst getting fit to row, not whilst rowing. Nevertheless there are specific rowing injuries and it is these that will be examined more closely. The aim of this chapter is to enable the oarsman/coach to understand and recognize the possible injuries that may occur and how to minimize the risk of a particular injury where possible (Fig. 11:1). For *prevention is better than treatment*.

Broadly speaking rowing injuries are either caused by over-use or poor technique.

An *over-use* injury is due to the repetitive stereotyped performance of a limited movement pattern compromising the

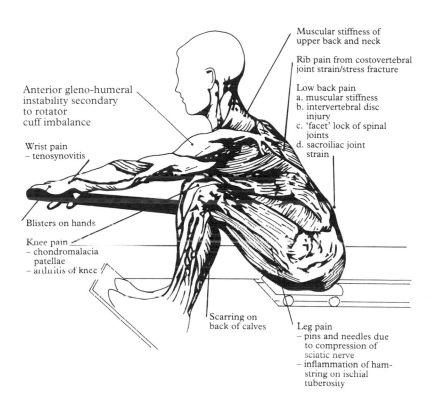

Muscular stiffness of
upper back and neck

Rib pain from costovertebral
joint strain/stress fracture

Low back pain
a. muscular stiffness
b. intervertebral disc
   injury
c. 'facet' lock of spinal
   joints
d. sacroiliac joint
   strain

Anterior gleno-humeral
instability secondary
to rotator
cuff imbalance

Wrist pain
– tenosynovitis

Blisters on hands

Knee pain
– chondromalacia
  patellae
– arthritis of knee

Scarring on
back of calves

Leg pain
– pins and needles due
  to compression of
  sciatic nerve
– inflammation of ham-
  string on ischial
  tuberosity

Fig. 11:1. Summary of the sites of injury in the rower.

tissues. This type of problem is often seen at key times in
an athlete's training calendar, usually in the build up to an
important race, trials for crew selection or on returning to
training after a holiday or period of illness when the athlete feels
he should do extra training to catch up. Over-use injuries
include tenosynovitis, rib joint strains and rib stress fractures.

Poor technique is easy to develop and very difficult to correct.
Sometimes poor technique is the consequence of a minor
physical abnormality that is magnified through the actions
required to row. It is common to find a person with a difference
in leg lengths having no daily symptoms except when active in
sport. In rowing this results in a torque occurring through the
pelvis and lower spine giving rise to a variety of symptoms in
the low back including, for example, sacroiliac joint strains,
intervertebral disc injury and facet locks of the spinal joints.

The common hazards of rowing

These conditions can safely be treated by the oarsman/coach with first aid, and in some cases minor changes to the equipment being used.

Blisters

Blisters occur because of the friction that develops between the skin of the palm of the hands and the surface of the oarhandle whilst taking the stroke. The friction separates the outer layer of the skin, the epidermis, from the inner layer, the dermis. The space created between the two layers becomes filled with a clear watery fluid.

Blisters occur in all rowers. In the novice rower they occur because the skin is soft and unaccustomed to the friction. In the hardened, more experienced rower they occur with a change in humidity.

Blisters should be tended to and not *ignored* as there is always the possibility that the blister will become septic.

It is generally agreed that once a blister has formed the fluid needs to be drained out if rowing is to be continued without extension of the existing blister. This may be done in a variety of ways:

1. Thread a piece of cotton through a sterile needle, pass the

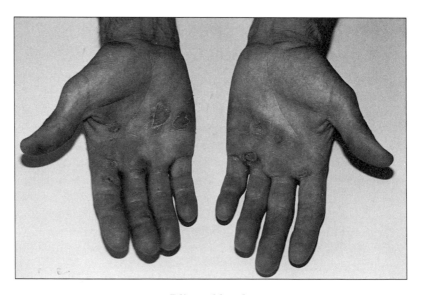

Blistered hands.

needle through the blister and allow the fluid to ooze out along the thread. Remove the thread and allow the skin to dry and flake off.

2. Puncture the blister with a sterile pair of scissors and trim away any loose skin carefully.

If training has to be resumed before the blisters have healed, strapping with Micropore or Elastoplast will help to protect the raw skin.

For blisters on the palm of the hand, where Elastoplast will not stick because of sweat production, a 'Tubigrip' mitten will provide good protection. Tubigrip is an elasticated tubular bandage that can be purchased at most chemists. To construct a Tubigrip mitten purchase wrist width Tubigrip, cut a length to fit from your wrist to the knuckles of the fist, and make a hole for the thumb.

As the blisters begin to heal by developing a new layer of epidermis, the new skin needs to be kept supple using a moisturizing cream, otherwise it will crack.

Once the hands have healed, new callosities occur with a change of equipment, a change in the humidity or a change in the intensity of training.

NB. Should any blister become septic or red tracking develop up the arm from the blisters, consult your general practitioner.

Scarring on the back of the calves

The construction of a rowing boat is such that for the majority when the feet are set at the correct position in the boat, sitting at backstops will cause the slidebeds to apply pressure to the back of the calves (Fig. 11:2).

Initially there may be no problem at this site, however through chronic irritation the skin thickens forming a scar. Sometimes the chronic irritation may actually abrade the skin giving rise to an acute inflammatory response in which the skin becomes red, hot and swollen and very tender. If this occurs the site should be bathed regularly with antiseptic and protected with Elastoplast until a healing scab has formed.

Sometimes it is possible to avoid this contact pressure by moving the slidebeds or shortening them.

Scarred hands and calves are the trademarks of an oarsman!

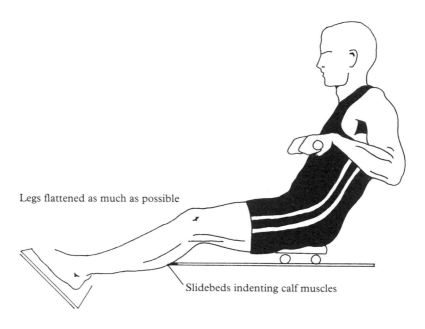

Legs flattened as much as possible

Slidebeds indenting calf muscles

Fig. 11:2. At the finish of the stroke the slidebeds may apply pressure to the calves causing scarring.

Pins and needles in the feet and legs

There are many causes of pins and needles in the legs but one in particular occurs in rowing and is easily prevented.

The standard rowing seat is constructed of wood bearing two circular holes. In Figure 11:3, x is the distance between the centre of one hole in the seat and the centre of the other hole. For the seat to be comfortable x should be equal to the distance between the ischial tuberosities of the person sitting on the seat. The ischial tuberosities are the bony prominences in the bottom that are rested on when sitting. If the distance x is not correct for the individual, then pressure develops on the sciatic nerve, because of the proximity of the nerve to the ischial tuberosity (Fig. 11:4).

Pressure on the sciatic nerve and/or piriformis muscle which crosses the buttock is painful and causes the development of pins and needles down the leg after sitting on the rowing seat for a length of time. The pins and needles do not occur immediately on sitting on the seat. Once out of the boat at the end of the outing, the pins and needles cease almost immediately, but the ache in the buttock may linger.

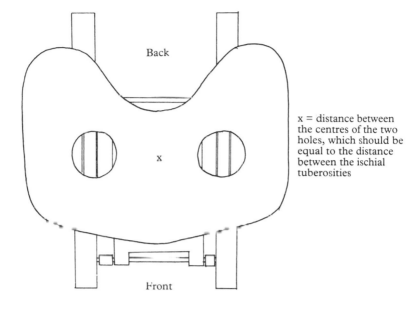

x = distance between the centres of the two holes, which should be equal to the distance between the ischial tuberosities

Back

x

Front

Fig. 11:3. A typical rowing seat.

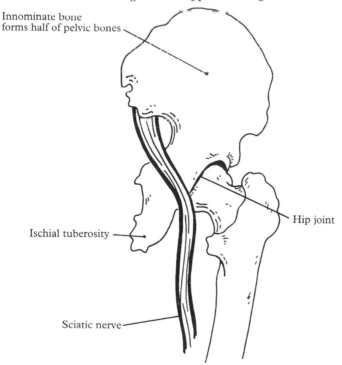

Innominate bone forms half of pelvic bones

Hip joint

Ischial tuberosity

Sciatic nerve

Fig. 11:4. Bones of lower limb – posterior view showing position of sciatic nerve.

There are two solutions:
1. If possible, enlarge the holes in the seat to suit your physique.
2. Use a Sorbathane or padded cover on your seat to prevent the pressure developing on the sciatic nerve. Remember that the seat cover will raise the height of the seat above the decking, and the height of the rigging may need to be adjusted accordingly.

NB. If pins and needles persist and do not respond to these measures, are associated with back pain or become continuous even when out of the boat, consult your general practitioner.

Muscular stiffness/lumbago

Lumbago is a dull muscular ache that usually occurs following unaccustomed exercise or with exercise overload when the body is unable to cope with the intensity. The symptoms in rowing may vary from bilateral mid lumbar pain i.e. low back pain, to pain that radiates up into the shoulders and through the legs, particularly the quadriceps and hamstrings.

Post-exercise stiffness is maximal 36 to 48 hours after training and responds well to hot baths and continued gentle training. If the pain is particularly uncomfortable an anti-inflammatory painkiller such as aspirin or Brufen (both of which are available from chemists without prescription) may be taken for a short period of time.

The cause of stiffness is still a controversial subject amongst exercise physiologists. Some argue that the pain is due to small tears in the muscle together with the release of chemicals that produce an acute inflammatory response, others believe it is due to the congestion of muscular tissue and the accumulation of chemical end-products of muscular activity such as lactic acid (for more information refer to Chapter 7: Training).

As a rule of thumb, if muscular stiffness of the back is not *beginning* to settle after 48 hours, it is advisable to consult a doctor or physiotherapist to rule out the possibility of an underlying problem that needs treatment.

The not so common hazards of rowing

The conditions in this section cannot be treated by the oarsman alone, but it is important that these conditions are recognized and early treatment sought from the appropriate practitioner. Where possible preventative measures should be implemented.

Tenosynovitis

Tenosynovitis is characterized by inflammation of a tendon sheath (Fig. 11:5).

Each of the tendons on the back of the wrist has a tendon sheath. These occur wherever a tendon passes under a non-elastic tight structure, in this case a fibrous band – the extensor retinaculum. The sheaths provide lubrication for the smooth passage of the tendons. The tendon sheath becomes inflamed through over use. The development of swelling and adhesions

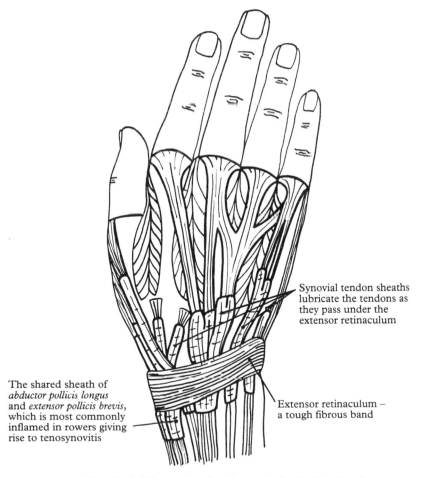

Synovial tendon sheaths lubricate the tendons as they pass under the extensor retinaculum

The shared sheath of *abductor pollicis longus* and *extensor pollicis brevis*, which is most commonly inflamed in rowers giving rise to tenosynovitis

Extensor retinaculum – a tough fibrous band

Fig. 11:5. The tendon sheaths on the back of the hand.

with continued activity causes a vicious cycle to develop in which the sheath then becomes an irritation in its own right.

Pain and grating – crepitus – over the tendon sheath involved and pain whenever the muscle group affected is used are early signs of this problem.

The tendons most commonly affected in rowing are those of *abductor pollicis longus* and *extensor pollicis brevis* over the back of the wrist, at the base of the thumb. These muscles share the same tendon sheath and are responsible for enabling the thumb to be held underneath the oar handle.

Gripping the oar handle too tightly predisposes the oarsman to tenosynovitis. Its prevalence in the cold weather of winter is probably due to the fact that when the hands are numbed by the cold, there is more tendency to grip the blade.

Treatment: the oarsman should take first-aid measures with the onset of pain in the wrist, placing an ice pack over the painful area but ensuring that the pack is not in contact with the skin to prevent the formation of ice burns. The application of ice will minimize the swelling that develops. Aspirin or Brufen are also useful for this purpose.

Physiotherapy and rest from rowing will usually settle the problem in a matter of days. However it is occasionally necessary to consider a minor operation to resolve the pain.

Prevention: loose grip should be encouraged and can be reinforced by playing the piano on the blade handle during the recovery. By this I mean releasing the grip of each hand in turn, stretching the fingers out straight, and repeatedly curling them back around the handle one finger at a time – similar to playing the keys of a piano! This forces you to let the grip off.

Relaxing the grip of the fingers on the recovery – the piano exercise.

Anterior knee pain – chondromalacia patellae (CMP)

Chondromalacia patellae is anterior knee pain believed to be caused by an imbalanced action of the quadriceps muscle of the thigh.

The quadriceps muscle group consists of four muscle bellies in the anterior thigh. On contraction the quadriceps pull the bent knee straight. A small rounded bone in the substance of the quadriceps tendon acts as a fulcrum for the muscle over the bent knee, and increases the efficiency of the muscles' contraction. This bone is known as the kneecap or patella (Fig. 11:6).

The four muscle bellies attach to the upper border of the knee cap. As the knee straightens the kneecap tracks along a groove on the anterior surface of the thigh bone (femur).

Balanced co-ordinated contraction of the four muscles of the quadriceps is required for normal tracking. The most medial muscle belly, *vastus medialis*, only contracts in the last 10 to 15 degrees of knee straightening, i.e., it is a muscle of predominantly straight-leg action rather than bent-leg action, unlike the other muscle bellies of the quadriceps.

In rowing it is common to find that at backstops when the legs are at their straightest, they are still flexed/bent to between 15 and 20 degrees. As a result there is no *vastus medialis* activity during the rowing stroke.

However the repetitive straightening of the bent knee during the stroke cycle causes the other three bellies of the quadriceps to become more powerful.

The combination of increasing the lateral quadriceps' strength, in the presence of the relatively diminishing medial quadriceps' strength produces an imbalance of pull on the knee cap, pulling it laterally over the buttress of the groove on the femur. The end result is erosion of the cartilage on the back of the kneecap which causes pain and eventually may lead to the development of arthritis behind the kneecap.

Chondromalacia patellae causes anterior knee pain that is made worse by walking downstairs, squatting, running and rowing. The pain is usually of gradual onset often preceded by stiffness of the knees after physical exercise.

Treatment and prevention: correction of the quadriceps imbalance will alleviate the pain behind the kneecap. This can be

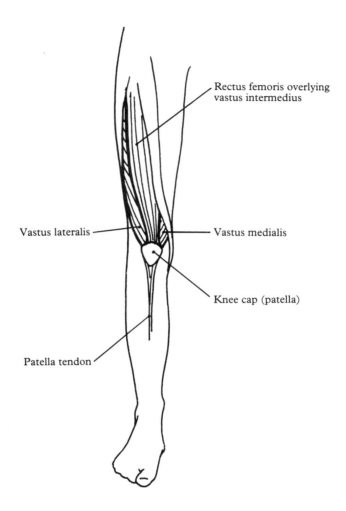

Fig. 11:6. The quadricep muscle of the anterior thigh and its relationship to the knee cap (patella).

Sit on the floor with one leg bent up. Turn the foot outwards, lock the knee straight and lift the leg 3 inches off the floor. Hold this position for a count of ten. Relax and repeat ten times. With time gradually increase the number of repetitions.

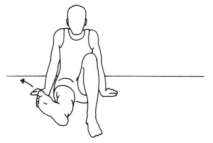

Fig. 11:7. Static quadriceps exercise for correcting an imbalance of anterior thigh muscles that give rise to CMP.

done by static quadriceps exercises which increase the strength of *vastus medialis* and correct the imbalance of the quadriceps (Fig. 11:7).

If the symptoms do not respond to correction of the quadriceps imbalance, referral to an orthopaedic specialist is advised.

Sacroiliac joint strain

There are two synovial sacroiliac joints, one on either side of the sacrum which articulate with the ilium of the pelvis (Fig. 11:8). The function of these joints is to transmit torque from leg movement to the spine and vice versa, and to allow the absorption of shock through the large blades of the ilia.

These joints unlike other joints of the body are not crossed by any muscles, movement through them is caused by momentum and ligamentous pull. When the bodyweight is placed through

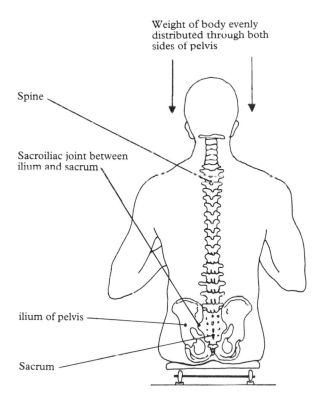

Fig. 11:8. Illustration of the spine and pelvis with boat level – weight is
evenly distributed through sacroiliac joints.

both legs the sacroiliac joints are very stable; once the body-weight is transferred to only one leg the joint of the other side opens up to allow movement, although small, to occur.

In a rowing boat sacroiliac strains arise for two reasons:

1. When one leg is shorter than the other. In a rowing boat the legs drive against a stretcher/footplate which assumes that the legs are of equal lengths. If the legs are of different lengths there is a tendency to push with only one leg or to push with a twist through the low back, both of which stress the sacroiliac joints unevenly.

2. In the presence of a constant or sudden balance problem. As the boat rolls to one side, more weight is placed through the sacroiliac joint on the opposite side, allowing the joint on the side of the roll to open and be susceptible to strain (Fig 11:9).

The joint strain arises because when one of the sacroiliac joints is transmitting the full force of the leg drive, the joint of

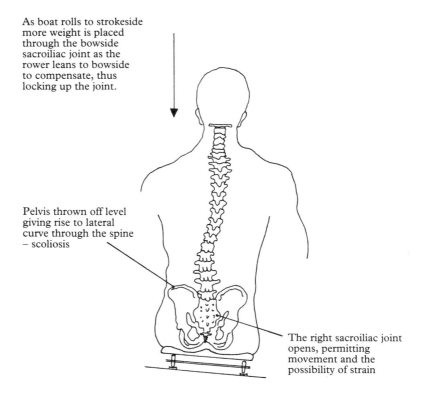

As boat rolls to strokeside more weight is placed through the bowside sacroiliac joint as the rower leans to bowside to compensate, thus locking up the joint.

Pelvis thrown off level giving rise to lateral curve through the spine – scoliosis

The right sacroiliac joint opens, permitting movement and the possibility of strain

Fig. 11:9. Illustration of the spine and pelvis with boat tilted to strokeside – the spine and pelvis compensate for the balance disturbance to keep the head and eyes on the horizontal.

Lie on floor with arms outstretched for balance. Bend knees up and rock over first to the left – hold for 10 seconds – then rock over to the right – hold for 10 seconds. As the body rocks, ensure the hips only just lift off the floor to prevent the torsion passing further up the spine. Repeat ten times for each side.

Fig. 11:10. Exercise for maintaining even mobility through the sacroiliac joints of pelvis.

that side locks up whilst the joint of the other side of the pelvis is able to move. The joint with mobility is susceptible to strain. Once a joint has been strained acute inflammation occurs in the overlying ligaments and this is the cause of the pain.

Sacroiliac joint strain is felt as unilateral low back and buttock pain, with specific aggravating activities that indicate it is these joints that are the cause of the back pain.

Treatment: manipulation to increase the mobility of the sacroiliac joint on the side being compressed, evening out the mobility across the pelvis helps to settle the pain. Inflammation of the overlying ligaments on the side of the strain responds well to the physiotherapy modalities and anti-inflammatory medication.

Prevention: in the presence of unequal leg lengths an extra insole in the shoe of the short leg will prevent the overstrain recurring.

Maintenance of even mobility across the sacroiliac joints may be achieved by tanking on the opposite side to the one being rowed on (i.e., if rowing on strokeside constantly, row in the tank on bowside) and by performing the exercise illustrated in Figure 11:10 on a daily basis.

Rib injuries

Rib problems have been, and continue to be, increasing in prevalence, which is perhaps a reflection on the intensity of today's training as they are essentially over-use injuries.

There are twelve pairs of ribs, all of which are attached posteriorly to the spine. The upper seven pairs are attached anteriorly to the sternum/breastbone by cartilage. The eighth, ninth and tenth pairs of ribs are attached anteriorly to each other and to the seventh rib by means of cartilages. The

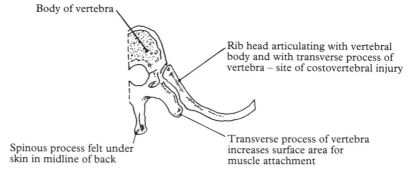

Fig. 11:11. Cross section of vertebra (thoracic) of rib-cage to show articulation with rib.

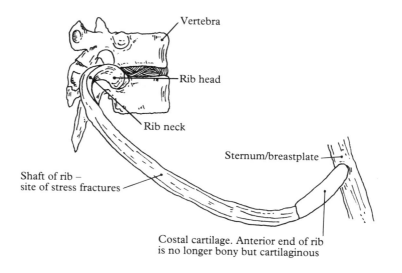

Fig. 11:12. Lateral view of rib and attachment to vertebra posteriorly, and to the sternum anteriorly.

eleventh and twelfth pairs have no anterior attachment and are known as the floating ribs (Figs 11:11 & 11:12).

Rib head joint strains (Costovertebral joint strains)

Inflammation of the ligaments supporting the articulation of the rib and its associated vertebra together with disturbance of the normal mechanics of the joint, cause pain to be felt in the upper spine. This pain is usually a dull background ache with a sharper pain on taking a deep breath, coughing, laughing and on taking the catch. The pain sometimes spreads around the chest wall, or may only be felt in the front of the chest due to the protective spasm of the muscles between the ribs.

How or why this problem arises is a matter of controversy, there are at present two lines of thought:

1. In a healthy spine the majority of movement in a rotatory or side-bending direction occurs through the apophyseal joints of the thoracic vertebrae and is limited in range by the presence of the rib-cage. The mechanics of rowing are such that unless *flexibility* is concentrated on in training, the thoracic spine stiffens. As it stiffens the rotation movement required in the rowing stroke is forced through the weakest link, through the joints of the rib head and vertebra, predisposing this site to strain.

2. The sudden onset of pain in this condition has provoked the second school of thought in which it is felt that local muscle pull is responsible for the strain of the rib head.

Treatment: if treated promptly the rib head strain will settle very quickly. Manipulation to restore the normal mobility of the area and release any muscle spasm, anti-inflammatory medication and 48 hours' rest are all that is necessary.

Occasionally strapping along the line of the rib may be required when training is resumed.

Sit in a chair with low back well supported. Clasp hands together and place over base of neck. Using elbows together as a pen, draw a figure of eight lying on its side. Ensure no movement occuring in lower back.
Spend a minimum of one minute daily doing this exercise.

Fig. 11:13. Figure-of-eight exercise for maintaining thoracic spine mobility.

Recurrence of the strain is usually caused by persistent restricted mobility through the thoracic spine.

Prevention: maintain mobility through the thoracic spine and rib-cage by regular figure-of-eight exercises (Fig. 11:13), and, when in intensive training, by loosening of the spine by manipulation every three months.

Rib stress fractures

A stress fracture is a fracture/break through normal bone due to localized repeated stress that weakens the normal architecture.

The rib-cage, being fixed both anteriorly and posteriorly, limits the movement of the thoracic spine. Bending forward (flexion) and bending backwards (extension) through the thoracic spine produces a twisting deformation through the longitudinal axis of the ribs.

In rowing this deformation is focused to one side by the rotation of the spine when preparing to take the catch (the left side if rowing on bowside, and the right if rowing on strokeside). This deformation occurs in everyone – but not every rower or sculler suffers from rib stress fractures. The formation of the stress fracture in rowers, in my opinion, is again predisposed to by stiffness through the spine which exacerbates the longitudinal torsion through the rib.

In scullers where there is no twisting to one side and the movement is more symmetrical, the formation of rib stress fractures is related to muscle-pull bending the rib, in particular the pull of serratus anterior and the rhomboids.

The focused stress occurs at approximately the mid-axillary line of the fourth to eighth ribs. The mid-axillary line is an imaginary line drawn vertically from the apex of the armpit downwards.

The rib stress fracture may start in a similar way to the rib head strain or it may begin with sudden severe pain at the site of the stress fracture. Breathing deeply is uncomfortable, as is any compressive force through the chest, e.g. lying on the affected side, sometimes even just lying in any position. General movement is difficult. The rib that has fractured is locally tender over the site of the crack.

A rib stress fracture is often not visible on an X-ray, the only conclusive evidence being a special investigation known as a bone scan.

Treatment: as the ribs are splinted by each other, a stress fracture is best treated by rest from the exercise that provoked the injury for four to six weeks. It is usually necessary to have total rest for three weeks, with introduction of maintenance fitness training, followed by gradual commencement of rowing when pain free.

Prevention: maintain mobility through the thoracic spine and rib-cage by regular figure-of-eight exercises (Fig. 11:13, p.215), and, when in intensive training, by loosening of the spine by manipulation every three months.

Low back pain

The majority of back problems feel very similar to the athlete. The causes of low back pain are numerous but as already stated if a muscular pain persists in the low back for 48 hours without showing signs of reducing, it is worth having the back examined to exclude any underlying problem.

I cannot emphasize enough that back pain should be treated with respect, it is a sign that there is something wrong – be it a pulled muscle, a ligament strain, a locked joint or an intervertebral disc injury.

Pain should *not* be masked with painkillers so that rowing/training may be continued, for this only leads to poor performance and aggravates the underlying injury.

Over the past ten years there has been a significant change in the type of back problems experienced by active rowers. This change has been from cases which were easily amenable to cure, did not interrupt training for more than a couple of days and, on the whole, did not carry long-term consequences, to those which are not easily cured, often necessitate weeks out of training and sometimes carry the risk of long-term damage. **Intervertebral disc herniation – slipped disc – is now the most prevalent cause of low back pain in rowers from the age of sixteen years onwards.** This is thought to reflect advances in modern technology which have allowed significant developments in the construction of rowing equipment. In addition, the greater understanding by coaches of the principles of training have enabled them to write training programmes culminating in ever-increasing boat speeds.

In effect the 'slipped disc' of the rower is an overuse injury resulting in degenerative changes in the substance of the disc which causes a bulge to develop, particularly during activities with sustained loading of the lower back in forward bending (flexion). Once a bulge exists, pressure on the surrounding structures causes pain which alerts the athlete to the often protracted and insidious progress of this injury (Fig. 11:14).

There is no typical presentation with this particular injury as the symptoms are determined by the actual position of the bulge. In general terms there is pain of some degree in the lumbar spine, the buttock and the posterior thigh of one leg. Leg pain may occur without preceeding back pain and initially may be wrongly diagnosed as muscular leg pain; alternatively the first symptom may be that of pins and needles in the leg or foot. Pain is usually worse in the morning, settling after a couple of hours, and is aggravated by coughing, sitting and any activity requiring forward bending.

There are specific tests performed by doctors/physiotherapists that help to diagnose this condition, and it is therefore imperative, as stated previously, to seek medical advice if symptoms persist for longer than 48 hours.

Treatment: physiotherapy and/or osteopathy to dissipate the swelling in the nucleus of the disc and thereby relieve the compression on surrounding structures. It is often necessary to take a short period of bedrest, together with the application of

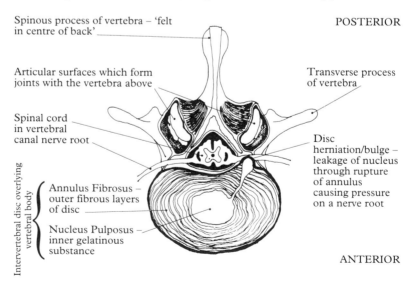

Fig. 11:14. Cross-section of an intervertebral disc to illustrate the anatomy and relation to other structures, and how nerve root compression may occur.

hot/cold packs to the lumbar spine and a course of anti-inflammatory medication. It may take up to three months to rehabilitate from an acute disc herniation. If conservative treatment fails to settle the condition, orthopaedic referral is sought and the spine assessed further by MRI Scan, a sophisticated X-ray techique which enables the soft tissues to be visualized, unlike plain X-rays which show only the bone. Occasionally surgery is required to settle this injury, but this line of treatment cannot always guarantee a pain-free back post-op.

Prevention: There is much debate about the recent increase in 'discogenic' pain in rowers, and a number of research projects examining the causes in depth are now underway. However, it will take several years to obtain hard data. For now it is generally accepted that the way to minimize the risk of this injury is to **reduce the loading of the lumbar spine in flexion** during training. This may be achieved by:

Land training

1. Do not land train after a long water session when the body is fatigued.
2. Do not incorporate lifts requiring good technique into competitive circuits.
3. Eliminate power cleans and dead lifts from land-training programmes.
4. Do appropriate exercises to:
    a. train the antagonist muscles
    b. improve coordination
    c. improve flexibility
    d. maintain hamstring length
5. Do not work continuously for more than 30 minutes on an ergometer without stopping to perform extension exercises which reverse the effect of sustained flexion on the disc.

Water work

1. Avoid consecutive outings of long low-rate steady state. Do not row for longer than one hour without a break to perform extension exercises (Fig. 11:15). If more endurance work is necessary consider cross training.

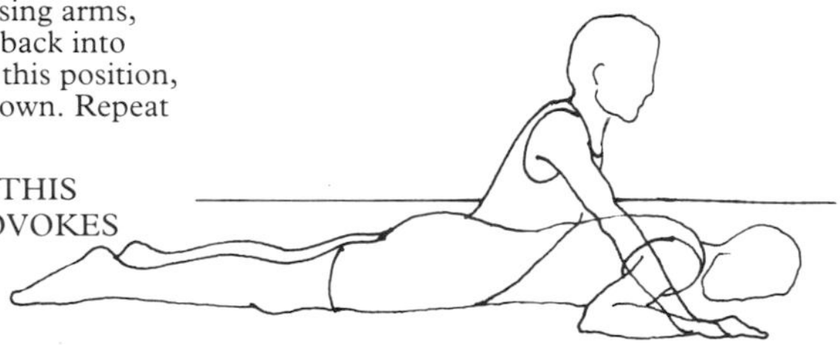

Lie on the floor face down with head turned to one side. Keep hips in contact with ground. Using arms, push up, arching lower back into extension. Do not hold this position, simply return to lying down. Repeat this action 10 times.

DO NOT PERFORM THIS EXERCISE IF IT PROVOKES LEG SYMPTOMS.

Fig. 11:15. Extension exercises to centralize and control swelling of the nucleus of the disc.

2. Macon blades are *safer* for long low-rate steady state. If you have to use hatchet blades – big blades – use them on a lighter gearing than you would use to race over 2,000 metres.

3. Use functional bracing of the spine. This is complicated to portray in print, but in essence involves protecting the discs of the lumbar spine at the point of loading, i.e. the catch, by contracting the abdominal corset. This controls the posture of the spine. If posture control is lost during an outing owing to fatigue, the training session should be terminated.

Swimming

1. It is advisable to incorporate one swimming session into the training schedule per week as it allows exercise without loading to the discs.

If in doubt do not row, seek advice!

12

DIET

Before looking at the diet and what fuel should be supplied to the body in order for it to function correctly, let's first take a quick look at the important processes that take place in the body itself during exercise.

Any strenuous physical activity such as rowing poses a considerable challenge to the body's numerous control systems. These control systems have to keep the environment within the body fluids constant and within very strict limits. Human cells can only tolerate small fluctuations in temperature or acidity and, therefore, the concentrations of substances required as fuel for exercise and the waste products produced during exercise must be kept almost constant. Nerve cells are particularly sensitive to changes in their environment. Muscle cells are *more* tolerant but they too have specific needs and will not function correctly if their surroundings change too much from the optimum.

The physiological changes that take place within the body during strenuous exercise are remarkable. The energy demand of muscle cells can increase twenty-fold within seconds, the total output of blood from the heart can increase five-fold, and the oxygen intake via the lungs can increase ten-fold. In order for these changes to take place the correct fuel must be provided.

Fuel

In the same way as a car engine requires petrol for its propulsion so the body requires fuel for muscle contraction in the form of glucose and fat. Glucose and fat are derived from the food that is eaten and stored in the body until needed.

Glucose is stored in all the body tissues. However, the two major storage organs are the muscles and the liver. It is stored in the form of glycogen (polymerized glucose).

Fat is stored in the adipose tissue of the body. Adipose tissue consists almost entirely of fat-filled cells held in a loose mesh of fibrous tissue and is mainly found packed around the abdominal organs, between the muscle bundles and in layers under the skin.

The body, when all its fat and glucose stores have been exhausted, may also utilize protein as a source of energy. This however is very damaging to the body structures of which protein is the main building block, and is only necessary in complete starvation.

The utilization of the fuels available for muscular contraction is dictated by the type, intensity and duration of exercise. Muscles contain sufficient fuel for short explosive bursts of exercise only. During longer sustained exercise the muscle glycogen is soon exhausted and the body has to call on the liver to release glycogen from its stores. This process is controlled by a large number of chemical substances called enzymes and happens in a slow, step-by-step fashion. When the liver starts to use its stores of glycogen, the hormone adrenalin is released by the adrenal glands to enable the body to convert stored fat into glycogen, and thereby replenish the stores of the liver.

During long endurance types of exercise in particular, the supply of glycogen to the muscles may fail if careful attention has not been paid to the diet. When the stores of glycogen become depleted there is energy starvation to the muscles and hard exercise cannot be continued. The athlete complains of fatigue.

Fatigue is associated with low levels of muscle glycogen.

To avoid or delay the onset of fatigue during exercise the glycogen stores of the body need to be full prior to exercise and replenished following exercise. This requires a diet high in carbohydrate foods.

Providing the correct fuel

Most people eat food from custom and habit with little real knowledge of what it does for their bodies. As most of us in the Western world have more than enough food to survive, we are rarely forced to think about our diet. However, there is a great difference between simply surviving and being really healthy. In fact there is growing evidence that many of us suffer from an imbalanced diet, not realizing the short- and long-term damage that this can do.

Although exercise is a means of relieving mental stress, it does increase physical stress, proportionate to the amount and intensity of the exercise being done.

The athletes' diet needs special attention, as they are constantly putting their bodies under abnormal conditions of stress by following hard training programmes. Stress puts nutritional demands on your body, when these demands are not met, the likelihood of injury increases and the probability of achieving your true athletic potential decreases. Many top sportsmen and women now recognize that they need to give extra attention to their diets, ensuring that they include all the essential vitamins and minerals as well as the three basics of carbohydrates, fats and proteins.

A healthy diet is one which supplies the body with the right amounts of energy and essential nutrients to keep it in good health and maximize physical performance. It should provide the right proportions of carbohydrate, fat, protein, vitamins and minerals, water and dietary fibre.

It is all very well being told that these are the elements of a healthy diet, but what exactly are the benefits of each part, and what foods provide a natural source?

Carbohydrates (the energy provider)

Carbohydrates come in several forms – the major categories being starches, cellulose and sugars.

a) Starch is the major ingredient of cereals, root vegetables and pulses (peas and beans).

b) Cellulose is indigestible but it is a very important form of fibre that is necessary to help the passage of waste products through the intestines. It can be found in whole grain cereal, fresh fruit and vegetables.

c) There are five main types of sugar:
Glucose: found in some fruit and plant juices and is the basic

sugar most carbohydrate is converted into by the digestive process.

Fructose: found in some fruit and vegetables and honey. It is the most sweet form of sugar.

Sucrose: is a combination of glucose and fructose and is what most people think of as 'sugar'. It is found in sugar cane, sugar beet and in most fruit and root vegetables, especially carrots.

Maltose: is formed when starch is broken down in the course of digestion or in the production of malt beer.

Lactose: is only found in milk or milk products.

The following foods are good sources of carbohydrates: sugar, syrup, jam, rice, flour, oatmeal, bread, raisins, dates, bananas, grapes, apples, pears, potatoes, baked beans, parsnips, cabbage, peas, spinach, milk, lambs' liver.

Most of these foods provide nutrients other than carbohydrates, with the exception of white sugar. White sugar is totally refined and is what is known as 'empty calories' – energy without nutrients. Therefore, white sugar should not be relied upon as your main supply of carbohydrates.

NB. It is recommended that carbohydrates should provide between half and two-thirds of the daily calorific content of an athlete's diet.

Fats (the energy conservers)

Fats have four important functions in our diet:

1. They are the most concentrated form of energy in food. They have twice as many calories per gramme as carbohydrates or protein. The body, ever efficient, prefers to store its energy in the form of fat, which is why excess carbohydrate is turned into fat before being stored.

2. Fat has the ability to make food more palatable, hence bread and butter. Potatoes tend to taste better with a little added butter and salads are more appealing with an oily dressing.

3. Fats act as an important delivery man to the body for essential fat soluble vitamins such as vitamins A, D, E and K.

4. Fats also provide three compounds that the body cannot manufacture for itself: linoleic acid, linolenic acid and arachidonic acid. These are vital for growth and help in the formation of sex and adrenal hormones.

The following foods are sources of fat: eggs, bacon, beef, lamb, chicken, fish, peanuts, bread, oatmeal, butter, cream, cheese, milk, oils, lard, margarine, ice cream.

Although as outlined there is a role for fat in our diet, it should always be kept to a minimum.

Protein (the body builders)

Proteins are essential for the creation and maintenance of all body cells. Proteins are made up of amino acids. These are chemical compounds combining nitrogen, hydrogen, carbon and oxygen. There are about twenty amino acids and they combine to form thousands of different permutations. Eight of these amino acids are considered essential for adults. They cannot be manufactured by the body itself and so must be provided in the food. Most protein-providing foods lack at least one of these essential acids.

The following are some examples of balanced combinations of proteins, i.e. combinations providing essential amino acids: beans on toast; fish and chips; cereals with milk; bread and cheese.

Since about 1–2 per cent of the body's tissue is being replaced every day, proteins are constantly needed for the rebuilding of cells. Different parts of the body require different amounts. Organs such as the heart, liver and kidneys which are in constant use require more than do muscles and bones whose protein turnover is slower. Protein is also needed to produce enzymes, the chemical substances needed by the body for various vital processes.

Proteins are found in the following foods: eggs, bacon, beef, lamb, chicken, liver, fish, milk, cheese, yogurt, bread, rice, potatoes, peas, beans.

Only two foods provide, on their own, a perfect balance of amino acids – eggs and mother's milk. Therefore for good health we should aim to eat a variety of protein foods simultaneously. The best diets provide meals which give a variety of protein foods at the same time. Baked beans on toast for example, is nicely balanced because while bread is low in amino acid lysine, it is rich in methionine, another amino acid. On the other hand, the beans are low in methionine but rich in lysine. Eat them together and you will have the right combination of amino acids with which to start the process of body building and repair.

The protein content of the diet should be 1.5g per kg of body weight per day. Any more than this will not produce any further benefit. A high protein diet will not, as is often believed, increase strength – only a strength training programme in conjunction with a healthy diet can do this.

Vitamins (essential nutrients)

Vitamins are organic substances essential to the normal functioning of our bodies. In their natural state, they are found in minute quantities in all organic food. We must obtain them from these foods or in dietary supplements. It is impossible to sustain life without all the essential vitamins. Many people think vitamins can replace food – they cannot. In fact vitamins cannot be properly assimilated by the body without ingesting food. A good all-round diet should provide us with all the vitamins that are required, but unfortunately due to the lifestyle and low budget of most sports fanatics convenience foods and junk foods tend to be used, or meals are skipped altogether. For these reasons it is often advisable for the athlete to supplement his diet with vitamins and minerals. Needless to say there is no substitute for well balanced, regular meals, and great attention should be paid to this if optimum health and strength is your aim.

1. **Vitamin A**

Occurs in two forms – preformed vitamin A, called retinol (found only in foods of animal origin) and provitamin A, called carotene (provided by foods of both plant and animal origin).

Carotene is converted by the body into vitamin A. It requires fats as well as minerals to be properly absorbed by the digestive tract. Vitamin A keeps the skin in good condition, counteracts night blindness and aids in the treatment of many eye disorders. It builds resistance to respiratory infections, shortens the duration of diseases, promotes growth, strong bones, healthy hair, teeth and gums. It will also help to heal acne and boils. Best sources: fish liver oil, liver, carrots, green and yellow vegetables, eggs, milk and dairy products, margarine and yellow fruits.

2. Vitamin B complex

There are now known to be fourteen B vitamins in this complex. They are all water soluble and cannot be stored by the body, therefore you need to make sure that you eat foods containing the B-complex each day. Any excess of these vitamins that you ingest will be passed out of the body in the urine. The B-complex function in the body as a group, each dependant upon the others. The need for the B-complex increases during stress situations (e.g. hard training/competition) as the body responds to these conditions by increasing its production of hormones in order to overcome the effects of stress. The hormones cannot be manufactured without the aid of the B-complex. Although a well-balanced diet should give adequate quantities of the whole complex, many factors can effect their potency, these include bad storage, over cooking of foods, food refining and processing, use of oral contraceptives, smoking and alcohol. A deficiency of the B-complex can cause anaemia, fatigue and muscular pains amongst other symptoms. If taking a supplement it is suggested that B-complex be taken 2–8 hours before exercise.

The main vitamins in this complex are:

B1 Thiamin: which promotes growth and aids digestion (especially of carbohydrates), keeps the nervous system, muscles and heart functioning normally and can improve mental attitude. A deficiency can cause tiredness, irritability, poor appetite, insomnia, nervous symptoms and mild depression. Best sources: yeast, whole grain rice and wheat, oatmeal, peanuts, pork, most vegetables, bran and milk.

B2 Riboflavin: which aids growth and reproduction, promotes healthy skin, nails and hair, can alleviate eye fatigue and is a very important factor in the metabolism of carbohydrates, fats and proteins. Best sources: milk, liver, kidney, yeast, cheese, leafy green vegetables, fish and eggs.

B3 Niacin: which promotes a healthy digestive system and skin; increases the blood circulation enabling more nutrients to be delivered to the cells and reduces the blood pressure and increases energy levels through the proper utilization of food. Niacin is necessary for a healthy nervous system and proper brain function. Best sources: liver, lean meat, whole wheat products, brewer's yeast, kidney, wheat germ, figs, eggs, roasted peanuts, the white meat of poultry, avocados, dates and prunes.

B6 Pyridoxine: which is required by the immune system for the production of antibodies necessary for fighting infection and red blood cells (vital for oxygen transport). Pyridoxine is necessary for the assimilation of protein and fats and to help transport amino acids directly to the sites where they are needed in the body. It helps to prevent various nervous and skin disorders, and is needed by the body for the synthesis of fifty different enzymes, for the conversion of glycogen to glucose, and to regulate the balance between sodium and potassium. A deficiency can produce muscle spasms, leg cramps and general muscular weakness. Best sources: yeast, wheat bran, wheat germ, liver, kidney, heart, cantaloupe melon, cabbage, black-strap molasses, milk, eggs and beef.

B12 Cobalamin: which is required by the body to form and regenerate red blood cells (vital for oxygen transport), to promote growth, to increase energy levels, and to help maintain a healthy nervous system. The body needs B12 to utilize fats, carbohydrates and protein properly. It can relieve irritability and improve concentration, memory and balance. Best sources: liver, beef, pork, eggs, milk, cheese and kidney.

B15 Pangamic Acid: which speeds recovery from fatigue and can offset the stress of heavy training. It's also very important to athletes who perform in extreme weather conditions, especially the cold. It aids in the synthesis of protein and can help relieve the symptoms of asthma. It stimulates immune responses and extends the cell life span. Best sources: brewer's yeast, whole brown rice, whole grains, pumpkin seeds and sesame seeds.

Folic acid: which promotes healthy skin and acts as an analgesic for pain. It helps to increase your appetite when you are run down and helps to ward off anaemia. Folic acid is essential for healthy blood and the body's utilization of protein. It is also essential for the correct functioning of the immune system – when folic acid is deficient so are your antibodies. Best sources: deep green leafy vegetables, carrots, brewer's yeast, liver, egg yolk, melon, apricots, pumpkins, avocados, beans, whole wheat, wheatgerm, soya flour and dark rye flour.

3. Vitamin C

This helps maintain healthy skin, ligaments and bones. It also promotes the absorption of iron and the body's utilization of folic acid. It aids in preventing many types of viral and bacterial infections. It accelerates the healing of wounds and is also a natural antibiotic. It is stored in the adrenal glands on a very short-term basis but can be depleted very quickly when the body is under any form of stress. Its enemies are cooking, water, heat, light, oxygen, smoking and the contraceptive pill. Best sources: citrus fruits, berries, green leafy vegetables, tomatoes, cauliflower, potatoes. It is easily lost from fruit and vegetables, so the fresher they are the better.

4. Vitamin D
This vitamin helps the body to utilize calcium and phosphorus necessary for strong bones and teeth and correct heart function. It aids in vitamin A assimilation. It also protects against muscular weakness. Best sources: fish liver oils, sardines, herring, salmon, tuna, milk and egg yolk.

5. Vitamin E
This supplies oxygen to the heart and other muscles therefore improving your endurance levels. It protects your lungs against pollution and helps alleviate fatigue. Best sources: wheat germ, soya beans, vegetable oils, broccoli, brussels sprouts, leafy green vegetables, spinach, whole grain cereals and eggs.

6. Inositol
This helps lower cholesterol levels. It promotes healthy hair, aids in preventing hair fall-out and helps to prevent eczema. It is needed for the growth and cell survival in bone marrow, eye membranes and intestines. It also is important to brain cell nutrition. Best sources: liver, brewer's yeast, dried lima beans, cantaloupe melon, grapefruit, raisins, wheat germ, unrefined molasses, peanuts and cabbage.

7. Choline
This helps control cholesterol build up. It aids in the sending of nerve impulses, specifically those in the brain used in the formation of memory and helps prevent memory loss. It aids liver function in eliminating poisons and drugs from your system. Best sources: egg yolks, brain, heart, liver, yeast, wheatgerm, green leafy vegetables, lecithin (from soya beans).

Minerals (the vital extras)
The body cannot manufacture its own mineral supply therefore

they must be supplied in the water we drink and the food we eat. Without minerals, all the vitamins we take in are useless as minerals liberate the vitamins to do their work. Actually, we are made of minerals. A person is a fleshy envelope of water, air and minerals, the average 150-pound human is composed of thirty trillion cells that are all dependant on proper mineral balance for normal functioning.

When minerals are in adequate supply, they provide for a strong healthy body but when they are lacking, individually or collectively, disease sets in. Surprisingly, malnutrition does exist in the well-fed Western world. It is not caused by a lack of food, but by a lack of nutrients in the food. This is due to mineral-poor soil, chemical fertilizers, food preservatives, and the refining processes used in food preparation.

1. Calcium
There is more calcium in the body than any other mineral and it works together with phosphorus to give healthy bones and teeth, and with magnesium for cardiovascular health. Twenty per cent of an adult's bone calcium is reabsorbed and replaced each year, when new bone cells form, as old ones break down. The body needs adequate supplies of vitamin D in order fully to absorb calcium from the gut. It keeps the heart beating regularly and helps to metabolize the body's iron. It aids your nervous system, especially in impulse transmission and can alleviate insomnia. Best sources: milk and milk products, all cheeses, soyabeans, sardines, salmon, peanuts, walnuts, sunflower seeds, dried beans and green vegetables.

2. Chromium
This works with insulin in the metabolism of sugar and helps to bring protein to where it is needed in the body. It aids growth and works as a deterrent for diabetes. Best sources: meat, shellfish, chicken, corn oil, brewer's yeast.

3. Copper
This is required to convert the body's iron into haemoglobin for oxygen transportation thereby keeping up energy levels. It is also essential for the utilization of vitamin C. Best sources: dried beans, peas, whole wheat, prunes, calf and beef liver, shrimp and most seafood.

4. Iodine

This is required by the thyroid gland, which in turn controls metabolism. It promotes growth and gives you more energy. It is essential for healthy hair, nails, skin and teeth and also improves mental alacrity. Best sources: kelp, vegetables grown in iodine-rich soil, onions and all seafood.

5. Iron

This is essential to life as it is necessary for the production of haemoglobin (red blood corpuscles), myoglobin (red pigment in muscles) and certain enzymes. An average 150-pound adult has about 4 g of iron in the body. Haemoglobin, which accounts for most of the iron, is recycled and reutilized as blood cells are replaced every 120 days. Women lose almost twice as much iron as men because of their monthly menstruation. Iron is necessary for the proper metabolism of B vitamins. It aids in growth and promotes resistance to disease. It prevents fatigue and anaemia and can help restore good skin tone. Best sources: liver, kidney, dried peaches, red meat, egg yolk, oysters, nuts, beans, asparagus, molasses and oatmeal.

6. Magnesium

This is necessary for calcium and vitamin C metabolism. It is essential for effective nerve and muscle function. It is important for converting blood sugar into energy and is also known as the anti-stress mineral. It promotes a healthy cardiovascular system and aids in fighting depression. Magnesium helps to keep teeth healthy and can help prevent harmful calcium deposits such as kidney stones and gallstones. Best sources: figs, lemons, grapefruit, yellow corn, almonds, nuts, seeds, dark green vegetables and apples.

7. Manganese

This helps activate enzymes, necessary for the body's use of biotin, B1 and vitamin C. It is important to the working of the thyroid gland, which controls metabolism and it is necessary for the digestion and utilization of food. It can help eliminate fatigue and is an aid to muscle reflexes. It can also improve memory and can reduce nervous irritability. Best sources: nuts, leafy green vegetables, peas, beetroot, egg yolks, whole grain cereal. Heavy milk drinkers and meat eaters need increased manganese.

8. Molybdenum

This aids in carbohydrate and fat metabolism. It is also a vital part of the enzyme responsible for iron utilization and can therefore help to prevent anaemia. Best sources: dark green leafy vegetables, whole grains and legumes.

9. Phosphorus

This is essential for the basic formation of the cells and for the production of energy within them. Vitamin D and calcium are needed for phosphorus to function correctly. B1 cannot be assimilated without it and it is important for normal functioning of the heart, the kidneys and nerve impulses. It aids in growth and body repair and produces energy and vigour by helping in the metabolism of fats and starches. Best sources: fish, poultry, meat, whole grains, eggs, nuts and seeds.

10. Potassium

This mineral works with sodium to regulate the body's water balance and normalize heart rhythms (potassium works inside the cells and sodium works outside them). Nerve and muscle functions suffer when the sodium/potassium balance is not correct. Both mental and physical stress can lead to a potassium deficiency. It can aid in clear thinking as it sends oxygen to the brain and assists in the disposal of body waste products. It is an aid in treating allergies and can assist in reducing blood pressure. Drinking large amounts of coffee and eating large quantities of sweet things can cause potassium loss which in turn leads to fatigue. Best sources: citrus fruit, watercress, all green leafy vegetables, mint leaves, sunflower seeds, bananas and potatoes.

11. Selenium

Males appear to have a greater need for selenium as half of their body's supply concentrates in the testicles. It aids in keeping youthful elasticity in the skin and acts as an anti-oxidant by slowing down hardening and ageing of tissues. It helps in the prevention of dandruff. Deficiency of selenium leads to a premature stamina loss. It works best when taken in conjunction with Vitamin E. Best sources: wheat germ, bran, tuna fish, onions, tomatoes and broccoli.

12. Sodium

Sodium and potassium were discovered together and both were found to be essential for normal growth. High intakes of sodium will result in a depletion of potassium, so it is important to try to balance the two. Sodium is required to help with the digestion of carbohydrates. It aids in preventing heat/sun stroke and helps nerve and muscle function. Best sources: salt, shellfish, carrots, beetroot, artichokes, brains, kidney and bacon.

13. Sulphur

This is essential for healthy skin, hair and nails. It helps to maintain the correct oxygen balance for brain function. It works with the B vitamins in energy conversion. It can help fight bacterial infections. Best sources: lean beef, dried beans, fish, eggs and cabbage.

14. Zinc

This is one of the most important minerals to the body as it tells other vitamins and minerals where to go and what to do. It governs the contractility of muscles. It is essential for the maintenance of the body's acid/base balance and for blood stability. Excessive sweating can cause a loss of as much as 3 mg of zinc per day. The majority of natural zinc is lost during food processing. Best sources: steak, lamb chops, pork loin, wheat germ, brewer's yeast, pumpkin seeds, eggs, non-fat dry milk and ground mustard.

As you can see from the preceding list of vitamins and minerals, the majority of them require the presence of one or sometimes several others, in order to do their own work effectively. This explains why a varied diet is so essential to good health.

Many of the vitamins are water soluble and cannot be stored. Foods containing water-soluble vitamins need to be eaten on a daily basis; any excess of these vitamins is lost from the body, if it is not required for use at the time of ingestion.

As you have already learnt, eating a good diet may not always be enough and you may want to supplement your diet with some vitamins and minerals in tablet or capsule form. Almost everyone will benefit by taking a good daily multivitamin/ mineral supplement with their breakfast. The supplements should always be taken with food, so that they are absorbed correctly, and never on an empty stomach. More sophisticated supplementation may be taken but only with the guidance of a qualified nutritionist.

Fluids

Drinking plenty of fluid is always advisable for the athlete, as so much is lost during strenuous exercise when the body perspires to keep cool. Fluids should be taken both before, during and after exercise. Mineral water is the best choice, with perhaps added fruit juice of your personal preference for extra minerals and vitamins.

Milk is a drink that is also a well-balanced fluid containing both vitamins and minerals. Milk shakes with added flavours or hot drinking chocolate made with milk can add variety.

Tea and coffee are acceptable in moderation, if they are not taken too strong, but remember coffee is also a diuretic and can actually cause the body to lose fluid along with vital vitamins and minerals.

If you think your diet is incorrectly balanced at the moment, you will feel an enormous improvement in energy levels, once you start eating correctly.

Remember you only have one body, only *you* can look after it. If you make changes to your diet for the better, your body will serve you well, recovery from exercise will be quicker and your capacity for endurance will be greater.

APPENDIX I
RIGGING CHARTS

INTERNATIONAL MEN		8+ EIGHT	4- COXLESS FOUR	4+ COXED FOUR	2- COXLESS PAIR	2+ COXED PAIR	4x QUAD SCULL	2x DOUBLE SCULL	1x SINGLE SCULL
MACON SHAPE BLADES oar/scull length	RANGE	384 – 385.5	384 – 386.5	382.5 – 386.5	381.5 – 386	378 – 386	300 – 302.5	298 – 300.5	298 – 302.5
	PREFERRED	385	385	385	385	385	300	300	300
spoon size	LENGTH	58.2	58.2	58.2	58.2	58.2	49.6	49.6	49.6
	WIDTH	20	20	20	20	20	18	18	18
	WIDTH AT TIP	18	18	18	18	18	14.5	14.5	14.5
BIG BLADE SHAPE oar/scull length	RANGE	376 – 378	375 – 377	375 – 377	374 – 377	374 – 377	290 – 293	289 – 292	288 – 292
	PREFERRED	377	377	377	377	377	291	290	289
spoon size	LENGTH	55	55	55	55	55	44	44	44
	WIDTH	25	25	25	25	25	21.5	21.5	21.5
oar/scull inboard	RANGE	113 – 115	114 – 117	114 – 117	113.5 – 117.5	113.5 – 118	87 – 88	86 – 89	86.5 – 89
	PREFERRED	113.5	114.5	115.5	116	117	87	87	88
spread/span	RANGE	83 – 84.5	83.5 – 86	83.5 – 85	83 – 86.5	83 – 87	156 – 159	158 – 162	157 – 161
	PREFERRED	83.5	84.5	85	86	86	158	160	160
pitch	RANGE	4° – 6°	4° – 6°	4° – 6°	4° – 6°	4° – 6°	5° – 8°	5° – 8°	5° – 8°
	PREFERRED	4°	4°	4°	4°	4°	6°	6°	6°
height of swivel	RANGE	16 – 18	16 – 18	16 – 18	16 – 18	16 – 18	15.5 – 18	15.5 – 18	15.5 – 18
distance through the work	RANGE	0 – 10	0 – 10	0 – 10	0 – 10	0 – 10	0 – 10	0 – 10	0 – 10
	PREFERRED	5	5	5	5	5	5	5	5
distance behind the work		66.5	67	67	67	67	66.5	66.5	67

All measurements except pitch are given in centimetres

CLUB MEN			8+ EIGHT	4- COXLESS FOUR	4+ COXED FOUR	2- COXLESS PAIR	2+ COXED PAIR	4x QUAD SCULL	2x DOUBLE SCULL	1x SINGLE SCULL
oar/scull length	MACON SHAPE BLADES	RANGE / PREFERRED	383–385 / 384	383–385 / 384	383–385 / 384	383–385 / 384	383–385 / 384	298–300 / 298	298–300 / 298	298–300 / 298
spoon size		LENGTH / WIDTH / WIDTH AT TIP	58.2 / 20 / 16.5	58.2 / 20 / 16.5	58.2 / 20 / 16.5	58.2 / 20 / 16.5	58.2 / 20 / 16.5	49.6 / 17 / 14	49.6 / 17 / 14	49.6 / 17 / 14
oar/scull length	BIG BLADE SHAPE	RANGE / PREFERRED	375–377 / 376	374–376 / 376	374–376 / 376	373–376 / 376	373–376 / 376	289–292 / 290	288–291 / 289	287–291 / 288
spoon size		LENGTH / WIDTH	52 / 25	52 / 25	52 / 25	52 / 25	52 / 25	44 / 21.5	44 / 21.5	44 / 21.5
oar/scull inboard		RANGE / PREFERRED	114–115.5 / 114.5	115–116.5 / 116	115.5–117 / 116.5	116.5–117.5 / 117	117–118.5 / 118	86.5–88.5 / 88	87–90 / 88.5	87–90 / 89
spread/span		RANGE / PREFERRED	83.5–84.5 / 84	84.5–85.5 / 85	85–86 / 85.5	85.5–86.5 / 86	86.5–88 / 87	157–159 / 158	158–160 / 159	157–160 / 159
pitch		RANGE / PREFERRED	4°–6° / 4°	4°–6° / 4°	4°–6° / 4°	4°–6° / 4°	4°–6° / 4°	6°–8° / 6°	6°–8° / 6°	6°–8° / 6°
height of swivel			16–18	16–18	16–18	16–18	16–18	15.5–18	15.5–18	15.5–18
distance through the work		RANGE / PREFERRED	0–10 / 5	0–10 / 5	0–10 / 5	0–10 / 5	0–10 / 5	0–10 / 5	0–10 / 5	0–10 / 5
distance behind the work			67	67	67	67	67	67	67	67

All measurements except pitch are given in centimetres

INTERNATIONAL LWT MEN			8+ EIGHT	4- COXLESS FOUR	4+ COXED FOUR	2- COXLESS PAIR	2+ COXED PAIR	4x QUAD SCULL	2x DOUBLE SCULL	1x SINGLE SCULL
MACON SHAPE BLADES	oar/scull length	RANGE	382 – 385	382 – 386	N/A	382 – 385	N/A	298 – 300	298 – 300	297 – 300
		PREFERRED	385	385		385		299	298	298
	spoon size	LENGTH	58.2	58.2	N/A	58.2	N/A	49.6	49.6	49.6
		WIDTH	20	20		20		17	17	17
		WIDTH AT TIP	16.5	16.5		16.5		14.5	14.5	14.5
BIG BLADE SHAPE	oar/scull length	RANGE	375 – 377	374 – 376	N/A	373 – 376	N/A	289 – 292	288 – 291	287 – 291
		PREFERRED	376	376		376		290	289	288
	spoon size	LENGTH	55	55	N/A	55	N/A	44	44	44
		WIDTH	25	25		25		21.5	21.5	21.5
oar/scull inboard		RANGE	114 – 117	114.5 – 117	N/A	116.5 – 117.5	N/A	86.5 – 88.5	86.5 – 90	87 – 90
		PREFERRED	114.5	116		117		88	88	88
spread/span		RANGE	83.5 – 85	84 – 86	N/A	85 – 87	N/A	157 – 159	158 – 160	158.5 – 162
		PREFERRED	84	85		86		158	159	160.5
pitch		RANGE	4° – 6°	4° – 6°	N/A	4° – 6°	N/A	6° – 8°	6° – 8°	6° – 8°
		PREFERRED	4°	4°		4°		6°	6°	6°
height of swivel		RANGE	15 – 17.5	15 – 17.5	N/A	15 – 17.5	N/A	15 – 17	15 – 17	15 – 17
distance through the work		RANGE	0 – 10	0 – 10	N/A	0 – 10	N/A	0 – 10	0 – 10	0 – 10
		PREFERRED	5	5		5		5	5	5
distance behind the work			66	66	N/A	66	N/A	66	66	66

All measurements except pitch are given in centimetres

CLUB LWT MEN

		8+ EIGHT	4- COXLESS FOUR	4+ COXED FOUR	2- COXLESS PAIR	2+ COXED PAIR	4x QUAD SCULL	2x DOUBLE SCULL	1x SINGLE SCULL
MACON SHAPE BLADES oar/scull length	RANGE	383 – 385	383 – 385	383 – 385	383 – 385	N/A	298 – 300	298 – 300	298 – 300
	PREFERRED	384	384	384	384	N/A	298	298	298
spoon size	LENGTH	58.2	58.2	58.2	58.2	N/A	49.6	49.6	49.6
	WIDTH	20	20	20	20	N/A	17	17	17
	WIDTH AT TIP	16.5	16.5	16.5	16.5	N/A	14	14	14
BIG BLADE SHAPE oar/scull length	RANGE	374 – 376	374 – 376	374 – 376	373 – 376	N/A	288 – 291	287 – 290	286 – 290
	PREFERRED	375	375	375	375	N/A	289	288	287
spoon size	LENGTH	52	52	52	52	N/A	44	44	44
	WIDTH	25	25	25	25	N/A	21.5	21.5	21.5
oar/scull inboard	RANGE	114.5 – 116	115.5 – 116.5	116 – 117.5	116.5 – 117.5	N/A	86.5 – 88.5	87 – 90	87 – 90
	PREFERRED	115	116.5	117	117	N/A	88	88.5	89
spread/span	RANGE	84 – 85	84 – 85.5	85 – 86	85.5 – 86.5	N/A	157 – 159	158 – 160	157 – 160
	PREFERRED	84	85	85.5	86	N/A	158	159	159
pitch	RANGE	4° – 6°	4° – 6°	4° – 6°	4° – 6°	N/A	6° – 8°	6° – 8°	6° – 8°
	PREFERRED	4°	4°	4°	4°	N/A	6°	6°	6°
height of swivel	RANGE	15 – 17.5	15 – 17.5	15 – 17.5	15 – 17.5	N/A	15 – 17	15 – 17	15 – 17
distance through the work	RANGE	0 – 10	0 – 10	0 – 10	0 – 10	N/A	0 – 10	0 – 10	0 – 10
	PREFERRED	5	5	5	5	N/A	5	5	5
distance behind the work		66	66	66	66	N/A	66	66	66

All measurements except pitch are given in centimetres

JUNIOR MEN

		8+ EIGHT	4- COXLESS FOUR	4+ COXED FOUR	2- COXLESS PAIR	2+ COXED PAIR	4x QUAD SCULL	2x DOUBLE SCULL	1x SINGLE SCULL
MACON SHAPE BLADES — oar/scull length	RANGE	383 – 385	383 – 385	383 – 385	383 – 385	383 – 385	298 – 300	298 – 300	298 – 300
	PREFERRED	384	384	384	384	384	298	298	298
spoon size	LENGTH	58.2	58.2	58.2	58.2	58.2	49.6	49.6	49.6
	WIDTH	20	20	20	20	20	17	17	17
	WIDTH AT TIP	16.5	16.5	16.5	16.5	16.5	14	14	14
BIG BLADE SHAPE — oar/scull length	RANGE	375 – 377	374 – 376	374 – 376	373 – 376	373 – 376	289 – 292	288 – 291	287 – 291
	PREFERRED	376	376	376	376	376	290	289	288
spoon size	LENGTH	52	52	52	52	52	44	44	44
	WIDTH	25	25	25	25	25	21.5	21.5	21.5
oar/scull inboard	RANGE	114.5 – 116	115.5 – 116.5	116 – 117.5	116.5 – 117.5	117 – 118.5	87 – 88.5	87 – 90	87 – 90
	PREFERRED	114.5	116	116	117	118	88	88.5	89
spread/span	RANGE	83.5 – 84.5	84.5 – 85.5	85 – 86	85.5 – 86.5	86.5 – 87.5	157 – 159	158 – 160	157 – 160
	PREFERRED	84	85	85.5	86	87	158	158	159
pitch	RANGE	4° – 6°	4° – 6°	4° – 6°	4° – 6°	4° – 6°	6° – 8°	6° – 8°	6° – 8°
	PREFERRED	4°	4°	4°	4°	4°	6°	6°	6°
height of swivel		15 – 17.5	15 – 17.5	15 – 17.5	15 – 17.5	15 – 17.5	15 – 17	15 – 17	15 – 17
distance through the work	RANGE	0 – 10	0 – 10	0 – 10	0 – 10	0 – 10	0 – 10	0 – 10	0 – 10
	PREFERRED	5	5	5	5	5	5	5	5
distance behind the work		66.5 – 65.5	66.5 – 65.5	66.5 – 65.5	66.5 – 65.5	66.5 – 65.5	66.5 – 65.5	66.5 – 65.5	66.5 – 65.5

All measurements except pitch are given in centimetres

J16 MEN		8+ EIGHT	4- COXLESS FOUR	4+ COXED FOUR	2- COXLESS PAIR	2+ COXED PAIR	4x QUAD SCULL	2x DOUBLE SCULL	1x SINGLE SCULL
oar/scull length	RANGE	381 – 384	381 – 384	381 – 384	381 – 384	N/A	296 – 298	296 – 298	296 – 298
	PREFERRED	382	382	382	382	N/A	298	296	296
oar/scull inboard	RANGE	114.5 – 116	115.5 – 116.5	116 – 117.5	116.5 – 117.5	N/A	86.5 – 88.5	88 – 89.5	87.5 – 90
	PREFERRED	115	116.5	117	117	N/A	88.5	88	88.5
spoon size	LENGTH	58.2	58.2	58.2	58.2	N/A	49.6	49.6	49.6
	WIDTH	20	20	20	20		17	17	17
	WIDTH AT TIP	16.5	16.5	16.5	16.5		14	14	14
spread/span	RANGE	84 – 85	84.5 – 85.5	85 – 86	85.5 – 86.5	N/A	157 – 159	158 – 160	157 – 160
	PREFERRED	84	85	85.5	86	N/A	158	158	158
pitch	RANGE	4° – 6°	4° – 6°	4° – 6°	4° – 6°	N/A	6° – 8°	6° – 8°	6° – 8°
	PREFERRED	4°	4°	4°	4°	N/A	6°	6°	6°
height of swivel		14.5 – 17	14.5 – 17	14.5 – 17	14.5 – 17	N/A	14.5 – 17	14.5 – 17	14.5 – 17
distance through the work	RANGE	0 – 10	0 – 10	0 – 10	0 – 10	N/A	0 – 10	0 – 10	0 – 10
	PREFERRED	5	5	5	5	N/A	5	5	5
distance behind the work		63	63	63	63	N/A	63	63	63

All measurements except pitch are given in centimetres

J14/J15 MEN		8+ EIGHT	4- COXLESS FOUR	4+ COXED FOUR	2- COXLESS PAIR	2+ COXED PAIR	4x QUAD SCULL	2x DOUBLE SCULL	1x SINGLE SCULL
oar/scull length	RANGE	378–382	378–382	378–382	378–382	N/A	296–298	295–298	294–297
	PREFERRED	380	380	380	380	N/A	296	296	295
oar/scull inboard	RANGE	114.5–116	115.5–116.5	116–117.5	116.5–117.5	N/A	86.5–88.5	88–89.5	87.5–88.5
	PREFERRED	115	116.5	117	117	N/A	88.5	88	88.5
spoon size	LENGTH	58.2	58.2	58.2	58.2	N/A	49.6	49.6	49.6
	WIDTH	19	19	19	19		16	16	16
	WIDTH AT TIP	16.5	16.5	16.5	16.5		13.5	13.5	13.5
spread/span	RANGE	84–85	84.5–85.5	85–86	85.5–86.5	N/A	157–159	157–159	156–159
	PREFERRED	84	85	85.5	86	N/A	158	158	158
pitch	RANGE	4°–6°	4°–6°	4°–6°	4°–6°	N/A	6°–8°	6°–8°	6°–8°
	PREFERRED	4°	4°	4°	4°	N/A	6°	6°	6°
height of swivel		14–16.5	14–16.5	14–16.5	14–16.5	N/A	14–16.5	14–16.5	14–16.5
distance through the work	RANGE	0–10	0–10	0–10	0–10	N/A	0–10	0–10	0–10
	PREFERRED	5	5	5	5	N/A	5	5	5
distance behind the work		58–60	58–60	58–60	58–60	N/A	58–60	58–60	58–60

All measurements except pitch are given in centimetres

INTERNATIONAL WOMEN		8+ EIGHT	4- COXLESS FOUR	4+ COXED FOUR	2- COXLESS PAIR	2+ COXED PAIR	4x QUAD SCULL	2x DOUBLE SCULL	1x SINGLE SCULL
MACON SHAPE BLADES oar/scull length	RANGE	380 – 383	380 – 382	380 – 382	380 – 382	N/A	297 – 299	298 – 300	297 – 299
	PREFERRED	381	380	380	380	N/A	298	298	298
spoon size	LENGTH	58.2	58.2	58.2	58.2	N/A	49.6	49.6	49.6
	WIDTH	20	20	20	20	N/A	18	17	17
	WIDTH AT TIP	18	18	18	18	N/A	14.5	14	14
BIG BLADE SHAPE oar/scull length	RANGE	373 – 375	372 – 374	372 – 374	371 – 374	N/A	288 – 291	287 – 290	287 – 290
	PREFERRED	374	374	374	374	N/A	290	289	288
spoon size	LENGTH	55	55	55	55	N/A	44	44	44
	WIDTH	25	25	25	25	N/A	21.5	21.5	21.5
oar/scull inboard	RANGE	114 – 115.5	115 – 116.5	115.5 – 117	116 – 117.5	N/A	85.5 – 88	86.5 – 88.5	87 – 89
	PREFERRED	114.5	115.5	116	116.5	N/A	87	87.5	88
spread/span	RANGE	83 – 85	84 – 85.5	84.5 – 86	85.5 – 87	N/A	156 – 158	157 – 160	158 – 160
	PREFERRED	84	85	85.5	86	N/A	157	158	159
pitch	RANGE	4° – 6°	4° – 6°	4° – 6°	4° – 6°	N/A	6° – 8°	6° – 8°	6° – 8°
	PREFERRED	4°	4°	4°	4°	N/A	6°	6°	6°
height of swivel		15 – 17.5	15 – 17.5	15 – 17.5	15 – 17.5	N/A	15 – 17	15 – 17	15 – 17
distance through the work	RANGE	0 – 10	0 – 10	0 – 10	0 – 10	N/A	0 – 10	0 – 10	0 – 10
	PREFERRED	5	5	5	5	N/A	5	5	5
distance behind the work		62.5	62.5	63	63	N/A	62.5	62.5	63

AS LAST USED IN 1988

All measurements except pitch are given in centimetres

CLUB WOMEN		8+ EIGHT	4- COXLESS FOUR	4+ COXED FOUR	2- COXLESS PAIR	2+ COXED PAIR	4x QUAD SCULL	2x DOUBLE SCULL	1x SINGLE SCULL
MACON SHAPE BLADES									
oar/scull length	RANGE	380 – 383	380 – 382	380 – 382	380 – 382	N/A	296 – 299	296 – 298	296 – 298
	PREFERRED	380	380	380	380		298	298	296
spoon size	LENGTH	58.2	58.2	58.2	58.2	N/A	49.6	49.6	49.6
	WIDTH	20	20	20	20		17	17	17
	WIDTH AT TIP	18	18	18	18		14	14	14
BIG BLADE SHAPE									
oar/scull length	RANGE	272 – 374	371 – 373	371 – 373	371 – 373	N/A	287 – 290	286 – 289	285 – 289
	PREFERRED	373	373	373	373		289	288	287
spoon size	LENGTH	52	52	52	52	N/A	44	44	44
	WIDTH	25	25	25	25		21.5	21.5	21.5
oar/scull inboard	RANGE	114.5 – 116	115.5 – 116.5	116 – 117	116.5 – 117.5	N/A	86.5 – 88.5	87 – 89	88 – 89.5
	PREFERRED	115.5	116	116.5	117		88	88	89
spread/span	RANGE	84 – 85	84.5 – 85.5	85 – 86	86 – 87	N/A	157 – 159	158 – 159	158 – 160
	PREFERRED	84	85	85.5	86		158	158.5	159
pitch	RANGE	4° – 6°	4° – 5°	4° – 6°	4° – 6°	N/A	6° – 8°	6° – 8°	6° – 8°
	PREFERRED	4°	4°	4°	4°		6°	6°	6°
height of swivel		15 – 17.5	15 – 17.5	15 – 17.5	15 – 17.5	N/A	15 – 17	15 – 17	15 – 17
distance through the work	RANGE	0 – 10	0 – 10	0 – 10	0 – 10	N/A	0 – 10	0 – 10	0 – 10
	PREFERRED	5	5	5	5		5	5	5
distance behind the work		62	62	62.5	62.5	N/A	62	62	62.5

All measurements except pitch are given in centimetres

INTERNATIONAL LWT WOMEN		8+ EIGHT	4- COXLESS FOUR	4+ COXED FOUR	2- COXLESS PAIR	2+ COXED PAIR	4x QUAD SCULL	2x DOUBLE SCULL	1x SINGLE SCULL
oar/scull length (MACON SHAPE BLADES)	RANGE	380 – 383	380 – 382	N/A	380 – 382	N/A	297 – 299	297 – 299	296 – 298
	PREFERRED	380	380		380		298	298	298
spoon size	LENGTH	58.2	58.2	N/A	58.2	N/A	49.6	49.6	49.6
	WIDTH	20	20		20		17	17	17
	WIDTH AT TIP	16.5	16.5		16.5		14	14	14
oar/scull length (BIG BLADE SHAPE)	RANGE	371 – 373	370 – 373	N/A	370 – 373	N/A	287 – 290	286 – 289	285 – 289
	PREFERRED	372	372		372		289	288	287
spoon size	LENGTH	55	55	N/A	55	N/A	44	44	44
	WIDTH	25	25		25		21.5	21.5	21.5
oar/scull inboard	RANGE	114.5 – 116	115.5 – 116.5	N/A	116.5 – 117.5	N/A	86 – 88.5	86.5 – 88.5	87.5 – 89
	PREFERRED	115	116		117		88	88	88.5
spread/span	RANGE	84 – 85	84.5 – 85.5	N/A	86 – 87	N/A	156 – 158	157 – 160	158 – 160
	PREFERRED	84	85		86		157.5	158.5	159
pitch	RANGE	4° – 6°	4° – 6°	N/A	4° – 6°	N/A	6° – 8°	6° – 8°	6° – 8°
	PREFERRED	4°	4°		4°		6°	6°	6°
height of swivel	RANGE	14.5 – 16.5	14.5 – 16.5	N/A	14.5 – 16.5	N/A	14.5 – 16	14.5 – 16	14.5 – 16
distance through the work	RANGE	0 – 10	0 – 10	N/A	0 – 10	N/A	0 – 10	0 – 10	0 – 10
	PREFERRED	5	5		5		5	5	5
distance behind the work		62	62	N/A	62.5	N/A	62	62	62.5

All measurements except pitch are given in centimetres

CLUB LWT WOMEN		8+ EIGHT	4- COXLESS FOUR	4+ COXED FOUR	2- COXLESS PAIR	2+ COXED PAIR	4x QUAD SCULL	2x DOUBLE SCULL	1x SINGLE SCULL
oar/scull length (MACON SHAPE BLADES)	RANGE	380 – 383	380 – 382	380 – 382	380 – 382	N/A	297 – 298	297 – 298	296 – 298
	PREFERRED	380	380	380	330		298	298	296
spoon size	LENGTH	58.2	58.2	58.2	53.2	N/A	49.6	49.6	49.6
	WIDTH	20	20	20	20		17	17	17
	WIDTH AT TIP	16.5	16.5	16.5	16.5		14	14	14
oar/scull length (BIG BLADE SHAPE)	RANGE	371 – 373	370 – 373	370 – 373	370 – 373	N/A	286 – 289	285 – 288	284 – 288
	PREFERRED	372	372	372	372		288	287	286
spoon size	LENGTH	52	52	52	52	N/A	44	44	44
	WIDTH	25	25	25	25		21.5	21.5	21.5
oar/scull inboard	RANGE	114.5 – 116	116 – 117	116.5 – 117.5	116.5 – 117.5	N/A	86.5 – 88.5	87 – 89	88 – 89.5
	PREFERRED	116	116.5	117	117.5		88	88.5	89
spread/span	RANGE	84 – 85	84.5 – 85.5	85 – 86	86 – 87	N/A	157 – 159	158 – 159	158 – 160
	PREFERRED	84	85	85.5	86		158	158.5	159
pitch	RANGE	4° – 6°	4° – 6°	4° – 6°	4° – 6°	N/A	6° – 8°	6° – 8°	6° – 8°
	PREFERRED	4°	4°	4°	4°		6°	6°	6°
height of swivel	RANGE	14.5 – 16.5	14.5 – 16.5	14.5 – 16.5	14.5 – 16.5	N/A	14.5 – 16	14.5 – 16	14.5 – 16
distance through the work	RANGE	0 – 10	0 – 10	0 – 10	0 – 10	N/A	0 – 10	0 – 10	0 – 10
	PREFERRED	5	5	5	5		5	5	5
distance behind the work		61.5	61.5	62	62	N/A	61.5	61.5	62

All measurements except pitch are given in centimetres

JUNIOR WOMEN		8+ EIGHT	4- COXLESS FOUR	4+ COXED FOUR	2- COXLESS PAIR	2+ COXED PAIR	4x QUAD SCULL	2x DOUBLE SCULL	1x SINGLE SCULL
MACON SHAPE BLADES — oar/scull length	RANGE	378 – 382	378 – 382	378 – 382	378 – 382	N/A	297 – 299	297 – 299	296 – 298
	PREFERRED	380	380	380	380		298	298	296
spoon size	LENGTH	58.2	58.2	58.2	58.2	N/A	49.6	49.6	49.6
	WIDTH	20	20	20	20		17	17	17
	WIDTH AT TIP	16.5	16.5	16.5	16.5		14	14	14
BIG BLADE SHAPE — oar/scull length	RANGE	372 – 374	371 – 373	371 – 373	370 – 373	N/A	287 – 290	286 – 289	285 – 289
	PREFERRED	373	373	373	373		289	288	287
spoon size	LENGTH	52	52	52	52	N/A	44	44	44
	WIDTH	25	25	25	25		21.5	21.5	21.5
oar/scull inboard	RANGE	114.5 – 116	115.5 – 116.5	116 – 117	116.5 – 117.5	N/A	87 – 89	87.5 – 89.5	88 – 89.5
	PREFERRED	116	116	116.5	117		88	88.5	89
spread/span	RANGE	84 – 85	84.5 – 85.5	85 – 86	86 – 87	N/A	157 – 159	158 – 159	158 – 160
	PREFERRED	84	85	85.5	86		158	158.5	158
pitch	RANGE	4° – 6°	4° – 6°	4° – 6°	4° – 6°	N/A	6° – 8°	6° – 8°	6° – 8°
	PREFERRED	4°	4°	4°	4°		6°	6°	6°
height of swivel	RANGE	14.5 – 17	14.5 – 17	14.5 – 17	14.5 – 17	N/A	14.5 – 16.5	14.5 – 16.5	14.5 – 16.5
distance through the work	RANGE	0 – 10	0 – 10	0 – 10	0 – 10	N/A	0 – 10	0 – 10	0 – 10
	PREFERRED	5	5	5	5		5	5	5
distance behind the work		61.5	61.5	62	62	N/A	61.5	61.5	62

All measurements except pitch are given in centimetres

J16 WOMEN		8+ EIGHT	4- COXLESS FOUR	4+ COXED FOUR	2- COXLESS PAIR	2+ COXED PAIR	4x QUAD SCULL	2x DOUBLE SCULL	1x SINGLE SCULL
oar/scull length	RANGE	376–380	376–380	376–380	376–380	N/A	296	296	295–296
	PREFERRED	378	378	378	378	N/A	296	296	295
oar/scull inboard	RANGE	114.5–116	115.5–115.5	116–117	116.5–117.5	N/A	87–89	87.5–89.5	88–89.5
	PREFERRED	115	115.5	116.5	117	N/A	88	88.5	89
spoon size	LENGTH	58.2	58.2	58.2	58.2	N/A	49.6	49.6	49.6
	WIDTH	19–20	19–20	19–20	19–20		16–17	16–17	16–17
	WIDTH AT TIP	16.5	16.5	16.5	16.5		14	14	14
spread/span	RANGE	83.5–84	84–85	85–85	36–87	N/A	156–158	158–159	158–159
	PREFERRED	83.5	84.5	86	86	N/A	158	158	158
pitch	RANGE	4°–6°	4°–6°	4°–6°	4°–6°	N/A	6°–8°	6°–8°	6°–8°
	PREFERRED	4°	4°	4°	4°	N/A	6°	6°	6°
height of swivel		14–16.5	14–16.5	14–16.5	14–16.5	N/A	14–16.5	14–16.5	14–16.5
distance through the work	RANGE	0–10	0–10	0–10	0–10	N/A	0–10	0–10	0–10
	PREFERRED	5	5	5	5	N/A	5	5	5
distance behind the work		58–60	58–60	58–60	58–60	N/A	58–60	58–60	58–60

All measurements except pitch are given in centimetres

J14/J15 WOMEN		8+ EIGHT	4- COXLESS FOUR	4+ COXED FOUR	2- COXLESS PAIR	2+ COXED PAIR	4x QUAD SCULL	2x DOUBLE SCULL	1x SINGLE SCULL
oar/scull length	RANGE	376 – 380	376 – 380	376 – 380	376 – 380	N/A	296	296	294
	PREFERRED	376	376	376	376	N/A	296	296	294
oar/scull inboard	RANGE	114.5 – 116	115.5 – 116.5	116 – 117	116.5 – 117.5	N/A	87 – 89	87.5 – 89.5	88 – 89.5
	PREFERRED	115	115.5	116.5	117	N/A	88.5	89	89
spoon size	LENGTH	58.2 – 56.2	58.2 – 56.2	58.2 – 56.2	58.2 – 56.2	N/A	48.6 – 49.6	48.6 – 49.6	48.6 – 49.6
	WIDTH	19	19	19	19		16	16	16
	WIDTH AT TIP	16.5	16.5	16.5	16.5		14	14	14
spread/span	RANGE	83.5 – 84	84 – 85	85 – 86	86 – 87	N/A	156 – 158	158 – 159	158 – 159
	PREFERRED	83.5	84.5	86	86	N/A	158	158	158
pitch	RANGE	4° – 6°	4° – 6°	4° – 6°	4° – 6°	N/A	6° – 8°	6° – 8°	6° – 8°
	PREFERRED	4°	4°	4°	4°	N/A	6°	6°	6°
height of swivel	RANGE	14 – 16.5	14 – 16.5	14 – 16.5	14 – 16.5	N/A	14 – 16	14 – 16	14 – 16
distance through the work	RANGE	0 – 10	0 – 10	0 – 10	0 – 10	N/A	0 – 10	0 – 10	0 – 10
	PREFERRED	5	5	5	5	N/A	5	5	5
distance behind the work		57 – 60	57 – 60	57 – 60	57 – 60	N/A	57 – 60	57 – 60	57 – 60

All measurements except pitch are given in centimetres

APPENDIX II
ARA Water Safety Code

1. Responsibilities of clubs

1. Every club shall appoint a competent member as Safety Officer. It shall be the duty of a Club Safety Officer to ensure that the ARA Code of Practice for Water Safety is implemented by all members of the club.

2. Clubs shall display prominently the ARA Code of Practice and any visual aids on water safety, life saving or resuscitation procedures as may be provided by the ARA, or by other organizations with the approval of the ARA.

3. Every Club shall draw up and display a local code of practice, which should include a plan of the local water, drawing attention to local rules of river/water use and to hazards. Attention should also be drawn to any variation in normal procedures which may be necessary due to the state of the tide or stream, high winds, or other climatic conditions.

4. A list of vital telephone numbers referable to water safety shall be displayed prominently in every Clubhouse, to include:
Doctor
Ambulance
Local hospital casualty department
Offshore or river rescue services
Local, river or harbour police
RNLI (for coastal waters)

If there is no telephone readily available at the Clubhouse, clear directions to the nearest available telephone must also be displayed.

5. Safety and first aid equipment shall be readily available in every Clubhouse, to include:
    First Aid Chest (to be fully stocked and regularly checked)
    Thermal Blankets/Exposure Bags (see section 8, paragraph 5d)
    Life rings/Buoys and line (see section 4, paragraph 3).

6. Clubs shall ensure that all equipment used for rowing and coaching is safe equipment (see sections 2 and 8).

7. Clubs shall provide adequate instruction in watermanship and rowing technique, and adequate supervision by coaches and experienced rowers, to ensure that no one boating from the Clubhouse puts themselves at risk when on the water. This applies particularly to single scullers and to juniors. Inexperienced coxswains should only be allowed out in boats with an experienced oarsman rowing in the crew and in charge of it.

8. Clubs should treat the coaching of coxswains and their education in watermanship and good safety procedures as being more important, from a safety aspect, than coaching oarsmen or scullers.

9. Clubs should take active steps to encourage members to become fully conversant with lifesaving and resuscitation procedures (see sections 10 and 11), by attending training courses and other appropriate means. In particular it is highly desirable that the Club Safety Officer and all regular Club Coaches should be so trained.

10. Club rowing activities shall be co-ordinated with those of other local water users to minimize clashes of interest and the possibility of additional hazards arising.

11. However carefully Club members observe the Safety Code, there is always the possibility that accidents will happen and injury or even loss of life will occur. All Clubs shall carry comprehensive insurance to cover personal injury to members on the water, and personal injury and damage to property of third parties.

12. All cases of accident involving injury to rowers (other than trivial incidents) shall be notified in writing to ARA Headquarters immediately by an Officer of the Club.

2. Safe rowing equipment

Rowing equipment should be maintained in good order to avoid the user being put in danger on the water. Particular attention should be paid to the following points:

1. So far as practicable, boats and equipment should be stored in well-lit premises in such a way that damage to boats and to people is avoided on removal and return.

2. When a boat is placed on the water, the crew or sculler should check that it is in safe condition and that the fittings are in good order:
   a) check for leaks;
   b) check that boats which are canvassed or decked are free of holes so the maximum buoyancy will be maintained if the boat sinks or capsizes;
   c) check that corks or bulkhead seals are in position before leaving the shore (especially important with boats built of non-buoyant material such as aluminium or plastic: such boats may need supplementary buoyancy);
   d) check that riggers are securely attached and that moving parts (swivels, sliding seats, stretchers) are in working order;
   e) coxswains and steersmen must always check that rudder-lines, steering gear, rudders and fins are in working order;
   f) check that oars and sculls are in good condition, particularly that the button is firm and the shaft of the blade free from damage.

3. Every boat must at all times carry firmly attached to its bows a white ball of not less than 4 centimetres diameter, made of rubber or material of similar consistency. (ARA Rule of Racing C2).

4. When it is necessary for outings to take place in the dark or in poor visibility the person in charge of the crew must carry a waterproof torch as a means of signalling and the boat must be

fitted with lights as required by the local water authority or, in the absence of such instructions, as recommended from time to time by the ARA.

5. Where boats are fitted with shoes, these should be of the 'quick-release' type. Make sure that 'quick-release' mechanisms work properly and give an immediate release when strain is put upon them. Make sure laces are properly in position and check that heel restraints are fitted and effective. If a 'Velcro' grip has become worn, do not use leather thonging to hold down quick release shoes – doing so will make them a trap for the rower if the boat capsizes. Fit a new 'Velcro' grip at once. Novices should not go out in boats with fitted shoes.

6. If rough water is likely during an outing, it is recommended that a baler and/or sponge is carried in the boat.

7. At the end of every outing, remove the corks or bulkhead seals and store them with the boat.

8. In order to ensure that equipment remains safe, a clear procedure should be set up in every Club whereby damage to equipment or failure in a boat is notified as soon as possible to a responsible Club official, and the defect repaired before the equipment is required again. It is recommended that damaged equipment should be clearly marked so that anyone intending to use the equipment is made aware of the damage.

9. Clubs are recommended to organize monthly boat maintenance sessions where the active members will clean and check all the boats they use. Clean equipment is far more likely to be safe equipment; and rowers who are made personally responsible for the condition of the boats they use are far more likely to notice and deal with wear and tear to equipment before it becomes potentially dangerous.

3. Oarsmen and scullers

1. All active club members shall satisfy the Club Safety Officer that they are in good health and can swim a minimum of 50 metres in light clothing (ROSPA recommended standard).

2. All oarsmen and scullers shall make themselves fully acquainted with the local code of practice displayed in their club (see Section 1, paragraph 5) and follow it at all times.

3. All oarsmen and scullers, before embarking on an outing, shall ensure that a responsible member of the club or any suitably qualified person is aware that the outing is taking place and its anticipated duration. Ideally a blackboard should be provided so that such information may be recorded when no one is available.

4. All active members should learn and practise capsize and accident drills (see Section 6). It is very desirable that they also learn lifesaving and resuscitation procedures (see Sections 10 and 11).

5. Every time a rower takes to the water, he/she should check that the condition of his/her boat and equipment is safe (see Section 2) and follow correct club procedure if damage occurs during the outing.

6. Active members should be taught the correct way to remove and replace boats on the boat racks, and the correct way to launch, embark and disembark, so that the risk of damage and capsizing is reduced. All active members should continue to use correct procedure every time they have an outing. Boats should be launched and brought back to shore in accordance with local practice.

7. Members starting to learn to row should not go onto the water without a coach or more experienced oarsman present.

8. Although the coxswain of a crew has responsibility by his/ her acts for the safety of that crew, coxes by reason of youth or inexperience are often not in overall charge of the boat. Except where a coxswain is mature and thoroughly experienced, it is essential that an experienced member of the crew is in charge and that the member is constantly aware of what is happening outside the boat to ensure that no accident occurs.

9. Single scullers (apart from beginners who are on the water under supervision) are solely and fully responsible for their own

safety, and must follow the appropriate procedures laid down elsewhere (Section 4, paragraph 2, 7, 10, 11, 12; Section 5, paragraph 2).

4. Coxswains

1. Every coxswain shall satisfy the Club Safety Officer that he/ she is in good health and can swim 50 metres in light clothing (ROSPA recommended distance). NB. This must be regarded as the absolute minimum.

2. No one who is subject to epileptic fits or blackouts should cox a boat. In cases of doubt, medical advice must be obtained.

3. All coxswains should wear a life-jacket of approved type (BS 3595) at all times when on the water.

4. Coxswains should always dress suitably for the prevailing conditions. Care should be taken to ensure warmth (particularly round the head and the lower back) and that clothing is sufficiently waterproof, including water-resistant outer gloves. Avoid heavy and bulky clothing. Never wear 'Wellington' type rubber boots in the boat.

5.Coxswains often carry voice projection equipment or a radio link with the coach. In racing a coxswain may have to carry deadweight. These items are to be attached to the boat and never to the coxswain. Any link to the coxswain must be fitted with a quick release device.

6. Coxswains must learn the simple commands for boat control, both on and off the water, so that they use them correctly, clearly and instinctively. They must also know and understand basic commands used by other water users – e.g. port and starboard.

7. Coxswains must understand and carry out all safety procedures and regulations applicable to the water they use, especially those relating to right of way, power boats, sailing craft, etc.
   a) Understand and observe local navigation rules of the river or water;
   b) On unfamiliar water, find out local regulations and

practices, and the existence of any particular hazards, before going out on the water;

c) Always recognize and respect the rights and needs of other water users, especially anglers; and show them the consideration and courtesy you expect them to show you;

c) Watch out for swimmers at all times. At best only a head will be visible, and a blow from a blade can kill. If in doubt, stop your boat.

8. Coxswains must know and ensure their crews carry out correct procedures for removing and replacing boats on the boat racks, and for launching, embarking and disembarking; and especially that boats are launched and brought in to shore in accordance with local practice.

9. Before every outing, the coxswain must make sure the rudder lines are in good condition and working fully and correctly, and that rudder and fin are in good order.

10. Manoeuvring racing boats is difficult because of their length. Coxswains are strongly recommended to spend their time in playboats and sculling boats to learn the basic principles of manoeuvring craft. In particular:

a) Learn to make full use of tide or stream when turning a boat;

b) Be aware that when a boat stops or 'easies', it is carried along by stream or tide. Never 'easy' just upstream of an obstacle such as a bridge or mooring. In particular when turning a boat, make sure it is well away from obstacles and preferably downstream of them.

c) On tidal water be constantly aware of the state of the tide, its effect on your craft and the danger of collision with others, particularly when the tide is changing.

d) Be aware of the effect on the stream from weirs, sluices and water inlets and outlets. Watch out for such hazards and avoid them.

11. Coxswains must be aware of danger from exceptional weather conditions or from changes in conditions during an outing. Some examples are:

a) Strong winds, particularly where wind and tide/stream are in conflict.

b) On tidal water, the possibility of conditions worsening if there is a strong wind and the tide changes during the outing.

c) The need to stay further out from the lee shore in strong wind.

d) The need to make ample allowance for the speed of the current when there is increased water flow.

The coxswain must recognize that an outing may have to be altered, postponed or even abandoned in the interest of safety.

12. Extremes of weather such as ice, fog or mist present further problems of which the coxswain must be aware. Thin slivers of ice floating on the water are capable of holing a racing shell. Fog and mist not only impair visibility but distort sound remarkably. A coxswain should never allow his/her boat to be paddled in such conditions at a speed at which he/she is unable to bring it to a complete halt if an obstacle appears. (See also Section 2, paragraph 4.)

13. All coxswains shall learn capsize and accident drills (see Section 6). It is also very desirable that they learn lifesaving and resuscitation procedures (see Sections 10 and 11).

5. Steersmen

Steersmen have a special responsibility for the safety of their crews. Not only must they observe the procedures for oarsmen (Section 3) but much of Section 4 (coxswains) also applies to them. And because a steersman is concentrating on his/her own rowing or sculling, and is tiring physically as the outing proceeds, he/she is more likely to overlook safety procedure than is the coxswain who is not using physical effort, and has the added advantage of facing the direction in which the boat is travelling.

1. Steersmen should look ahead once in every 10 strokes throughout the outing, irrespective of the work that the crew is doing. However sure you are that the water ahead is clear, it is easy to miss seeing a partly submerged obstacle, a lone swimmer or other craft making unexpected changes in direction.

2. Before leaving the shore for an outing check that the steering gear is in good condition and working fully and correctly.

3. The following paragraphs of Section 4 apply equally to steersmen: 2; 6; 7; 8; 10; 11; 12.

6. Capsize and accident drill

By their design, racing boats when sat properly will not capsize. However, the smaller the boat, the more easily it will capsize; and in rough conditions or when an accident occurs, even an eight can capsize. Panic is the greatest danger, and practising the drill to be followed when the boat capsizes is a great help in controlling panic, and in disciplining rowers who find themselves in an emergency into simple procedures which provide them with the maximum protection.

1. All rowers should take part in organized and controlled capsize practices; when they have done this several times, they will know just what to expect if their boat capsizes accidentally. Even a very experienced oarsman who has been lucky enough never to have fallen in may lose his/her self-control if his/her boat should capsize.

2. Drill Procedure – whenever possible the drill should be carried out in open water as this most closely resembles the real-life situation. However it must not be practised without a suitable, fully equipped safety launch under the control of a very competent driver for every sculler afloat. Also the precise procedure will need to be modified dependent upon local conditions and water pollution; it may also need modification in the light of the ability and experience of the group.

Open water

1. Get into the boat and scull well clear from intended landing area; well upstream and into the wind (with strong flowing stream it may be necessary to go much further than at first appearance).

2. Push one scull out parallel to boat at finish.

3. Roll into space left by scull. Put head under water.

4. Release shoes as necessary – keeping knees straight.

5. Surface alongside boat.

6. Turn boat right way up as necessary/appropriate by pushing down on the nearside rigger with feet and one hand whilst reaching other arm over hull to grip far-side rigger to pull over and up. Watch top scull as boat turns over.

7. Check sculls are not jammed.

8. Swim to bows of boat maintaining contact by having one arm hooked over hull. NB. Don't lean on boat.

9. Grip bows of boat in both hands above chest and in front of chin (as in lifesaving – two handed carry).

10. Tow boat to landing point decided by drill organizer.

11. Land using appropriate method and empty the boat with assistance of one other.

Swimming pool

1. Get into boat in shallow end and scull to deep end.

2. Carry out capsize as in open water.

3. Tow boat to shallow end then back to deep end.

4. Climb out in deep end using the boat if necessary.

5. Empty boat with help of one other person.

6. Carry boat back to shallow end.

3. If the boat begins to fill with water, paddle it to the bank or into shallow water, take out the blades and empty it out.

4. If the boat fills with water so that it begins to sink before you can get it to the shore, get out of it carefully into the water, hold on to the boat and tow it to the shore. The weight of a crew in a water-logged boat will probably cause it serious damage, whereas with the crew out of it, it will continue to float at water

level and provide the crew with buoyancy whilst they tow it to safety.

5. If you capsize, the only situation in which you should let go of your boat and swim to the shore is if the stream, wind or tide are carrying it on to a hazard, such as a mooring or weir, too fast for you to paddle it to the shore and you are certain you can swim to safety. If you are likely to be carried on to a weir or similar danger, your chances of survival are better if you continue holding on to the boat and go onto the weir supported by it.

6. If his/her boat capsizes, a coxswain must resist panic, free himself/herself immediately from all loose equipment (rudder lines, microphone cable, clogs etc.), get out and hold on to the boat once he/she is free.

7. When a boat capsizes, the coxswain and/or senior member of the crew should take control and make sure all members are following correct capsize procedure. Every member of the crew who stays in control of himself/herself lessens by his/her example the risk that other members of the crew will panic.

8. If a rower has lost consciousness, support him/her in the water until a rescue craft arrives, or help him/her to the bank as fast as possible if no rescue craft is at hand. The desirability of all those who row knowing lifesaving procedure cannot be over-emphasized. If necessary, resuscitation (Section 10) should be applied immediately, even while the rower is still in the water. An ambulance should be summoned by the quickest method available.

9. The water on which you row is rarely free from pollution. If your boat capsizes, try to keep your mouth closed and avoid swallowing water. If you do swallow water, obtain medical advice without delay, even if you do not feel unwell. Your local hospital will know if you are in danger of pollution and will give you any treatment that is necessary.

7. Coaches

1. A coach is not only concerned to teach his/her crews how to

row better or faster; he/she is also responsible for their safety. Coaches using launches must also be aware at all times of other water users; must ensure that neither their coaching launches nor their crews place anyone else using the water in difficulty or danger; and should always be alert to give help to other users who may be in danger and without help.

2. A coach shall ensure that every member of his/her crew he/she coaches follows the appropriate safety procedures at all times, and he/she shall himself/herself apply them to ensure his/her crew's safety. In particular coaches should:

   a) Be aware of local codes of practice (Section 1, paragraph 5).

   b) Ensure that his/her crew is using safe rowing equipment (Section 2).

   c) Be aware of weather and water conditions and arrange the outing to avoid any danger (Section 4, paragraph 11 and 12 apply equally to coaches).

   d) Watch out for any hazards his/her crew may meet. It is often easier for the coach, who is higher above the water than members of the crew, to see swimmers or similar hazards ahead. He/she must draw the attention of the cox or steersmen to such hazard and not merely attempt to influence any steering decision that has been made.

   e) Showing consideration for other water users is very much the responsibility of the coach, both in regard to his/her coaching launch and to the boats he/she is coaching.

3. Coaches of young children shall ensure that the whole crew, and not just the coxswain, are dressed suitably as youngsters are unlikely to be able to generate a high level of body warmth during their first outings.

4. When his/her crew is rowing away from their home water, the coach shall ascertain the local code of practice and, at regattas, any special traffic rules to be observed, and ensure his/her crew fully understands them.

5. Coaches should pay particular attention to the coaching of coxswains. Not only is a competent coxswain important to his/her crew's success; his/her competence is essential to their safety on the water.

6. Every coach should know capsize and accident drills (Section 6). If a crew he/she is coaching has an accident or capsizes, he/she should check that every member is following correct capsize procedure and be prepared to assist or rescue any member who is in difficulties, is injured, or appears to be suffering from hypothermia or exposure. Every time he/she goes out in a coaching launch he/she should check that it is fully equipped with safety equipment (See Section 8, paragraph 5) and know how to use this.

7. Every coach should learn lifesaving and resuscitation procedures (see Sections 10 and 11). This knowledge may literally make the difference between life and death for someone he/she is coaching.

8. Coaches using launches, even where they are not themselves driving are responsible for ensuring the Section 8 of this Safety Code is fully observed.

9. Coaches of beginners and especially of crews of young children have an extra responsibility. Those who are new to the sport are likely to concentrate on their own rowing to the exclusion of all else, and are thus less likely to be aware of approaching danger. Coaches of school crews, when dealing with several crews of young novices on the water together, must be especially concerned with their safety. It is very easy for the first crew that gets boated to get into difficulties whilst the coach is supervising further crews getting into the water. Beginners, whether in crews or sculling boats, should never be allowed on the water unsupervised.

8. Coaching launches

Coaching from a launch or inflatable craft has now become commonplace. The presence of the launch gives far better safety protection to a crew than a coach on a bike, on the bank, but raises the need to ensure competent driving, safety of those on board the coaching craft, and the effect upon the other water users of the coaching craft's activities.

1. Training Drivers – to take out an engine-powered boat without previous tuition is to put the driver, any passengers and

other water users at risk. The Royal Yachting Association, many local authorities and the boating centres hold courses in handling powered boats and issue certificates of competence. It is strongly recommended that no one should drive a launch without first having taken a course of instruction. At the very least the Club shall ensure that an experienced driver goes out with a new driver until he/she has shown that he/she is fully in control of the launch. NB. The manner in which launches are manoeuvred and generally handled may create unnecessary problems for other water users. Excessive washes create impossible conditions for other water users and can cause accidents to smaller boats. Thoughtless driving often causes damage to moored boats and to river banks. To use launches and coaching, rescue and other purposes, all on the same water, requires drivers to be fully aware of the effect of the washes they cause and the risk that the very sport they are seeking to assist cannot take place because their manner of driving their boats has made the water unusable.

2. All coaching launches and safety boats shall carry the following safety aids:
   a) A bailer and, for inflatables, a suitable pump and spare valve.
   b) A klaxon horn or similar warning device, capable of attracting attention over a distance of at least 200 metres.
   c) A grab line at least 30 metres (100 feet) long with a large knotted tie in one end to assist in throwing.
   d) Thermal blankets/exposure bags to counteract hypothermia. Make use of proprietary items; and not woollen blankets which only absorb moisture but do not retain heat. In the absence of recognized equipment, polythene sheets cut to the size of a commercially available exposure bag will provide the necessary level of heat retention until proper treatment can begin.
   e) Life rings/life buoys. These are essential when several people are in the water and the launch can attend to only one at a time.
   f) A basic first aid kit.
   g) A sharp knife.
   h) A paddle.
   i) Simple hand holds fitted to the side of a launch to give help to any person being rescued and provide self-help

should the driver fall overboard.

3. When it is necessary for an outing to take place in the dark or in poor visibility the launch must carry a waterproof torch and klaxon horn or similar device as a means of signalling and the boat must be fitted with lights as required by the local water authorities or, in the absence of such instructions, as recommended from time to time by the ARA.

4. Life jackets (BS 3595) should be worn at all times and are essential for launches going out to sea or on very wide stretches of water. Those which depend on oral inflation should be worn partly inflated; those which have auto-inflation must be checked at intervals suggested by the manufacturers.

5. Maintenance of the boat and its engine is vital, since the possible consequences of failure are too great. The driver and his/her passengers are dependent on the efficient working of the engine and the good condition of the launch for the proper execution of their duties. Driver and coaches should know how the engine works, and a box with basic tools and spare parts (in particular spark plugs and a spark-plug spanner) should always be carried to enable running repairs to be done and simple replacement to be made. The tool/spares box should be kept dry and should be checked regularly (an extra can of pre-mixed fuel is also a vital spare). It is a wise precaution to check that the engine is securely fixed to the hull and that the secondary safety fixing is properly attached every time the boat is used.

6. Choice of launch, its hull size and its shape, must be matched to an engine suitable to the work it is to undertake and the load to be carried. In particular, launches to be used for coaching on rivers or enclosed waters must be of a design which will enable a launch to accompany a crew rowing at speed without causing a wash that makes the water unusable for everyone else.

9. Safety at regattas (including processional races)

1. All regattas shall appoint a suitably competent person as

Safety Officer, whose duty shall be to ensure that the ARA Code of Practice for Water Safety is fully implemented.

2. No regatta, processional race or sponsored row shall take place without full prior consultation between the organizers, the local water authority and, as appropriate, the police, life saving organizations and other bodies as may be necessary, to ensure that adequate safety measures are taken.

3. All regattas shall appoint a person to be Medical Officer. Whilst it is not essential that such a person be a qualified Medical Practitioner, he/she shall be responsible for ensuring that medical support is accessible to the regatta. First aid facilities must always be available.

4. Where practicable, safety boats manned by trained professionals and equipped with adequate safety aids should be available throughout the regatta. These should be sufficient in number and so placed that rapid assistance can be provided wherever the need occurs.

5. All officials and competitors shall be informed of local hazards and traffic rules, and a plan of the course and launching areas identifying hazards and traffic rules shall be displayed and brought to the notice of the competitors before they embark. The telephone numbers of police, ambulance, medical and fire services shall be prominently displayed, together with the location of the nearest telephone.

6. Where practicable the racing course should be marked with clearly visible buoys. Guard boats should be stationed at each end of the course to advise competitors and to direct other water users away from the course. If this is practicable, such information should be displayed on notice boards suitably placed at each end of the course.

7. Where races are umpired from launches, the instructions to umpires shall clearly state that in the event of an accident, the umpire's first duty is to abandon the race and render all possible assistance if anyone's safety is at risk.

8. Umpire's launches shall carry a life ring and line, thermal

blanket and first aid equipment; and should where possible comply fully with Section 8, paragraph 2.

9. All officials shall be informed of accident and safety procedures, and details of these shall, so far as is practicable, be brought to the notice of competitors.

10. Resuscitation

1. To be effective resuscitation must be started immediately, even while the patient is in the water, otherwise irreversible damage or death may occur within a few minutes. Many thousands of lives have been saved by ordinary citizens who have known what to do and have had the courage to do it at the critical time.

2. The saving of a life during a medical emergency depends on the accurate assessment and proper management of the ABC of the resuscitation.
   A – AIRWAY
   B – BREATHING
   C CIRCULATION
On finding a person requiring resuscitation:
   i. Approach
   ii. Airways
   iii. Breathing
   iv. Circulation

3. APPROACH
   1. Establish there is no danger to yourself or the patient. If you see someone in difficulties in the water DO NOT go into the water after him/her.
      Remember there may be a neck or a back injury requiring extra care when removing the patient.
   2. a) Look for something to help pull him/her out – stick, rope, clothing.
      b) Lie down to prevent yourself from being pulled in.
      c) If you cannot reach him/her, throw any floating object – football, plastic bottle – for him/her to hold on to, then fetch help.
      d) If you are in a safety launch carefully approach him/her if it is safe to do so.

REACH TOW THROW ROW

3. Is the patient conscious?
Establish consciousness by shouting 'WAKE UP' loudly 2–3 times, and gently shaking the shoulder.
– If conscious:
Place in recovery position.

Kneel to one side of the patient. Straighten arm and leg furthest from you. Place arm nearest to you across the patient's chest. Bend his/her nearest knee and with hand on knee and on his/her nearest shoulder, turn the patient away from you, on to his/her side.
– If unconscious:
Proceed to establish an Airway.

4. A – AIRWAYS

1. Open the Airway.
The rescuer should place one hand beneath the patient's neck and the palm of the other hand on the patient's forehead. By lifting the neck and pressing the forehead the Airway is opened. The jaw may also need support – remove the hand from behind the neck to hold the chin forward.
2. Inspect the Airway.
Remove blood, vomit, loose teeth or broken dentures but leave well-fitting full dentures in place.

5. B – BREATHING

Is the patient breathing?
Check for breathing by holding your ear close to the patient's mouth. Listen and feel for breathing. Also look for breathing; see if the chest is rising and falling.
– If breathing:
Place in recovery position.
Continue to observe – Airway
                              – Breathing
– If NOT breathing:
Patient requires artificial breathing/mouth to mouth breathing/expired air respiration (EAR).

Kneel beside patient and open Airway. Open his/her mouth and pinch his/her nose closed. Open your mouth, take a deep breath, seal his/her mouth firmly with yours and breathe out into the patient. Breathe out just enough to raise the patient's chest. Remove your mouth from the patient's and allow chest to fall. Repeat 4 times. If breaths are difficult to get in check Airway for obstruction and try again. If breathing returns place in recovery position.

Vomiting often occurs when breathing returns and placing the patient in the recovery position will prevent him/her from choking.

If breathing does not return proceed to circulation.

6. C – CIRCULATION

Is there a pulse?

Check for presence of the pulse in the neck (CAROTID PULSE).

– If pulse present:

Either continue breathing/EAR at 12 breaths per minute or place in recovery position and observe ABC

– If pulse not present:

Patient needs heart massage/heart compressions/external cardiac compressions (ECC).

To commence External Cardiac Compressions (ECC) place patient flat on his/her back. Place hands over lower half of breast bone. With arms held straight and hands on the chest at all times compress the chest one and a half to two inches (4–5 cm) and then release.

Compress the chest 15 times and then give two artificial breaths (EAR) at a rate of 80 compressions per minute. If assistance is present compress the chest 5 times (at a rate of 60 compressions per minute) for every artificial breath by assistant.

Check for breathing and pulse every two minutes. Continue until pulse and breathing have returned or until experienced medical help arrives. If patient recovers a pulse and/or breathing place in recovery position and observe ABC.

7. Remember that effective resuscitation training is essential; the foregoing being only a guide/*aide memoire* to the practice of resuscitation.

11. Hypothermia

1. In hypothermia the whole of the body has been chilled to a much lower than normal temperature, below 35 degrees C compared with the normal 37 degrees C.

Note: A lesser degree of chilling is less dangerous and may not affect the inner core temperature but can still be very damaging. In the case of an already chilled person continued exposure can produce hypothermia very quickly.

2. Be alert to the warning signs of cold both in yourself and others. In water, the body loses heat rapidly. Wind and exposed arms, legs and head heighten the risk.

3. Do not take alcohol when boating or swimming or go for dare swims after drinks parties. Alcohol causes heat loss as well as impairing judgement.

4. Sudden immersion in cold water can have a shock effect which can disrupt normal breathing and reduce even a proficient swimmer to incompetence.

5. First Aid treatment for hypothermia differs from the treatment for drowning and it is therefore essential to recognize the signs. If the person is unconscious or apparently dead –
If the rescue had been made within a few minutes of the victim going into the water there is a strong presumption of drowning. If the evidence suggests a lengthy wait for rescue, the victim may be suffering from hypothermia.

6. The following are the most usual symptoms and signs, but all may not be present:
   a) Unexpected and unreasonable behaviour possibly accompanied by complaints of coldness and tiredness.
   b) Physical and mental lethargy with failure to understand a question or orders.
   c) Slurring of speech.
   d) Violent outburst of unexpected energy and violent language, becoming uncooperative.
   e) Failure of, or abnormality in, vision.
   f) Twitching.
   g) Falling and complaining of numbness and cramp.
   h) General shock with pallor and blueness of lips and nails.
   i) Slow weak pulse, wheezing and coughing.

7. A very dangerous situation is still present when a person who has been in the water for some time is taken out. Further

heat loss must be prevented. The victim should be protected against wind and rain if possible.

8.There can be risks in resuscitating a seriously hypothermic victim too energetically, i.e. the heart may beat abnormally or stop if stimulated too vigorously, and heat can be lost from the skin if the victim is massaged too energetically. This is less likely in milder cases of cold injury.

Here then is a guide:

A young and previously fit person, who has not been in the water for very long can be treated fairly vigorously – dry, then change their clothes. Their trunk could be immersed in a warm bath (approximately 44 degrees C).

A very young or adult person who has been in the water for a long time – treat more carefully. After removing from exposure, generally dry off wet clothing and cover with blankets, and allow to re-warm passively, preferably in a warm room.

Re-warming can also be effected by:
   i) Putting the victim in a sleeping bag or plastic bag.
   ii) Others placing their warm bodies against the victim.

9. Where treatment on the spot effects revival, the golden rule is to get the victim to hospital. Delayed, or secondary drowning, affects the lungs and heart. Delayed effects of hypothermia may cause deterioration and even death after successful resuscitation.

10. PREVENTION IS ALWAYS THE BEST POLICY.

Reproduced by kind permission of the Amateur Rowing Association.

APPENDIX III
USEFUL ADDRESSES

United Kingdom
England
Berkshire

Eton College Boat House
Brocas Street
Eton
Windsor
Berkshire SL4 6BW
Tel: (0753) 860072

Boats (racing and recreational)
Coaching boats

Matt Wood
Brocas Street
Eton
Windsor
Berkshire SL4 6BW
Tel: (0753) 858449
Fax: (0753) 855757

Fittings and accessories
Riggers and accessories
Timing devices
Training devices

Phoenix Boats
79 Priors Way
Braywick
Maidenhead
Berkshire SL6 2EN
Tel: (0628) 71145

Boats (racing)

Simon Johnson International
Unit 14 Sheeplands Farm
High Street
Wargrave
Berkshire RG10 8DL
Tel: (0734) 404755
Fax: (0734) 404755

Oars and sculls
Fittings and accessories
Riggers and accessories
Ergometers
Trailers and transport
Timing devices
Trophies

Cambridgeshire

Burgashell
67A The Row
Sutton Ely
Cambridgeshire CB6 2PB
Tel: (0353) 777184
Fax: (0353) 777184

Boats (racing and recreational)

Davies Racing Boats
The Firs
Main Street
Southwick
Nr Oundle
Peterborough PE8 5BL
Tel: (0832) 274782
Fax: (0832) 274782

Boats (racing)
Riggers and accessories
Timing devices

Hi-tech Racing
Units 3 & 4
Cedars Industrial Park
Broughton
Huntingdon
Cambridgeshire PE17 3AS
Tel: (0487) 823783
Fax: (0487) 823783

Boats (racing)

Cheshire

H.S. Sports Ltd
Unit 5
Radnor Park Industrial Estate
Congleton
Cheshire CW12 4XN
Tel: (0260) 275708
Fax: (0260) 278352

Timing devices

Durham

Brown's Boathouse Ltd
Elvet Bridge
Durham DH1 3AF
Tel: (091) 386 3779

Boats (racing and recreational)

Hampshire

Spartan Racing Boats
Herriard Old Station
Herriard
Hampshire RG25 2PY
Tel: (0256) 83501

Boats (racing and recreational)
Trophies

Kent

G. Pullern Esq
(Mike Pullern & Associates)
10 Gazelle Glade
Riverview Park
Gravesend
Kent DA12 4PU
Tel: (0474) 363480

Fittings and accessories

London and Greater London

Ainsworth
76 The Green
Twickenham
Middlesex TW2 5AG
Tel: (081) 898 4839
Fax: (081) 755 0981

Boats (racing and recreational)
Oars and sculls

Amateur Rowing Association
The Priory
6 Lower Mall
Hammersmith
London W6 9DJ
Tel: (081) 748 3623
Fax: (081) 741 4658

Coaching booklets and videos
The National Rowing Magazine

George Sims (Racing Boats)
Eel Pie Island
Twickenham
Middlesex TW1 3DY
Tel: (081) 892 8844

Boats (racing)
Oars and sculls
Clothing and accessories

Jackmate Trophies
56 Staunton Road
Kingston Upon Thames
KT2 5TL
Tel: (081) 546 5616

Trophies

Vandeleur Antiquarian Books
69 Sheen Lane
London SW14
Tel: (081) 878 6837
Tel: (081) 393 7752

Books, magazines and art

Nottinghamshire

Concept II
151–153 Nottingham Road
Old Basford
Nottingham NG6 0FU
Tel: (0602) 421925
Fax: (0602) 422302

Ergometers

Godfrey Textiles
Mundella Works
Mundella Road
The Meadows
Nottingham NG2 2EQ
Tel: (0602) 864600
Fax: (0602) 862018

Clothing and accessories

Raymond Sims Ltd
Trentside North
West Bridgeford
Nottingham NG2 5FA
Tel: (0602) 810992

Boats (racing)

Oxfordshire

F. Collar Ltd
Isis Works
South Hinksey
Oxford OX1 5AZ
Tel: (0865) 735493
Fax: (0865) 326189

Oars and sculls

George Harris Racing Boats
Isis Boathouse
Iffley
Oxford OX1 4UW
Tel: (0865) 243870

Boats (racing)

Glyn Locke (Racing Shells) Ltd
Bolney Court Farm
Henley on Thames
Oxon RG9 3NL
Tel: (0491) 571177
Fax: (0491) 579698

Boats (racing)
Timing devices
Trophies

Microstroke
3 Sudbury Court
Faringdon
Oxon SN7 8AF
Tel: (0367) 22202

Timing devices

Richard Way Booksellers
54 Friday Street
Henley on Thames
Oxon RG9 1AH
Tel: (0491) 576663

Books, magazines and art

Rock the Boat (Athletic Designs)
7 Badgemore Lane
Henley on Thames
Oxon RG9 2JH
Tel: (0491) 578525

Clothing
Original artwork

Shropshire

Celebrity Glass
Preston Montford Lane
Montford Bridge
Shrewsbury SY4 1DU
Tel: (0743) 850851
Fax: (0743) 850146

Trophies

South Yorkshire

A.E. Ellis & Co. Ltd
16–20 Sidney Street
Sheffield S1 4RH
Tel: (0742) 722703

Trophies

Corivo Products
190 Rockingham Street
Sheffield S1 4ED
Tel: (0742) 754168

Trophies

Suffolk

David Cartwright Boatbuilder
Church Farm Cottages
Linstead Magna
Halesworth
Suffolk IP19 0QN
Tel: 098 685 302

Boats (racing and recreational)
Coaching boats

Surrey

Aylings Racing Boats Ltd
The Rowing Centre
Bessborough Works
7 Molesey Road
West Molesey
Surrey KT8 0BF
Tel: (081) 979 8249
Fax: (081) 979 6754
Tlx: 926434

Boats (racing and recreational)
Oars and sculls
Fittings and accessories
Riggers and accessories
Ergometers
Trailers and transport
Coaching boats
Magazine
Private instructor
Equipment hire

Carl Douglas Racing Shells
'Kanalia' Wildwood Close
Pyrford
Woking
Surrey GU22 8PL
Tel: (09323) 42315
Tlx: 928570

Boats (racing and recreational)
Fittings and accessories

Coaching Advisory Services
Consultancy
117 Kingsmead Avenue
Worcester Park
Surrey KT4 8UT
Tel: (081) 979 8249
Fax: (081) 979 6754
Tlx: 262092

Riggers and accessories
Coaching books and videos
Private instructor
Coaching consultancy

CPA Systems Philip Walker
PO Box No: 111C
Esher
Surrey KT10 8EU
Tel: (081) 398 8501

Electrical and timing devices
Radio-link between coach and boat

Janousek Racing Boats
1a Abbot Close
Byfleet
Weybridge
Surrey KT14 7JN
Tel: (0932) 353421
Fax: (0932) 336381

Boats (racing)

Jerry Sutton
Racing Oars & Sculls
Laleham Reach
Chertsey
Surrey KT16 8RP
Tel: (09325) 60270

Boats (recreational)
Oars and sculls
Fittings and accessories

Neaveo Rowing Fittings
43a Dennis Road
East Molesey
Surrey K18 9AJ
Tel: (081) 979 4086
Fax: (081) 979 1328

Fittings and accessories
Riggers and accessories

Rowing Supplies International
Mail Order
PO Box 49E
Worcester Park
Surrey KT4 8UN
Tel: (081) 337 2176
Fax: (081) 330 7732

Boats (racing and recreational)
Oars and sculls
Fittings and accessories
Riggers and accessories
Ergometers
Trailers and transport
Books, magazines and art
Clothing and accessories
A full directory of rowing items

Worcestershire

Spartan Clothing (Malvern) Ltd
32 Graham Road
Malvern
Worcestershire WR14 2HL
Tel: (0684) 568208/565966
Fax: (0684) 572808

Clothing and accessories

Scotland
Ayrshire

Peveril Manufacturing Co
1 Campbell Street
Darvel
Ayrshire KA17 0DL
Tel: (0560) 21965

Clothing and accessories

West Lothian

Russell Athletic
Russell Corp UK Ltd
1 Dunlop Square
Dean's South West Industrial
Estate
Livingston
West Lothian EH54 8SB
Tel: (0506) 419444
Fax: (0506) 419494

Clothing

Wales

Gwent

Nekton-Wye
Unit 1 (D)
The Old Laundry
Hadnock Road
Monmouth
Gwent NP5 ENC
Tel: (0600) 4864
Fax: (0600) 4507
Tlx: 94011497

Boats (recreational)
Oars and sculls

Other Countries

Australia

New South Wales

Carbonlite Rowing Shells
PO Box 312
Brookvale
Sydney 2100
NSW
Australia
Tel: (2) 9052 532
Fax: (2) 9050 624

Boats (racing)
Fittings and accessories

Croker Oars
Remo, Cowans Lane
Oxley Island
NSW 2430
Australia
Tel: (065) 532 473
Fax: (065) 532 544

Oars and sculls
Fittings and accessories

Melba Racing Shells Pty Ltd
Rear – 443 Victoria Road
Gladesville
NSW 2111
Australia
Tel: (612) 817 1916
Fax: (612) 816 2509

Boats (racing)
Oars and sculls
Fittings and accessories
Riggers and accessories
Ergometers
Timing devices

Rough Trade Rowing Clothing
PO Box 34
Split Junction 2088
Sydney
NSW
Australia
Tel: (61) 2 451 5443
Fax: (61) 2 905 0604

Clothing and accessories

Sargent & Burton
5 Bertam Street
Mortlake
NSW 2137
Australia
Tel: (02) 743 1105
Fax: (02) 736 3787

Boats (racing)
Coaching boats

Ted Hale Racing Boats
PO Box 833
Tweed Heads
NSW 2485
Australia
Tel: (075) 364 922
Fax: (075) 364 716

Boats (racing and recreational)
Oars and sculls
Fittings and accessories

WM Racingshell Pty Ltd
Henley Marine Drive
PO Box 335
Drummoyne
NSW 2047
Australia
Tel: (02) 819 7314
Fax: (02) 819 6224

Boats (racing)
Fittings and accessories

South Australia

William Hay Pty Ltd
PO Box 636
Norwood
SA 5067
Australia
Tel: (08) 362 8616
Fax: (08) 363 0554

Boats (racing and sculling)
Oars and sculls
Coaching boats

Victoria

Jeff Sykes & Associates
Riversdale Road
Newtown
Geelong
Victoria 3220
Australia
Tel: (052) 213 655
Fax: (052) 212 596

Boats (racing)
Oars and sculls
Fittings and accessories
Ergometers

Austria

Max Schellenbacher
AM Winterhafen 15
4020 Linx
Austria
Tel: (0732) 284 686
Fax: (0732) 284 696

Boats (racing and recreational)

Josef Swoboda
Schickgasse 13
1220 Wien
Austria
Tel: (0222) 228 798

Boats (racing and recreational)
Oars and sculls

Canada
British Columbia

Eric. G. Jennens
1978 McDouall Street
Kelowna
BC V1Y 1A3
Canada
Tel: (604) 763 2273
Tel: (604) 763 1705
Fax: (604) 762 5242

Oars and sculls
Art
Trophies
Scale models shell and oar replicas

Exer-tech Services
31–36 West 10th
Avenue Vancouver
BC V6K 2K9
Canada
Tel: (604) 731 7117
Fax: (604) 228 5785

Fittings and accessories
Ergometers

Okanagan Rowing Craft
PO Box 1125
Kelowna
BC V1V 7P8
Canada
Tel: (604) 763 2920

Boats (recreational)

Ontario

Adventure Fitness
12 Queens Street
PO Box 1285
Lakefield, ON K0L 2H0
Canada
Tel: (705) 652 7986

Boats (recreational)
Oars and sculls
Fittings and accessories
Books, magazines and art
Clothing and accessories

Crew *d
36 Dalhousie Avenue
St Catharines
Ontario
Canada
Tel: (416) 646 0160

Clothing and accessories

Dan's Rowing Machines
114 Page Street
St Catharines
Ontario
ON L2R 4A9
Canada
Tel: (416) 684 8492

Ergometers

Hudson Boat Works Inc
RR #3
Komoka
ON N0L 1R0
Canada
Tel: (519) 473 9864
Fax: (519) 473 2861

Boats (racing)
Oars and sculls

Kaschper Racing Shells Ltd
PO Box 40
Lucan
ON N0M 2J0
Canada
Tel: (519) 227 4652
Fax: (519) 227 4247

Boats (racing)

Paluski Boats Ltd
Country Road #18 R.R. #3
Lakefield
ON K0L 1H0
Canada
Tel: (705) 652 7041

Boats (recreational)
Oars and sculls
Fittings and accessories

Regattasport
38 Lakeport Road
St Catharines
ON L2N 4P5
Canada
Tel: (416) 937 5130
Fax: (416) 937 4941

Books and magazines
Clothing and accessories
Timing devices

Rowing Canada Aviron   *Coaching books and videos*
1600 James Naismith Drive   *Books and magazines*
Gloucester   *Clothing and accessories*
ON K1B 8H9 5N4   *Trophies*
Canada
Tel: (613) 748 5656

Sport Book Publisher   *Books and magazines*
278 Robert Road
Toronto
ON M5S 2 K8
Canada
Tel: (613) 748 5656
Fax: (613) 748 5712

Stevenson Canada   *Clothing and accessories*
Div. of Boathouse Row
Sports Ltd
PO Box 284 Station 2
Toronto
ON M5N 2Z4
Canada
Tel: (416) 482 2694

Denmark

Jorgen Andersen   *Boats (racing and recreational)*
Uggelose Bygade 148   *Oars and sculls*
3540 Lynge   *Fittings and accessories*
Denmark
Tel: (452) 188 289

Ole Bloch   *Coaching books and videos*
Rylevaenget 33
2880 Bagsvaerd
Denmark
Tel: (44) 989 689
Fax: (44) 989 689

Willy Modest & Son Reimer   *Boats (racing and recreational)*
Modest   *Fittings and accessories*
Vandtarnsvej 110   *Ergometers*
2860 Soborg
Denmark
Tel: (45) 3156 5054
Fax: (45) 3156 1960

Finland

Oy Lahnakoski AB   *Oars and sculls*
Pbb 3/ Lahnakoski 25
67100 Karleby
Finland
Tel: (358) 682 9213
Fax: (358) 682 9364
Tlx: 19101672

France

Jean-Marc Fage
21 rue Arnoult Crapotte
78700 Conflans Sainte-Honorine
France
Tel: (16) 1 4768 7530
Fax: (16) 1 4768 9703

Boats (racing and recreational)
Oars and sculls
Fittings and accessories
Ergometers

Joel Jullien
Puech de Soulie
30650 Saze
France
Tel: 90 31 45

Boats (racing)

Plastan
7, avenue d'Ares
33510 Andernos-les-Bains
France
Tel: 56 26 08 79

Clothing and accessories

Roche Nautic France
38 rue Gagrine
39100 Dole
France
Tel: (84) 726 479
Tel: (44) 715 712

Oars and sculls

Sylk S.A.R.L.
1 rue de l'Industrie
59820 Gravelines
France
Tel: (028) 653 701

Boats (racing and recreational)
Fittings and accessories

Germany

B.H. Mayer's Kunstprägeanstalt
Turnplatz 2
7530 Pforzheim
Germany
Tel: (07231) 92310
Fax: (07231) 26442
Tlx: 783696 gold d

Trophies

Behr – Bootshandel
Siegburger Strasse 130
5330 Konigswinter 21
Oberpleis
Germany
Tel: (02244) 81240
Fax: (02244) 81428

Boats (racing and recreational)
Oars and sculls
Fittings and accessories
Riggers and accessories
Ergometers
Trailers and transport
Coaching boats

Bootsbau Berlin GmbH
Muggelseemamm 40–70
1162 Berlin
Germany
Tel: 645 5374
Fax: 656 9380
Tlx: 112709

Boats (racing and recreational)
Fittings and accessories

Bootswerft Empacher GmbH Rockenauer Strasse 7 Postfach 1541 6930 Eberbach Germany Tel: (06271) 8000-0 Fax: (06271) 8000-99 Tlx: 466234 empac d	*Boats (racing and recreational)* *Oars and sculls* *Fittings and accessories* *Ergometers* *Coaching books and videos* *Trailers and transport* *Coaching boats* *A full range of rowing accessories*
Bootswerft Helmut Rehberg Im Nordfeld 7 3101 Nienhagen Germany Tel: (05144) 3393 Fax: (05144) 5283	*Boats (racing and recreational)* *Oars and sculls* *Fittings and accessories* *Riggers and accessories*
Concept II Ruderergometer Alex Bootshaus Allermoher Deich 64 2050 Hamburg 80 Germany Tel: (040) 737 3092 Fax: (040) 737 3092	*Oars and sculls* *Fittings and accessories* *Ergometers*
FISO – Werft (Formerly) W. Karlisch Goerlitzer Ring 24 2410 Molln (Waldstadt) Germany Tel: + BTX (04542) 2219 Fax: (02154) 42444	*Boats (racing)* *Oars and sculls* *Fittings and accessories* *Riggers and accessories* *Coaching boats*
Heipcke Bootsbau GmbH Weseler Strasse 60 4330 Mulheim an der Ruhr Germany Tel: (0208) 590 855 Fax: (0208) 599 0933	*Boats (racing and recreational)* *Oars and sculls* *Fittings and accessories* *Ergometers* *Trailers and transport* *Boat repair*
Hermann Techau GmbH Bayernstrasse/Hohweg W-2800 Bremen 1 Germany Tel: (0421) 384 104-17 Fax: (0421) 391 972 Tlx: 245583	*Trailers and transport*
Leich D. Gruenguertelstrasse 10 PO Box 501605 5000 Köln 50 Germany Tel: (0221) 394 382 Tlx: 889275	*Fittings and accessories*

Loewe Rowing Shells
Bochumer Bootsbauverein
Vosskuhlstrasse 74
4630 Bochum 1
Germany
Tel: (0234) 791 297
Tel: (02323) 83 637

Boats (racing and recreational)
Oars and sculls
Fittings and accessories
Ergometers
Books
Timing devices

Magazine RUDERSPORT
Limpert Verlag GmbH
Redaktion 'Rudersport'
Postfach 2869, Stiftsallee 40
4950 Minden
Germany
Tel: (0571) 432 42
Fax: (0571) 410 17

Magazine

New Wave Inh.H.Borchert
Seeburger Strasse 9–11
1000 Berlin 20
Germany
Tel: (030) 332 7161
Fax: (030) 332 8446

Oars and sculls
Clothing and accessories

Oarsmaker Hans Ziegler
Nikolausstrasse 9
8700 Wurzburg
Germany
Tel: (0931) 867 25

Oars and sculls

Werner Kahl
'Die Ruderwerkstatt'
Schiffenberger Weg 43
6300 Giessen
Germany
Tel: (0641) 77302
Fax: (0641) 77369

Boats (racing and recreational)
Oars and sculls
Riggers and accessories
Ergometers
Timing devices
Boat repair

Wolloner Dynamic Bootsbau
GmbH
Rheinhorststrasse 37
6700 Ludwigshafen am Rhein
Germany
Tel: (0621) 679 021
Fax: (0621) 672 717

Boats (racing and recreational)
Oars and sculls
Fittings and accessories

Italy

Cantiere Nautico
Donoratico 'Tre'
Via Matteottie 82
57024 Donoratico (Livorno)
Italy
Tel: (0565) 777 353
Fax: (0565) 777 762 Dono 3

Boats (racing and recreational)

Cantiere Navale Filippe Lido   *Boats (racing)*
Via Matteotti 113   *Oars and sculls*
57024 Donoratico (Livorno)   *Coaching boats*
Italy
Tel: (0565) 777 311
Fax: (0565) 777 483

Ciolli S. N. C.   *Oars and sculls*
Piazza Bartelloni N43
57122 Livorno (LI)
Italy
Tel: (0586) 405 276

Martinoli di Bernasconi Luigia   *Fittings and accessories*
& C. S.n.c.
Via Cavour, 3
21032 Caravate (VA)
Italy
Tel: (0332) 602791
Fax: (0332) 602791
Tlx: 316893 ASARVA I

Salani Costruzioni Nautiche di L   *Boats (racing)*
Via A Ponchielle n 3   *Oars and sculls*
PO Box 980   *Fittings and accessories*
50050 Limite sull 'Arno (FI)
Italy
Tel: (0571) 57 062
Fax: (0571) 57 062

STS Studio Tecnologie Sportive   *Oars and sculls*
di Bertelli
Via Cisa 146
46030 Virgilio
Mantova
Italy
Tel: (0376) 440 353
Fax: (0376) 440 353

Japan

Delta Shipyard Co Ltd   *Boats (racing and recreational)*
8-26-23, Higashiogu   *Oars and sculls*
Arakawa-ku   *Fittings and accessories*
Tokyo   *Riggers and accessories*
Japan   *Training manuals*
Tel: (03) 3894 4411   *Coaching boats*
Fax: (03) 3894 4494

Kuwano Shipyard Co Ltd   *Boats (racing)*
4-3-25 Hamachtsu
Ohtsushi
Shigaken
Japan
Tel: (0775) 22 4367
Fax: (0775) 22 4320

Yamaha Motor Co Ltd
3380-67 Mukojima
Araicho Hamanagun
Shizuokaken 431-03
Japan
Tel: (05359) 4 6511
Fax: (05359) 4 6510

Boats (racing)

Netherlands

Bootbouwery J.A. Busman BU
Ysseldyk Nrd.273
3935 B.R. Ouderkerk a/d Yssel
Netherlands
Tel: (01808) 3257
Fax: (01808) 3243

Boats (racing and recreational)
Oars and sculls
Riggers and accessories

CIC
Jan Vroegopsingel 8–10
1096 CN Amsterdam
Netherlands
Tel: (035) 233 093

Fittings and accessories

De Vrieseborch Publishing Co
Postbus 274
2000 AG Haarlem
Netherlands
Tel: (23) 325 620
Fax: (23) 322 504

Books and magazines

New Zealand

Kruetzmann Skiffs
Victoria Road
RD1 Cambridge
New Zealand
Tel: (071) 278 087

Boats (racing and recreational)

Norway

Arne Hasle A.S.
1800 Askim
Norway
Tel: (09) 882 366

Boats (racing and recreational)

Spain

Sportecniks
c/.de los Amézqueta, 10 entlo. E
20010 San Sebastian
Spain
Tel: (34) 43 472396/472144
Fax: (34) 43 472271

Boats (racing)
Oars and sculls
Ergometers
Trailers and transport
Coaching boats
Training devices

Switzerland

FISA (Federation Internationale des
Societés d'Aviron)
3653 Aberhofen am Thunersee
Switzerland
Tel: (41) 33 43 5053
     (41) 33 43 5073

Markus Graf Rennruderboote   *Boats (racing)*
Bleichestrasse 55
8280 Kreuzlingen
Switzerland
Tel: (072) 753 037

PMI Sport AG   *Boats (racing)*
Fabrikstrasse 2   *Ergometers*
4708 Luterbach   *Coaching boats*
Switzerland
Tel: (65) 42 40 48
Fax: (65) 42 22 77

Staempfli Racing Boats AG   *Boats (racing and recreational)*
Seestrasse 497   *Oars and sculls*
8038 Zurich   *Fittings and accessories*
Switzerland   *Ergometers*
Tel: (01) 482 9944   *Trailers and transport*
Fax: (01) 482 0503   *Clothing and accessories*

Susanna Staempfli Racing   *Boats (racing)*
PO Box 4308
8022 Zurich
Switzerland
Tel: (01) 715 2911
Tlx: 811050 TX KB CH

Weitnauer and Macherel   *Boats (racing)*
Ruderrennboote
Hintere Rueti
8820 Waedenswil
Switzerland
Tel: (01) 781 2422
Fax: (01) 780 7705

United States of America
California

Glide Sportswear Inc   *Clothing and accessories*
999C Edgewater Boulevard
Suite 201
Foster City
CA 94404
United States
Tel: (415) 341 8812
Fax: (415) 341 8812

Maas Rowing Shells
1453 Harbour Way South
Richmond
CA 94804
United States
Tel: (415) 232 1612

Boats (recreational)

Michael Weissenberger
28 Lupine Avenue
San Francisco
CA 94118
United States
Tel: (415) 386 0994
Fax: (415) 386 0995

Timing devices

Row Magazine
401 West Washington Street
Suite D
Petaluma
CA 94952
United States
Tel: (707) 762 6297
Fax: (707) 762 0705

Magazine

Schooner Gulch Boats
PO Box 226
Point Arena
CA 95468
United States
Tel: (707) 882 2244

Boats (recreational)
Oars and sculls
Fittings and accessories

Sol Oar Cycle
PO Box 1786
Oceanside
CA 92054
United States
Tel: (619) 434 5185

Clothing and accessories

Connecticut

Advance USA
East Haddam
Industrial Park
PO Box 452
East Haddam
CT 06423
United States
Tel: (203) 873 8643

Boats (recreational)

Mystic River Oar Company
59 Brunswick Avenue
Moosup
CT 06354
United States
Tel: (203) 564 2751
Tel: (800) 428 7305

Oars and sculls

Vespoli USA, Inc
385 Clinton Avenue
New Haven
CT 06513
United States
Tel: (203) 773 0311
Fax: (203) 562 1891

Boats (racing)
Fittings and accessories
Riggers and accessories
Trailers

Florida

Little River Marine Company
250 S E 10th Avenue
PO Box 986
Gainesville
FL 32602
United States
Tel: (904) 378 5025
Fax: (904) 378 5044

Boats (racing and recreational)
Oars and sculls
Videos

Shells for Rowing
5302 Clifton Road
Jacksonville
FL 32211
United States
Tel: (203) 536 9153 Summer
Tel: (904) 725 7573 Winter

Boats (racing and recreational)
Electrical devices
Sculling and rowing school

Idaho

Landrower Inc
4928 S 5th West
Idaho Falls
ID 83404
United States
Tel: (208) 524 3712

Ergometers

Illinois

Hurka Racing Shells
41 W042 Colson Drive
St Charles
IL 60174
United States
Tel: (708) 377 7532

Boats (racing and recreational)
Oars and sculls
Fittings and accessories

Indiana

US Rowing
201 South Capitol Avenue
Suite 400
Indianapolis
IN 46225
United States
Tel: (317) 237 5656
Tel: (317) 237 5656

Coaching books and video
The national rowing magazine
Clothing and accessories

Maine

Martin Marine Co
PO Box 368
Eliot
ME 03903
United States
Tel: (207) 439 1507
Fax: (207) 439 1507

Boats (recreational)
Oars and sculls

The Arundel Point Publishing
House
PO Box 1058Z
Kennebunk Port
ME 04046
United States
Tel: (207) 985 6134
Fax: (207) 985 7633

Art

Maryland

Westend Enterprises
5018 Sangamore Road
Bethesda
MD 20816
United States
Tel: (301) 229 3373
Fax: (301) 229 3373

Clothing and accessories
Specialize in blazer badges

Massachusetts

Garofalo High Performance
Shells
660 Franklen Street
Worcester
MA 01604
United States
Tel: (508) 755 1457

Boats (racing and recreational)
Oars and sculls

Lowell's Boat Shop
(Onboard Products)
459 Main Street
Amesbury
MA 01913
United States
Tel: (508) 388 0162
Fax: (508) 388 6408

Boats (recreational)
Oars and sculls
Fittings and accessories

Miller Design
PO Box 2060
Duxbury
MA 02331
United States
Tel: (617) 934 6192

Rowing strength machine

Northeast Sculling & Rowing
Center
PO Box 2060
Duxbury
MA 02331
United States
Tel: (617) 934 6192

Rowing and sculling school

Piantedosi Oars Inc
PO Box 643
West Acton
MA 01720
United States
Tel: (508) 263 1814

Boats (recreational)
Oars and sculls
Fittings and accessories

The Better Motion
PO Box 669
South Hadley
MA 01075
United States
Tel: (413) 534 0930

Fittings and accessories
Clothing and accessories

The Rower's Bookshelf
PO Box 440-F
Essex
MA 01929-0008
United States
Tel: (508) 468 4096
Fax: (508) 468 6388

Coaching books and video
Books and art

Van Dusen Racing Boats
Composite Engineering Inc.
277 Baker Avenue
Concord
MA 01742
United States
Tel: (508) 371 3132
Fax: (508) 369 3162

Boats (racing)

Michigan

Rowing Awards & Jewelry
PO Box 152
Buchanan
MI 49107
United States
Tel: (616) 695 9637

Trophies

The Potomac Company
29908 South Stockton
Farmington Hills
MI 48336-3560
United States
Tel: (313) 471 4448
Fax: (313) 478 4409

Riggers and accessories
Books
Clothing and accessories
Timing devices

New Hampshire

Durham Boat Co
264 Newmarket Road
Durham
NH 03824
United States
Tel: (603) 659 2548
Fax: (603) 868 5109

Boats (racing and recreational)
Oars and sculls
Fittings and accessories
Riggers and accessories
Books and videos
Clothing and accessories
Timing devices

Independence Rowing Club
C/O Thomas G. Kudzma
PO Box 1412
Nashua
NH 03061-1412
United States
Tel: (603) 888 2875

Art

Shell & Oar Restoration
Old Antrim Road
RFD 1, Box 578
Hancock
NH 03449
United States
Tel: (603) 525 4069

Boat repair

New York

Al Borghard Inc
14 Windham Drive
Huntingdon Station
NY 11746
United States
Tel: (516) 427 6884

Oars and sculls

Coffey Racing Shells
918 Addison Road
Painted Post
NY 14870
United States
Tel: (607) 962 1982
Fax: (607) 962 1974

Boats (racing and recreational)
Oars and sculls
Ergometers
Training devices

Sullivan Flotation Systems Inc
Kings Hwy Box 639
Warwick
NY 10990
United States
Tel: (914) 986 7377
Tel: (914) 986 8531

Rowing dock

Ohio

Simuletics
1218 Kinnear Road
Columbus
OH 43212
United States
Tel: (614) 486 7741

Ergometers

Pennsylvania

American Sculling
250 Conway Street
Carlisle
PA 17013
United States
Tel: (717) 249 3781
Fax: (717) 249 3781

Boats (racing and recreational)
Oars and sculls
Fittings and accessories
Riggers and accessories
Ergometers

Boathouse Row Sports Ltd
1021 Ridge Avenue
Philadelphia
PA 19123
United States
Tel: (215) 236 1883
Fax: (215) 236 1897

Videos
Clothing and accessories

Nielsen-Kellerman Co
201 East 10th Street
Marcus Hook
PA 19061
United States
Tel: (215) 494 0602
Fax: (215) 494 9537

Timing devices

Texas

Felker Boat Co
PO Box 33280 Suite 248
Austin
TX 78736
United States
Tel: (512) 263 5994

Boats (racing)

Vermont

Concept II Inc
RR #1 Box 1100
Morrisville
VT 05661–9727
United States
Tel: (802) 888 7971
Fax: (802) 888 4791

Oars and sculls
Ergometers

Craftsbury Sculling Center
Box 31-F
Craftsbury Common
VT 05827
United States
Tel: (802) 586 7767

Coaching books and videos
Sculling school

Mad River Canoe Inc
PO Box 610
Mad River Green
Waitsfield
VT 05673-0610
United States
Tel: (802) 496 3127
Fax: (802) 496 6247

Fittings and accessories
Ergometers

Sparhawk Model Oars
222 Porters Point Road
Colchester
VT 05446
United States
Tel: (802) 658 4799 June–Nov
Tel: (407) 798 1093 Nov–June

Trophies

Washington

Pocock Racing Shells Inc
2212 Pacific Avenue
Everett
WA
United States
Tel: (206) 252 6658
Fax: (206) 259 6802

Boats (racing and recreational)
Oars and sculls
Fittings and accessories

Trimline by Graham
2351 Hwy 28
Quincy
WA 98848
United States
Tel: (509) 787 4404

Boats (recreational)

INDEX